European Security Governance

This book focuses on the problems of, and prospects for, strengthening the global system of security governance in a manner consistent with the aspirations and practices of the EU. The EU approach to security governance has been successful in its immediate neighbourhood: it has successfully exported its preferred norms and principles to applicant countries, thereby 'pacifying' its immediate neigh-bourhood and making all of Europe more secure. The EU governance orientation ultimately seeks to enlarge the European security community and expand the geopolitical area within which armed conflicts are inconceivable, and where state and private actors converge around a set of norms and rules of behaviour and engagement.

The EU's success along its immediate boundaries has not yet been replicated on a global scale; it remains an open question whether the EU system of governance can be exported globally, owing to different normative structures (for example, a tolerance of armed conflict or non-democratic governance internally), great-power competition (such as US–China), or ongoing processes of securitization that has made it difficult to find a commonly accepted definition of security. Moreover, the EU system of security governance clashes with the continuing unwillingness of other major powers to cede or pool sovereignty as well as varying preferences for unilateral as opposed to multilateral forms of statecraft. This edited volume addresses both the practical and political aspects of security governance and the barriers to the globalization of the EU system of security governance, particularly in the multipolar post-Cold War era.

This book will be of great interest to students of security governance, EU politics, European Security and IR in general.

Charlotte Wagnsson is Associate Professor in the Department of Strategic and Security Studies at the Swedish National Defence College. **James A. Sperling** is Professor of Political Science at the University of Akron, Ohio, USA. **Jan Hallenberg** is Professor of Political Science at the Department of Security and Strategic Studies, Swedish National Defence College.

Contemporary security studies
Series Editors: James Gow and Rachel Kerr
King's College London

This series focuses on new research across the spectrum of international peace and security, in an era where each year throws up multiple examples of conflicts that present new security challenges in the world around them.

NATO's Secret Armies
Operation Gladio and terrorism in Western Europe
Daniele Ganser

The US, NATO and Military Burden-sharing
Peter Kent Forster and Stephen J. Cimbala

Russian Governance in the Twenty-first Century
Geo-strategy, geopolitics and new governance
Irina Isakova

The Foreign Office and Finland 1938–1940
Diplomatic sideshow
Craig Gerrard

Rethinking the Nature of War
Edited by Isabelle Duyvesteyn and Jan Angstrom

Perception and Reality in the Modern Yugoslav Conflict
Myth, falsehood and deceit 1991–1995
Brendan O'Shea

The Political Economy of Peacebuilding in Post-Dayton Bosnia
Tim Donais

The Distracted Eagle
The rift between America and old Europe
Peter H. Merkl

The Iraq War
European perspectives on politics, strategy, and operations
Edited by Jan Hallenberg and Håkan Karlsson

Strategic Contest
Weapons proliferation and war in the greater Middle East
Richard L. Russell

Propaganda, the Press and Conflict
The Gulf War and Kosovo
David R. Willcox

Missile Defence
International, regional and national implications
Edited by Bertel Heurlin and Sten Rynning

European Security Governance

The European Union in a Westphalian world

**Edited by Charlotte Wagnsson,
James A. Sperling and Jan Hallenberg**

Routledge
Taylor & Francis Group

LONDON AND NEW YORK

First published 2009
by Routledge
2 Park Square, Milton Park, Abingdon, Oxon OX14 4RN

Simultaneously published in the USA and Canada
by Routledge
711 Third Avenue, New York, NY 10017

Routledge is an imprint of the Taylor & Francis Group, an informa business

First issued in paperback 2012

Typeset in Times by Wearset Ltd, Boldon, Tyne and Wear

British Library Cataloguing in Publication Data
A catalogue record for this book is available from the British Library

Library of Congress Cataloging in Publication Data
European security governance : the European Union in a Westphalian
world / edited by James Sperling, Charlotte Wagnsson and Jan Hallenberg.
p. cm.
1. European Union. 2. Security, International–European countries. I.
Sperling, James. II. Wagnsson, Charlotte. III. Hallenberg, Jan.
JN30.E9143 2009
355'.03304–dc22   2008054168

ISBN13: 978-0-415-49352-9 (hbk)
ISBN13: 978-0-415-69157-4 (pbk)
ISBN13: 978-0-203-87597-1 (ebk)

Contents

Illustrations

Contributors

Rafael Biermann is an Associate Dean of Academics at the George C. Marshall European Center for Security Studies in Garmisch, Germany.

Malena Britz is Assistant professor in political science at the Swedish National Defence College. Her PhD dissertation in political science is *The Europeanization of Defence Industry Policy*, 2004.

Arita Eriksson is Lecturer in Political Science at the Swedish National Defence College.

Jan Hallenberg is Professor of Political Science at the Swedish National Defence College and Guest Professor at the Department of Political Science, Stockholm University.

Bertil Nygren is Associate Professor of Political Science at the Swedish National Defence College and the Department of Political Science, Stockholm University.

Hanna Ojanen is Programme Director of the European Union research programme at the Finnish Institute of International Affairs. She is also Adjunct Professor in International Politics at the University of Helsinki.

Andrew L. Ross is Director of the Center for Science, Technology, and Policy, and Professor of Political Science at the University of New Mexico and Chair of the New Mexico Nuclear Study Group.

James A. Sperling is Professor of Political Science at the University of Akron.

Charlotte Wagnsson is Associate Professor of Political Science at the Swedish National Defence College.

Alison M. S. Watson is Professor of International Relations at the University of St Andrews, Scotland.

Preface

This volume focuses on the prospects for an increasingly global system of security governance and on the role of the European Union in such a system. It is yet another book from a group of scholars based at the Department of Security and Strategic Studies at the Swedish National Defence College. As such, it follows two previous books on transatlantic relations and global security that we published with Routledge: in 2006 Hallenberg and Karlsson (eds): *Changing Transatlantic Security Relations: Do the US, the EU and Russia Form A New Strategic Triangle?* and in 2008 Engelbrekt and Hallenberg (eds): *The European Union and Strategy: An Emerging Actor*. As was the case in the previous volumes, our closely knit research group has once again been fortunate to cooperate with scholars from outside Sweden: two from the United States, and one each from Finland, Germany and the United Kingdom.

As editors, we particularly would like to thank our co-editor, Professor James A. Sperling of the University of Akron, Ohio. Jim has been a truly excellent scholar and friend to work with during the course of our labour with this volume and he has materially improved the book in many ways.

Apart from Jim, we thank our colleague Dr Arita Eriksson, whose theoretical thinking about governance has inspired our project. We are very also grateful to our US colleague, Professor Andrew L. Ross, Director, Center for Science, Technology, and Policy and Professor of Political Science at the University of New Mexico for contributing a chapter to this volume. Likewise, we wish to thank Associate Professor Hanna Ojanen of the Finnish Institute of International Affairs for her co-operation with our own Dr Malena Britz on Chapter 1 of this book. Dr Rafael Biermann has been a Visiting Professor at the Center for Contemporary Conflict at the Naval Postgraduate School in Monterrey, CA, while contributing his chapter to our book, for which we are grateful. We also wish to thank Professor Alison M. S. Watson of the School of International Relations, University of St. Andrew's for her contribution of Chapter 6 in this volume.

As editors, Jan Hallenberg and Charlotte Wagnsson wish to thank each other for good cooperation throughout our work on this book. Editor Hallenberg, in particular, wishes to acknowledge the leading role that editor Wagnsson has consistently played throughout our work on this volume. We also wish to thank one more person who has helped us a lot in completing this volume. She is Lisa Larsson, Master of Political Science, who has very ably served as an assistant to the editors throughout our work on this volume.

Finally, as always, Jan Hallenberg wishes to thank his wife Professor Ulrika Mörth for her love and support during his work on this volume. Charlotte Wagnsson wishes to thank her husband Fredrik Allard for enthusiastically sharing with her the experience of managing three quite autonomous kids – Nadine, Louise and Nathan – an exercise that continually provides new insights into the complexities of governance.

Jan Hallenberg
Charlotte Wagnsson

Abbreviations

AFSOUTH	Allied Forces in Southern Europe
BTC	Baku–Tbilisi–Ceyhan (Pipeline)
BTE	Baku–Tbilisi–Erzurum (Pipeline)
CFSP	Common Foreign and Security Policy (of the EU)
CIA	Central Intelligence Agency
CIAT	International Committee in Support of the Transition
CIS	Commonwealth of Independent States
CSCA region	Caspian Sea and Central Asian region
CSCE	Commission on Security and Cooperation in Europe
DDR	Disarmament, demobilization, reintegration
DG ECHO	(EU's) Directorate-General for Humanitarian Aid
DRC	Democratic Republic of Congo
EFTA	European Free Trade Association
ESDI	European Security and Defence Identity
ESDP	European Security and Defence Policy
ESS	European Security Strategy
EU	European Union
EUSR	European Union Special Representative
IAEA	International Atomic Energy Agency
ICC	International Criminal Court
ICISS	International Commission on Intervention and State Sovereignty
ICRC	International Committee of the Red Cross
IEC	Independent Electoral Commission
ILO	International Labour Organization
IMF	International Monetary Fund
IPAP	Individual Partnership Action Plan
IPU	Integrated Police Unit
ISAF	International Security Assistance Force
MLF	Multilateral Nuclear Force
MNC	Multinational corporation
MONUC	United Nations Mission in the Democratic Republic of Congo
NATO	North Atlantic Treaty Organization
NGO	Non governmental organization

OCHA	Office for the Coordination of Humanitarian Affairs (United Nations)
OECD	Organization for Economic Cooperation and Development
OEF	Operation Enduring Freedom
OPEC	Organization of the Petroleum Exporting Countries
OSCE	Organization for Security and Co-operation in Europe
PNC	National Congolese Police
PfP	Partnership for Peace
R&D	Research and development
RFE/RL	Radio Free Europe/Radio Liberty
RIA *Novosti*	Russian News and Information Agency *Novosti*
SACEUR	Supreme Allied Commander Europe
SCO	Shanghai Cooperation Organization
SDI	Strategic Defense Initiative
SG/HR	Secretary-General/High Representative for the CFSP
SSR	Security Sector Reform
TCGP	Trans-Caspian gas pipeline
UN	United Nations
UNCRC	United Nations Convention on the Rights of the Child
UNHCR	United Nations High Commissioner for Refugees
UNICEF	United Nations Children's Fund (United Nations International Children Emergency Fund)
UNESCAP	United Nations Economic and Social Commission for Asia and the Pacific
UNSAS	United Nations Standby Arrangements System
USSR	Union of Soviet Socialist Republics
WEU	Western European Union
WHO	World Health Organization
WMD	Weapon of mass destruction
WTO	World Trade Organization

Introduction

Security governance in a Westphalian world

James A. Sperling[1]

Why do highly institutionalized and normatively conditioned systems of security governance emerge in some geopolitical regions of the world, but are episodic or absent in others? An answer to this question may be found in the emergence of late- and post-Westphalian states. The dominant system-level theories of international relations generally treat state attributes as given and homogeneous. This homogeneity assumption no longer comports with the contemporary international system. Westphalian, late-Westphalian and post-Westphalian states each possess a unique set of characteristics and identities facilitating or impeding cooperation, or leading some states to adopt a narrow security agenda, while compelling others to adopt a broadened definition of security. Moreover, the porousness of states, the (in)voluntary abnegation of sovereignty, and the emergence of malignant non-state actors has affected these states in different measure and created new categories of threats which target the vulnerabilities of late- and post-Westphalian states. Although these new threats resist unilateral solutions, the character of individual states places a constraint on the form(s) of security governance available.

This perspective raises three additional questions: What implications do the emergence of the late- and post-Westphalian state have for developing effective responses to the challenges of security governance? How has the complexity of the current threat environment complicated the task of security governance? How much conceptual and empirical value is added by substituting security governance for state-centric forms of security multilateralism? Each of these questions will be addressed in turn.

The post-Westphalian state

There has been a sustained debate about the importance of domestic constitutional orders as the determinant of international order. Phillip Bobbitt (2002) linked the historical evolution of the European state system to changes in domestic constitutional form. The democratic peace hypothesis, which ignited one of the most heated post-Cold War debates, holds that democratic constitutional orders present the best guarantee of global or regional peace and stability (Owen 1994; Lipson 2003). Stochastic analyses generally support the hypothesis, but the data supporting the hypothesis are largely drawn from the European and Anglophone worlds (Ward and Gleditsch 1998; Russet and Oneal 2001).[2] This particular use of the European state system as the primary benchmark for testing theories of international relations has become hazardous, particularly when the hypothesis is supported by a circumscribed empirical base and precludes from consideration the more fundamental change that is taking place – the rise of the post-Westphalian state. Domestic democratic governance, an essential characteristic of the post-Westphalian state, is a necessary but insufficient condition for explaining the emergence and nature of the security communities that have arisen within Europe and the wider transatlantic area. Conversely, the persistence of the Westphalian state, rather than the persistence of underdeveloped or non-democratic states, better explains the continuing force of anarchy and the continued reliance on the familiar forms of security multilateralism – the balance of power, concerts, impermanent alliances.

The post-Westphalian hypothesis challenges the assumption that states can be treated as functionally non-differentiated actors. Rather, states fall along a continuum bounded by the Westphalian and post-Westphalian forms: each practices an alternative statecraft, instrumentally and substantively. Post-Westphalian states are more vulnerable to the influence of non-state actors – malevolent, benevolent, or benign – in international politics. Non-state actors fill or exploit the gaps left by the (in)voluntary loss or evaporation of sovereignty attending the transformation of the state, while others are purposeful repositories for sovereignty ceded, lent, pooled or forfeited. Moreover, the changing nature of the security agenda, particularly its functional expansion and the changing agency of threat, necessitates a shift from coercive to persuasive security strategies (Kirchner and Sperling 2007a).

Westphalian sovereignty forms a significant barrier to security cooperation – even in the transatlantic area. John Herz (1957) identified territoriality as the key characteristic of the Westphalian state and characterized it as the 'hard shell' protecting states and societies from the external environment. Territoriality is increasingly irrelevant, particularly in Europe. States no longer enjoy the 'wall of defensibility' that leaves them relatively immune to external penetration. The changed salience and meaning of territoriality has not only expanded the number and type of security threat, but increased the effectiveness of 'soft' power and rendered less effective 'hard' power, relatively and absolutely. Westphalian states are preoccupied with protecting autonomy and independence, retaining a gate-keeping role, and avoiding external interference in domestic constitutional arrangements. Post-Westphalian states, while not indifferent to territorial integrity, have largely abandoned their gate-keeper role owing to the network of interdependencies formed by economic openness, the political imperative of welfare maximization, and democratic political principles. Autonomy and independence have been devalued as sovereign imperatives; sovereign prerogatives have been subordinated to the demands of the welfare state and the preferences of individual agents.

Stephen Krasner's challenge of the post-Westphalian hypothesis is contingent on the validity of three claims: 'the principles of territoriality and autonomy' had never been sacrosanct in practice (Krasner 1995–6: 123); states have never been able 'to regulate perfectly transborder flows'; and the EU (and presumably the states constituting it) may be dismissed as a 'neutral mutation' without apparent consequence for the international system (Krasner 2001: 234, 244; see also Krasner 1999; Osiander 2001). These claims cannot withstand superficial scrutiny. First, the violation of the principles of territoriality and autonomy is distinct from the voluntary acceptance of mutual governance and loss of autonomy attending it. Second, the question is not simply whether states have been able to control transborder flows historically, but instead whether the nature and volume of those flows now makes it prohibitively expensive for a state to limit those flows. And finally, Krasner is, at a minimum, suppressing the inconvenient with his dismissal of the EU as a 'neutral mutant'.

The presence of states with fundamentally different characteristics poses a significant barrier to a unified system-level of theory of international relations (Powell 1991: 1305). The existence of states with different *kinds* of preference structures and vulnerabilities lacks theoretical elegance, but many states do approximate the post-Westphalian ideal-type. The structural characteristics of the post-Westphalian state propel governments to favour highly institutionalized and normatively constituted forms of security governance, while the persistence of the Westphalian state in much of the world explains the continuing reliance upon forms of security governance where the norms are extrinsic rather than intrinsic to the calculation of interest and institutions are absent or merely serve as ciphers for reconciling narrowly defined national interests.

The success of the European project in the post-war period reinforced Europe's material, ideational, and cultural interconnectedness (March and Olsen 1998: 944–947; Schimmelpfennig 2008). Geography, technological innovations, the convergence around the norms of political and economic openness, and a rising dynamic density amongst them have progressively stripped away the prerogatives of sovereignty and eliminated the autonomy once afforded powerful states by exclusive territorial jurisdiction. The ease with which domestic disturbances are transmitted across national boundaries *and* the difficulty of deflecting those disturbances underline the strength and vulnerability of the post-Westphalian state: the ever expanding spectrum of interaction provides greater levels of collective welfare than would otherwise be possible, yet the very transmission belts facilitating those welfare gains serve as diffusion mechanisms handicapping the state's ability to inoculate itself against exogenous shocks or malevolent actors (Hanrieder 1978; Most and Starr 1980; Siverson and Starr 1990). Those actors, in turn, are not only largely immune to sovereign jurisdiction, but are not adequately protected by the Cold War security strategies of dissuasion, defence, and deterrence (Freedman 2003). Consequently, broad and collective milieu goals have been substituted for particularistic national security goals, conventionally conceived. Perforated sovereignty has rendered post-Westphalian states incapable of meeting their national security requirements alone. This development, in conjunction with the emergence of failed states along Europe's periphery and the growing autonomy of non-state actors has also produced a changed threat environment that, in turn, has required a reconceptualization of security and the introduction of security governance as an alternative conceptual framework.

Security governance

Why security governance? The fundamental problem of international politics – and security provision in particular – is the supply of order and the regulation of conflict without the resort to war. Anarchy – and the benefits afforded the state by it – precludes by definition the emergence of either a global or even regional government to manage its attending liabilities. The regulation of international politics, particularly the management of disorder, can be best considered as a problem of governance as well as non-governance.[3] Alternative forms of security multilateralism are mutually exclusive (collective defence or concert) and are defective for the purpose of understanding the problem of security today, largely owing to their inherent limitations, the most important of which is a preoccupation with the military aspect of security and the persistent assumption that all states are essentially Westphalian in character.

The Westphalian state system was well served by the conceptual reliance upon alliances for understanding interstate interactions under conditions of anarchy and unqualified sovereignty. Alliances, as either formal or informal institutions, have been rightly regarded as mechanisms for regulating disequilibria in the international system, but the underlying concern with maintaining systemic equilibrium among the great powers is not particularly relevant to understanding the security dilemma facing late- or post-Westphalian states or the choice of alternative forms of security governance.[4] Not only have the source of threat and the security objectives of the state changed in fundamental ways, but the nomenclature security analysts have employed is less relevant to the task of clarifying the appropriate statecraft in a heterogeneous international system.

A change in nomenclature is required for a number of reasons: the international system – or minimally the European and North American subregions – can no longer be treated within a simple state-centric framework; the conceptual preoccupation with mitigating power disequilibria adds marginal value to understanding European or even Atlantic interactions; and there is little empirical evidence supporting the contention that states have *not* subcontracted many of their security tasks to international or supranational institutions, particularly those falling outside the traditional concern with territorial defence.

Thus, the formulation and execution of security policy cannot be disciplined or translated into the traditional rubric of sovereign jurisdiction or assessments of the capabilities and intentions of identifiable adversaries with a state identity. Only by relying on an alternative concept – security governance – can we capture the challenges and instruments of attaining within group security as well as security from 'out' groups. Thus, the regulation of international politics can be best thought of as a problem of governance.

Security governance has received increasing attention since 1989 (Rosenau 1992, 1997; Young 1999; Keohane 2001; Jervis 2002; Webber 2002; Krahmann

2003, Sperling 2003; Webber *et al.* 2004; Kirchner 2006; Kirchner and Sperling 2007a, 2007b). Security governance has been treated as a general theory (Webber 2002; Webber *et al.* 2004); as a theory of networks (Krahmann 2003); as a system of international and transnational regimes (Young 1999); and as a heuristic device for recasting the problem of security management in order to accommodate the different patterns of interstate interaction, the rising number of non-state security actors, the expansion of the security agenda, and conflict regulation or resolution (Sperling 2003, 2008). Relying upon security governance as a heuristic device permits an investigation of the role institutions play in the security domain, particularly the division of labour between the state and institution, the proscribed and prescribed instruments and purposes of state action, the consolidation of a collective definition of interest and threat, and does not privilege any particular method or general theory of international relations. It is elastic enough to accommodate theoretical frameworks treating institutions as mechanisms employed by states to further their own goals (Koremenos *et al.* 2001: 761–799), states as the primary actors in international relations where some states are more equal than others (Waltz 1979; Gilpin 1981), power relationships determined not only by underlying material factors, but norms and identities (Checkel 1998; Hopf 1998; Barnett and Duvall 2005), or states as constrained by the rules and norms of institutions (Martin and Simmons 1998; March and Olsen 1998).

Security governance has been expansively defined as 'the coordinated management and regulation of issues by multiple and separate authorities, the interventions of both public and private actors ... formal and informal arrangements, in turn structured by discourse and norms, and purposefully directed toward particular policy outcomes' (Webber *et al.* 2004: 4). This definition serves as the foundation for categorizing alternative *forms* of governance; it also possesses several virtues: it allows for hierarchical and heterarchical patterns of interaction as well as the disparate substantive bundling and normative content of security institutions; it neither precludes nor necessitates the privileging of the state or non-state actors in the security domain; and lastly, it leaves open the question of whether states are able to provide security across multiple levels and dimensions unilaterally or whether states are compelled to work within multilateral or supranational institutional frameworks.

The study of security governance, which with a few exceptions has been limited to geographical Europe, has generally focused on two distinct features: first, the institutional characteristics of governance, with particular attention directed to the geographical boundary of those governance structures; and second, a marked tendency to reserve the military aspects of security to NATO. Less attention has been given to identifying and establishing the relative importance of common interests, shared and divergent cultural identities, and the norms and rules giving rise to and 'binding' the European governance structure.[5] The transition to the post-Westphalian state and the concurrent broadening of the contemporary security agenda are the key rationales for adopting the concept of governance rather than the more established frameworks and concepts in the security field. Moreover, the emergent role of the EU as a security actor – and a corresponding erosion of state prerogatives in this policy domain – requires a more plastic framework allowing the simultaneous consideration of the entire range of Westphalian and post-Westphalian states, both in terms of instruments and goals.

Governance functions

The complexity of the contemporary threat environment has made security governance profoundly challenging, in theory and practice. It is clear that security threats are no longer limited to the existential questions of national survival or territorial integrity. Threats may be usefully categorized according to two salient variables: the agent of threat (state and non-state actors) and the target of threat (state, society, and regional milieu). These variables, which provided the basis for categorizing the entire spectrum of potential security threats (Kirchner and Sperling 2002), identify the overwhelming majority of probable threats facing states in the contemporary international system, particularly those posed by non-state actors targeting social infrastructure and civilian populations (see Table I.1). The threats European states confront today are generally aimed 'above' and 'below' the state. Many of the new security challenges target society, threatening societal structures or cohesion. Other security challenges target the European governance structures or the milieu goals of its member-states, particularly a continent dedicated to democracy and the market. In both cases, the state itself is largely bypassed as a target of threat. As, problematically, states are the least likely source of threat. This change in the nature of security places into question not only the ability of the state to discharge its protective function in isolation, but the utility of traditional forms of governance, including a collective defence arrangement like NATO, in meeting the challenges of the contemporary threat environment. This threat environment, made possible by the confluence of post-Westphalian states and non-governance in weak or failed Westphalian states, requires a reconceptualization of the governance functions served by any system of security governance.

Table I.1 Threat typology

		Target of threat		
		State	*Society*	*Regional milieu*
Agent of threat	State	Conventional war Nuclear attack	Cyberwarfare against economic infrastructure	Macroeconomic instability
	Non-state	Terrorism	Migratory pressures Cybervandalism Trafficking in humans, drugs, small arms	Environmental degradation

One approach to the problem of disentangling and understanding the current threat environment is a focus on how those threats are manifested. In this case, security challenges may be defined by the arena of conflict (state, society or regional/global milieu) and the range of policy instruments (coercive to persuasive). These two variables produce a typology presenting four categories of security challenge: interstate and intrastate conflicts, state-building, and the construction of the institutions of a civil democratic society (see Table I.2). These four governance challenges overlap in many instances and are inseparable in practice. In some cases they require the simultaneous application of the coercive and persuasive instruments of statecraft; in many cases the distinction between intra-and interstate conflicts is unhelpful; and in still others, the policy challenges and tasks of threat mitigation are sequential.

Although this typology provides a window on the changing nature of security threats, a functional categorization of security policy not only provides a typology that captures both the external and internal tasks of governance, but can make the critical distinction between pre- and post-conflict interventions. Such an approach combines the functional and instrumental requirements for meeting the security challenges facing Europe today. Security governance performs two functions – institution-building and conflict resolution – and employs two sets of instruments – the persuasive (economic, political and diplomatic) and the coercive (military intervention and internal policing). Taken together, four categories of security governance suggest themselves: assurance, prevention, compellence and protection (see Table I.3).[6]

Table I.2 Challenges of governance

		Instruments of statecraft	
		Coercive	Persuasive
Arena of conflict	State	Avoidance of interstate conflict by coercive means	State-building
	Society	Criminalization of economy	Institutionalization of democratic norms
	Regional or Global Milieu	Avoidance of inter- and intra-state conflict by coercive means	Strengthening institutions of global or regional civil society

Table I.3 Policies of governance

		Instruments	
		Persuasive	Coercive
Functions	Institution-building	Prevention	Protection
	Conflict resolution	Assurance	Compellence

Policies of assurance identify efforts aimed at post-conflict reconstruction and attending confidence-building measures. Policies of prevention capture efforts to prevent conflict by building or sustaining domestic, regional or international institutions that contribute to the mitigation of anarchy and the creation of order. Policies of compellence capture the tasks of conflict resolution via military intervention, particularly peace-making and enforcement. And policies of protection describe multilateral efforts to fulfil the traditional function of protecting society from external threats. These four tasks of security governance are oftentimes pursued concurrently; it is also clear that economic and military instruments can be used to achieve not dissimilar objectives. Arguably there *is* an elective affinity between policy instruments and a specific form of governance challenge; and post-Westphalian states exhibit a substantive normative reliance upon the civilian instruments of statecraft and disinclination to rely upon military force.

Systems of governance: towards a typology[7]

Any form of security governance has five components: sovereign prerogatives; the security referent; the regulator; the normative framework; and the interaction context (see Table I.4). Sovereign prerogatives indicate whether the authority relations within the international or regional system are hierarchical or heterarchical or some admixture of both, particularly with respect to the balance between the state and international institutions and between the state and individual agents (e.g. NGOs or global corporations). In an ideal-type Westphalian system of security governance, the claims of the state as the sole source of authority remain

Table I.4 Constituent elements of security governance systems

	Identifies	*Range of values*
Sovereign prerogative	Authority relations within system	Hierarchical to heterarchical relations of authority
Security referent	Target of security concern	Within group, external 'other' and/or external milieu
Regulator	Mechanism for conflict resolution	Warfare to binding arbitration within well-defined institutional framework
Function of norms	Role of norms in defining national or group interests and governing sanctioned behaviour	Instrumental and extrinsic (contingent impact on state behaviour or interest formation) to substantive and intrinsic to the definition of interest (constitutes state interests and governs behaviour)
Interaction context	Intensity of the security dilemma, the level of amity and enmity	Enmity and intense security dilemma to amity and the absence of a security dilemma

unchallenged and contingently circumscribed by either international institutions or individual agents. In an ideal-type post-Westphalian system of security governance, international institutions have an equal claim on authority vis-à-vis the state and the sovereign control of the state over individual agents is fundamentally qualified and subject to alternative sources of authority.

The security referent identifies the target(s) of the security arrangement; it may be directed inwardly towards the contracting states or outwardly towards an 'other' or the regional milieu.[8] The referent is determined by the identity shared by individual states and the preferred form of statecraft. Depending upon the constellation of those states interacting, the security referent may be within the group (a collective security arrangement or Westphalian security community), may be directed towards an antagonistic other (a collective defence arrangement or informal alliance), or may be directed internally and externally (a post-Westphalian security community). The security referent is determined by three general factors: first, the nature of the state; second, the interaction of identity and interest; and third, the utility of force. Where identity moves from the egoist to other-regarding, states are more likely to enter into governance arrangements that focus primarily upon the within-group dynamic and secondarily on the external dynamic; as the utility of power wanes (or normative prohibition on the use of gains waxes), the transformation of identity will accelerate and reinforce the within-group orientation. Yet where power defines the content and form of interstate relations, even among states sharing a common identity, security arrangements will primarily be directed outwardly towards an 'other'. These two forms of Westphalian interaction are also joined to the post-Westphalian security community where a common identity and the prohibitionary norm against the use of force are conjoined to a preoccupation with the external milieu owing to the vulnerabilities attending the post-Westphalian condition.

The regulator identifies the range of mechanisms – spanning the continuum bounded by the rule of war and the rule of law – relied upon to resolve conflicts or meet security challenges, and those mechanisms. The regulator identifies the (il)legitimacy of war as a dispute settlement mechanism. As the utility or legitimacy of war or force declines, states will seek alternative mechanisms for conflict regulation. In a post-Westphalian context, conflicts between states are regulated by norms and rules as well as compulsory adjudication; these states operate according to the 'logic of appropriateness' rather than the Westphalian 'logic of consequentiality' where interstate conflict sometimes leads to war (March and Olsen 1998).

The normative component identifies the role that norms play in the definition of state interests and acceptable behaviours. The mere existence of international norms does not reveal whether norms are intrinsic or extrinsic to state calculations or if they govern behaviour reflexively or tactically. The relevance of system-level norms is closely linked to the strength of the sovereignty principle. If sovereignty is jealously guarded, then states will presumptively act according to domestic ambitions and desires independent of the 'rules of the game'; where the sovereignty norm has weakened, international norms will shape national interests and behaviour. In other words, Westphalian states adhere to the 'logic of consequentialism', while post-Westphalian states follow the 'logic of appropriateness' (March and Olsen 1989, 1998; Hyde-Price 2001). Where system-level norms govern within-group interactions, outcomes are likely to be inconsistent with material interests or the structure of power; where interests are driven by reference to national norms and ambitions, interests and behaviour closely track material interests and the distribution of power

The interaction context, the final component, identifies the level of intramural amity and enmity as well as the intensity of the security dilemma. Where states have lost sovereign control and discounted sovereign prerogatives, states develop a positive affect for one another owing to the positive externalities associated with openness. Amity is reinforced when the loss of sovereignty initiates the pooling or ceding of sovereign prerogatives to international or regional institutions. The security dilemma will be most acute where war remains a viable option, normatively and instrumentally, and states retain an egoist national interest. Where states share a common set of interests (or identity) and war becomes normatively proscribed, the security dilemma will dissipate and create an enabling condition for the advanced forms of security governance.

There are four highly institutionalized forms of security governance: collective defence, collective security, a Westphalian security community, and a post-Westphalian security community.[9] The collective defence arrangement represents one of the most evolved systems of effective security governance in the Westphalian system. A collective defence arrangement, where the security referent is outwardly directed, may only emerge when one group of states identifies another state or group of states as a common threat. Within group conflicts are mediated by institutionalized procedures of dispute management and decision-making, while deterrence and defence mediate conflicts with the adversary. A binding normative framework is required to offset the required abnegation of sovereignty: military forces are likely to be aggregated at some level, defence acquisition and expenditures become a matter of common concern, and strategy is likely to serve the collective rather than the particularistic interests of its members. Yet, each state retains the right to decide whether an act of aggression has occurred and whether it constitutes a threat. Moreover, when an act of aggression does occur, the member-states have the option, rather than the obligation, to intervene on behalf of their ally (Wolfers 1963: 182–183; Kelsen 1948: 793–794). A collective defence arrangement emerges in the context of internal amity and external enmity; the security dilemma gives the arrangement its *raison d'être*.

Collective security arrangements differ fundamentally from collective defence. In a collective security arrangement, the security referent is inwardly directed at a contracting state that initiates an act of aggression. Any party to a collective security arrangement is contractually and normatively obligated to assist any other contracting state that is the victim of aggression and to punish the aggressor. A collective security arrangement makes provision for the compulsory adjudication of within-group conflicts. Finally, in a collective security system, the use of force – except in cases warranting immediate self-help measures – must be wielded and legitimized by a quasi-sovereign entity (Kelsen 1948: 784–790; Wolfers 1963: 182–186).

The Westphalian security community has been advanced as the most fully developed form of security governance institutionally and normatively (Deutsch *et al.* 1957; Adler and Barnett 1998a) and the most relevant to understanding security governance in Europe. Such a system of security governance exists where states have replaced 'the military enforcement of rules (politics based on power) with the internalization of socially accepted norms (politics based on legitimacy)' (Harnisch and Maull 2001: 4). Five conditions must be met: there are normative constraints on the use of force and an unwillingness to rely on it for resolving conflicts; international law serves as the basis for conflict resolution; formal institutional mechanisms must exist to adjudicate within-group conflict; decision-making is participatory; and sovereignty plays an instrumental rather than substantive role in the calculation of interest (Harnisch and Maull 2001; Eberwein 1995: 350–352). The security referent is predominately within the group, conflict is regulated by rule of law, the normative framework is binding and codified, and an abiding amity complements the absence of a security dilemma. The European system of security governance, as opposed to the transatlantic governance system, goes beyond this form, however.

The post-Westphalian security community is approximated by the EU system of security governance. The EU security referents are both inwardly and outwardly directed, although there is no adversarial 'other'. The inward orientation of the EU focuses on the non-traditional aspects of security that arise from the post-Westphalian character of the member-states; the outward orientation is directed towards a broad and consistent set of regional milieu goals in its self-declared neighbourhood. The EU members share a collective identity reinforced by supranational institutions that have muted asymmetries of power and in certain instances renders them inoperative. Power does not play a significant role in EU relations with its neighbouring states, attributable in large measure to a benign external environment (which it has assiduously sought to nurture) as well as geopolitical good fortune.

The EU member-states have pooled or ceded considerable sovereignty to supranational institutions and have forged a collective identity. While a European collective identity has not superseded the national identities of its citizens, there nonetheless exists a denationalized understanding of threats and the response to them. War between the EU states has become unthinkable; no other state or group of states currently constitutes a military threat, although the Russian–Georgian conflict in 2008 demonstrates the persistence of Westphalia along its outer periphery. A willingness to rely on force remains, but is restricted to executing the Petersberg tasks of peacekeeping, humanitarian intervention, rescue tasks, crisis-management and conflict prevention. These permissive internal factors in combination with a settled external environment have enabled the EU to institutionalize conflict resolution to a degree only exceeded within states: intramural conflicts are resolved within the Council of Ministers and European Council, the European Commission drafts policies meeting common needs, and the European Court of

Table I.5 Characteristics of formally institutionalized systems of security governance

	Security referent	Regulator	Function of Norms	Context of interaction
Collective defence	Identifiable enemy out-side the group	Balancing, deterrence, defence, or war	Alliance norms are substantive and intrinsic to interests along a narrow range of issues	Amity within group, enmity without, security dilemma intact
Collective security	Within group	Collective, compulsory adjudication of Conflicts, collective enforcement of violations of group norms	Norms replace sovereign prerogatives in issues of war and peace. Renunciation of war is intrinsically and substantively valued	Amity, security dilemma resolved
Westphalian security community	Within group	International law, institutional conflict resolution mechanisms	Norms replace sovereign prerogatives across a wide range of issues, constitute state interests, are substantively and intrinsically valued.	Deep amity derived from a positive or collective identity, a common set of norms have been internalized, security dilemma atrophied
Post-Westphalian security community	Within group and external milieu	Highly institutionalized and binding adjudication of conflict	Norms determine interests and action adheres to logic of appropriateness	Lack of differentiation between states with respect to security, absence of internal security dilemma and concern with external milieu

Justice adjudicates conflicts and the plaintiffs expect voluntary compliance with the court's decisions.

The norms governing the EU states are substantive and intrinsic to the calculation of interest. National interests are themselves subject to the solidarity principle; namely the expectation that national security policies will serve not only the particularistic interests of the member-state, but the collective interests of the Union. The erosion of the sovereignty principle, the absence of force in mediating intramural conflicts, and a broad and deep normative framework progressively institutionalized as hard law create a context where EU norms constitute the definition of interest.

Amity and the absence of a security dilemma characterize the EU interaction context. While the rationale for the European project may have been initially instrumental (Milward 1992), it could only persist and broaden if accompanied by intramural trust and amity. This same dynamic altered the calculus of interest from the particular to the collective, a process unhindered by the prospect of war. By the time that the EU acquired a security writ in the late 1980s, the fear of a renascent Germany and the corresponding security dilemma perceived by its neighbours (the original motivation for the Brussels Treaty Organization) had evaporated.

Thus, the EU generally meets the criteria of a civilianized security community. This conclusion should not come as a surprise since the category was created to accommodate the EU as a system of security governance. The defining characteristic of the EU is the post-Westphalian status of its member-states and the post-Westphalian system dynamic that pushes states towards collective security governance (Falk 2002). Yet, classifying the EU is not as important as understanding why the EU developed into a security community since the answer to that question has policy implications for those wishing to reproduce the number of security communities across the globe.

Conclusion

There are two competing, overlapping forms of European security governance: the post-Westphalian security community institutionalized in the EU; a collective defence arrangement underpinning a Westphalian security community institutionalized in NATO. The coexistence of these two forms of governance, and the minimal socialization of the Russian Federation into either form, reflects, first, the participation of late- and post-Westphalian states in the latter and the participation of primarily post-Westphalian states in the former; and second, the ossification of the post-war division of labour between the governing of security and the governing of the economy that reflects, in turn, an outmoded and overly restricted definition of security. The interaction of these two forms of security governance are conditioned by the underlying barriers to implementing advanced governance structures in the transatlantic area, notably the persistence of Westphalianism in the United States and the corresponding transatlantic divergence in the targets and instruments of security governance polices.

European Security Governance: The European Union in a Westphalian World considers the consequences of the overlapping systems of security governance for the European Union as an effective security actor and the prospects for externalizing or extending the post-Westphalian security community regionally (or globally) that evolved from the process of European economic integration and the dynamic of the Soviet–American competition for European hegemony. In their respective contributions, Malena Britz and Hanna Ojanen, Rafael Biermann, and Arita Eriksson investigate the institutional dimension of security governance. Britz and Ojanen compare the modes of governance represented by the EU and UN towards determining whether these two distinct governance systems are complementary or competing. Biermann, in turn, questions the consequences of NATO's persistence and Westphalian character for the completion of the EU governance project and its externalization. Eriksson, in turn, focuses on the role of the EU as a provider of 'hard' security in the Democratic Republic of the Congo, differentiating between limited and comprehensive security and placing the EU as a security actor into the context of an emerging, universal system of security governance. These contributions seek to provide an answer to an important question: What are the prospects for regional and global security governance on the EU model?

The chapter contributions of Bertil Nygren, Alison M. S. Watson, and Andrew L. Ross consider two categories of structural barriers to global security governance on the EU model, the persistence of a Westphalian hegemon and incorrigibly Westphalian policy domains. In his chapter, Ross considers the implications of American foreign policy for the EU approach to security governance, particularly the incompatibility of America's post-11 September 'malgovernance' domestically with reinforcing and practising good governance internationally. Nygren and Watson consider in their chapters, respectively, the challenges to good governance posed by the intractability of specific policy sectors, specifically energy and human security. Nygren explores the paradox that the energy sector, although underpinned by enforceable commercial contracts on the demand side of the equation, one hallmark of effective global governance, remains nonetheless vulnerable to the impulses of the Westphalian pursuit of unilateral advantage on the supply-side. Watson considers the consequences of nongovernance with respect to the role of children in conflict and post-conflict environments, comparing the limited role of children in international law and in practice or in the post-conflict strategies of intervening states. Each chapter, in identifying significant barriers to security governance, questions the ability of the EU to generalize its system of governance globally or within Europe expansively defined.

In the conclusion Charlotte Wagnsson and Jan Hallenberg address two questions at the core of this collection: Can the European Union's post-Westphalian security community be exported or expanded in geographic scope? Does the persistence of Westphalian states and forms of security governance pose a threat to the viability of the EU system of security governance itself? In answering these questions, Wagnsson and Hallenberg explore whether states and regions suffering nongovernance can 'skip Westphalia' and become embedded in a multilateral system of security governance where the failure of domestic governments to provide security is remedied with a system of post-Westphalian governance. If the liabilities of sovereignty outweigh the ascribed de facto and *de jure* advantages it once conferred upon states and societies in the contemporary international system, it then allows us to redirect our conceptual attention from the potentially self-defeating preoccupation with strategies of state- or nation-building to the more constructive strategies of seeking mechanisms for by-passing the pathologies of the Westphalian state that constitute barriers to individual and societal security.

Notes

1 Thanks are owed to the following individuals for their comments on this chapter: Rafael Biermann, Arita Eriksson, Jan Hallenberg, Maria Hellman, Bertil Nygren, Andy Ross, and Charlotte Wagnsson.

2 Edward Mansfield and Jack Snyder (2007) also demonstrate that states in the early stages of democratization are as likely to be war prone as not. Kal Holsti (1995) rejects the emphasis on democratic constitutional orders and suggests that the absence of domestic legitimacy, regardless of constitutional form, is the better indicator of bellicosity.

3 Special thanks are owed to Haruhiro Fukui, who suggested that the presence of non-governance outside Europe creates the permissive context generating these new categories of threat.

4 For the period 1648–1945, see Langer (1950), Taylor (1954), Holsti (1991) and Schweller (1998). For the post-war period, see Wolfers (1959), Osgood (1962), Liska (1962) and Walt (1987).

5 Important exceptions are Risse (1995), Gheciu (2005), Sjursen (2004) and the chapter by Rafael Biermann in this volume.

6 This model is applied in Kirchner and Sperling (2007) and Dorussen, Kirchner and Sperling (forthcoming).

7 This argument is fully developed in Sperling (2008).

8 This is drawn from Sperling (2004); for the classic statement on goal referents, see Wolfers 1963.

9 A Westphalian security community corresponds to Karl Deutsch's pluralistic security community, while the post-Westphalian security community occupies the space between a pluralistic security community and an amalgamated one (Deutsch *et al.* 1957).

Part I

The institutional dimension of security governance

EU, NATO and the UN

1 Multilateral security governance

Comparing the UN and the EU

Malena Britz and Hanna Ojanen

This chapter starts from the basic assumption that the European Union (EU) and the United Nations (UN) are both not only parts of a system of security governance but indeed actively and intentionally create security governance or use governance as a tool to enhance international security. Yet, there might be important differences between the two organizations beyond the obvious ones of geographic reach (regional versus global) and decision-making (partially supranational versus intergovernmental). This chapter delineates the similarities and differences between the modes of governance of these organizations in order to assess whether they can be said to be part of the same system of security governance or, indeed, represent two different systems.

This matter is important because it affects both the present and future relationship between the two organizations, an issue that raises debate. To what extent should the EU base its international role on a system that has its own weaknesses, the UN system, or should it rather invest in autonomous capacity? Does increasing autonomy mean decreasing legitimacy? Is the EU credible and influential as an actor within the UN system? Are the two organizations' conceptions of security governance in line with today's developments towards a multipolar world, and, if they can co-operate, is it at the expense of other actors such as the USA or NATO? The chapter concludes that there is mutual willingness in the two organizations to work for the same system of global governance, and that their modes of governance are becoming more similar. Ideally, the EU as an actor with considerable material capacities and considerable ideational influence, but also legal authority over its member-states, is exactly what the UN needs to enforce its norms and reach its goals. Yet, willingness and capacity are not sufficient for an effective joint security governance to emerge. The chapter shows that due to the organizations' diverging characters, they differ in their ability to influence both their own member-states and non-member-states.

The comparison of the organizations is based on six features that define and characterize governance, that is, six different components of governance deriving from a definition of governance specified below. The 'power' of governance can be said to be both material and ideational, therefore our analysis of the UN's and the EU's modes of security governance compares both material and ideational components, all relating to security. These components are: the function of security for the organization; the organization's threat perception; the organization's means to create security; security-linked norm creation that the organization undertakes; the importance of membership in the organization (exclusion and inclusion: influence over non-members, legitimacy in the eyes of outsiders); and finally the role of supranationality (which affects both the material and ideational power of the organization). The comparison reveals similarities and differences but also tells about the respective development of the two organizations and the extent to which they have come to resemble each other more closely.

From the outset, the EU distinguishes itself as an organization that is more dynamic than the UN. The EU evolves and changes its nature: it has become more like the UN in that it also engages in crisis management and peace support operations, extending its realm well beyond its own territory to a global reach, and emphasizing norm-making beyond its own members. But it also moves further apart from the UN by further constitutionalization and increasing its autonomy as an actor. Meanwhile, the long-awaited UN reform has not shown much progress.

When explaining the two organizations' approaches to security governance, special attention is paid to the nature of the member-states as an important factor illuminating both what unites and what separates the two. This links to constitutionalization of the EU. As argued by Sperling in this volume, states in Europe are no longer homogeneous. In fact, there is now in the international system a type of state that could be called the 'EU member-state', a post-Westphalian state, in some crucial ways different from the traditional Westphalian state or nation-state that we know from textbooks on international relations. If UN membership was earlier seen as something that 'creates' a (Westphalian) state as a recognized actor in international relations, it now seems that the EU has an almost comparable function of 'recreating' a (post-Westphalian) state as an EU member-state. This, moreover, is a status that is actively sought, as the constant enlargement shows. The central new feature is that the EU member-state is part of a political union, something that the other states are not. The EU has different – deeper and stronger – relations to its member-states than other organizations. Thus, one difference between the two modes of governance stems from the different relationships the organizations have with their member-states. As pointed out by Kirchner and Sperling (2007: 21), also the interactions produced by Westphalian and post-Westphalian states are qualitatively different.

The difference becomes even clearer when the EU and the UN are compared with other organizations such as NATO. One could speak about three different types of governance. The UN is in itself not a formally institutionalized system of security. Perhaps it is best described as a regulative security organization in that its purpose is to create security through regulating the behaviour of its member-states towards each other. The EU, then, can be described as a formally institutionalized system of security in the form of a post-Westphalian security community (cf. Introduction by Sperling in this volume, Kirchner and Sperling 2007). Compared to these, NATO could be characterized as a functional security organization; (see Chapter 2 by Biermann in this volume). As such, it does not change the statehood of its members, and it does not aim at regulating the behaviour of its members towards each other. Rather, it takes their peaceful behaviour for granted and there-fore only affects the policies of member-states relating to their capacity to fulfil their obligations towards the other members of the organization. Such differences in the nature of the organizations and in that of their member-states may lead the organizations' security governance also to occasionally clash.

Defining security governance

As Webber *et al.* (2004: 25) point out, 'governance' can be understood as a research method or theory, but also as a phenomenon, an observable fact. In other words, governance can be a perspective from which to look at reality or a trend observed in international relations. In this chapter, governance is taken as a fact or an observable trend. More specifically, it could be an interim phase in time between the phase of state-centred government and that of something new, resembling organization-centred government of some kind.

Krahmann (2003: 11) gives the following definition of governance: 'Governance denotes the structures and processes which enable a set of public and private actors to coordinate their interdependent needs and interests through the making and implementation of binding policy decisions in the absence of a central political authority'. Even though not totally applicable here, this functions as a starting point. Starting from this, the EU and the UN can first of all be seen as structures which enable policy decisions and policies in the field of security. European integration, moreover, qualifies well as a process that enables various actors to coor-dinate their needs and interests. In the process of integration, public and private spheres interact.

And yet, the UN and the EU cannot be seen *only* as structures or processes within which or whereby other actors make decisions. They are also among the very actors that act within certain structures and are part of certain processes as makers of (even binding) decisions. There is, thus, also a need to look at the intentionality of governance: do some actors actively produce governance or aim at governance? Or is governance something that emerges from their unintended actions, from the fact that there is no central political authority in the field?

The question of intentionality leads, in turn, to the question of whether inter-national organizations such as the EU and the UN can be strategic actors in the first place. It is still debated, and many – including Webber *et al.* (2004: 6) – see that states are still the (real) agents. Even though the EU is an acknowledged actor in some policy fields, it is still somewhat controversial to see it as an actor in security policy. Thus, while Webber *et al.*, to take an example, see that the 'Europeanization of security' (without, however, defining the notion) has been the great political revolution of the late twentieth and early twenty-first centu-ries, they still also argue that 'NATO is the key agent in building security governance in Europe' (Webber *et al.* 2004: 14, 19).

Differences in the degree to which the organizations are regarded as actors also have to do with the role of the states within them. Here, the difference between the UN and the EU is again visible: the EU is gradually building up an actorness that affects the international actorness of its member-states in a way that does not take place in the UN. It is taking away some of the elements of sovereignty of its members.

Ortega (2007) understands global governance as the management of global problems and the pursuit of global objectives through the concerted efforts of states and other international actors. Against this definitional background, Ortega sees the EU contributing to the global order both as an actor, and as a model (Ortega 2007: 91). This chapter chooses to regard both the EU and the UN as strategic actors that actively aim at regional and global security through their own policies (building governance with material and ideational tools), but who, moreover, are central elements of the structures and processes of security governance.

Comparing the EU and the UN

Starting then to analyse the security governance of the EU and of the UN, six aspects are looked at. First, the function of security for the organization, that is, whether security is the main function of the organization, or one of its goals, how important success in security is for the overall success of the organization, and how other policy fields that the organization is involved in contribute to security governance. Second, the way security and security threats are perceived and analysed. In the introductory chapter by Sperling, a typology of contemporary threats to European stability has been presented. This typology differentiated between the agent of the threat (the state or a non-state) and the target of a threat (state, society or above state). However, in this typology nothing is said of the threat perceptions. It can be assumed that strategic actors engaging in security governance do so based partially on their threat perception. Therefore, an analysis assuming that both the EU and the UN are strategic actors aiming at building security through governance needs to look at threat perceptions. Are they similar in the two organizations? Are they similar within the organizations? The first question relates to the organizations' capacity to cooperate, the second to their nature and also mode of governance.

A central dichotomy here is between 'mutual recognition of threats' (*à la* Kofi Annan, see below) versus shared threat perception (*à la* classical military alliance). The shared threat perception is straightforward in that there, cooperation between the states is from the outset based on the existence of a common threat or a common enemy. Ideas on the means used to counter the threat may, then, give rise to debates.[1] Mutual recognition of threats, instead, means that different states' subjective threat definitions are the ground for common security thinking. The threats themselves may not be the same for all the countries, but there is a basic understanding that a member country needs to get assistance by the other members regardless of what kind of a security threat or problem it is under. The basic understanding may also include a shared view on what needs to be safeguarded[2] and on the means used, that is, on how crises should be dealt with. Interestingly, mutual recognition is on the rise more broadly speaking also as a mode of governance (see Nicolaïdis 2007).

Third, the spectrum of means used to create security governance is analysed. This is a very important part of the comparison, because here both the structural capacity of the organizations to enable policy in the field of security governance and their capacity to be direct (autonomous) actors in security governance is visible. The means may belong to any of the persuasive and coercive instruments: prevention, protection, assurance, and compellence – the policies of security governance discussed by Sperling in the introductory chapter. Sperling also discusses norms as one constituent element of security governance systems. The fourth part of the analysis will therefore look at security-linked norm creation in the two organizations. These norms relate both to the organizations themselves (the security culture and values guiding the use of force), and to their members (the content of statehood and values guiding the use of force).

Given the discussion above about the differences in statehood that the EU and the UN bring, the analysis will also take into account two issues that have to do with membership in the two organizations. The fifth point of comparison will therefore be the balance between inclusion and exclusion. This could take place on several levels: on the level of choice between regional and global reach, and on that between members and non-members (Webber *et al.* 2004: 23), where the enlargement/accession perspective can be seen as one way of extending governance beyond the member countries. The point is the extent to which the organization is perceived as legitimate. The sixth and final point of comparison is the organizations' relations to their member-states, notably the supranational character that the EU but not the UN has. Bailes (2005) states that global governance can be seen as an enforceable system that can both serve and constrain sub-state, trans-state and traditional state players. A supranational character of one organization might mean that it differs from organizations without that supranational character, because efficiency of the organization can be measured as a capacity to influence both member-states and non-member-states.

The function of security for and within the organizations

The UN

The UN has been a security organization from the start, envisaged to engage in security measures to create peace between states and thus the creation of global security is its *raison d'être*. The UN is basically the world's only universal body with a mandate to address security, development and human rights issues. The UN was created after the end of the Second World War. As a global security organization it was not a new phenomenon. It had a predecessor in the League of Nations which was created after the First World War. The League of Nations, however, failed to prevent a new war and thereby ceased its activities. In 1945, 50 countries met up to finalize the Charter of the United Nations. The organization the United Nations was formally created when the charter had been ratified by a majority of its signatory countries, including the permanent members of the

Security Council (China, France, the UK, the US and the Soviet Union) (Karns and Mingst 2004: 97–99).

The UN, thus, was a security actor from its creation. Obviously, this is reflected in the organization's means for security governance which can be said to consist both of bodies and activities. Some of these have been there from the beginning, whereas others have evolved over time. The UN Security Council is an important body and can partially be seen as its own actor in security governance. Under article 24 of the UN Charter it has primary responsibility for the maintenance of international peace and security and is authorized to act on behalf of all UN members. Chapters vi and vii of the UN Charter lay out this role, chapter vi deals with the peaceful settlement of disputes and chapter vii deals with the possibilities to use force. Before 1992, all UN peacekeeping forces were authorized under chapter vi, but after the end of the Cold War, the Security Council's use of chapter vii increased dramatically (Karns and Mingst 2004: 110–114).

Article 39, chapter vii of the Charter states that:

> The Security Council shall determine the existence of any threat to the peace, breach of the peace, or act of aggression and shall make recommendations, or decide what measures shall be taken in accordance with articles 41 and 42, to maintain or restore international peace and security.

Article 42 continues that: 'should the Security Council consider the non-military measures inadequate, it may take such action by air, sea, or land forces as may be necessary to maintain or restore international peace and security'.

Despite being envisioned as the central organ of the UN by the founders of the organization, and despite taking more action than previously on armed conflicts after the end of the Cold War, the Security Council has not always been an efficient actor. Compared to the possibilities laid down in the UN Charter, the Security Council as an actor has been more or less lame. The Charter edicts on all members being committed to provide armed forces to have at its disposal and, for instance, holding immediately available national air force contingents for combined international enforcement action. This has not become a reality any more than has the decision of a Military Staff Committee (articles 43–47, consisting of the chiefs of staff of the five permanent members of the Security Council) to plan the employment of forces placed at its disposal. The member-states, by invoking the right to self-defence, have taken care of countering threats themselves as best they see fit without always giving the UN a possibility to act. During the Cold War some conflicts were never brought to the Security Council at all (Findlay 2002: 9–10; Karns and Mingst 2004: 127).

The Secretary-General has an extensive task of both managing the UN secretariat and being a global diplomat, and has been especially important when it comes to the UN's ability to contribute to peaceful settlements of disputes as prescribed under chapter vi of the charter. According to Karns and Mingst (2004), the 'UN secretaries-general have been a key factor in the emergence of the UN itself as an autonomous actor in world politics' (2004: 119). In this way, the secretaries-general have, for example, articulated principles for the organization's involvement in peacekeeping, resolved specific conflicts as an intermediary, and pushed for the development of the organization after the end of the Cold War (Karns and Mingst 2004: 118–122). However, the commander-in-chief function that the Secretary-General has played in the absence of a Military Staff Committee has also meant that the Secretary-General has become involved in command decisions when force has been used, sometimes making the final decisions on tactics such as the application of air power or the disposition of ground forces (Findlay 2002: 10; Rosenau 1995).

While the UN can be seen as having failed in putting in place the advanced security mechanisms and means that were envisaged in the UN Charter, it has also had difficulties in adjusting its formal structures to the fact that it now has almost 200 members; and adjusting to today's geopolitical and demographic realities. One of the main issues when UN reforms are discussed is the composition and proceedings of the Security Council. There is agreement that the Security Council is no longer representative of the current membership of the organization. Criticism has also arisen as to the openness and the efficiency of this body. As changes in the Security Council membership requires an amendment of the UN Charter (which, in turn, requires a vote of two thirds of the General Assembly and ratification of two thirds of the members including all present members of the Security Council) so far only changes in the working procedures of this Council have been successful. Changing its membership has proved to be very difficult even though there exist a number of suggestions of how it could be done (Karns and Mingst 2004: 139–142). In all, as Bailes (2005) puts it, the UN is unique in global security governance, but it is not all-encompassing: it never sought or possessed authority over all security-related transactions in world governance (like commerce). In addition to difficulties in reforming its structures, it also suffers from a lack of resources. Thus Bailes concludes that what is needed is synergy and complementarity between the UN and other processes and actors, such as the EU (Bailes 2005: 27).

The EU: not an explicit actor in security governance at the start

Contrary to the UN, the EU's developing into a proper actor in security governance is a recent phenomenon. Security was first defined as comprising only the political and economic aspects (the Single European Act 1986). The EU's security role has been widening step by step from first creating internal security, i.e. assuring peace among the member-states, to regional security (through enlargement and neighbourhood policies but also trade) and then to international security. In this way, the EU has gone from being an implicit actor to an explicit actor in security governance (Ekengren 2007).

Some of the important steps towards a formal role in security governance include the Amsterdam Treaty and the European Security Strategy (ESS). The Amsterdam Treaty came into force in 1999 adding the crisis management tasks, or the Petersberg tasks,[3] to the repertoire of the Union, eventually leading to the start of the first crisis management operations – also military – in 2003. The European Security Strategy of December 2003[4] put forward not only a shared analysis of threats and ways of encountering them, but also a global role for the Union and a definition of its relations with the UN. It states that 'Europe should be ready to share in the responsibility for global security and in building a better world'. The immediate reason seems to be self-interest: the strategy affirms that 'A European Union which takes greater responsibility and which is more active will be one which carries greater political weight'. It is also acknowledged that 'the United Nations Security Council has the primary responsibility for the maintenance of international peace and security'.

The Lisbon Treaty, which was signed in December 2007 but has not come into force, further enhances the EU's role as an explicit actor in security governance. It includes many security and defence-related aspects, some of which have been put into place already. This treaty widens the scope of security-related tasks of the Union, and explicitly refers to the Common Security and Defence policy (the CSDP, more commonly called the ESDP – the European Security and Defence Policy). When it comes to foreign policy, the EU has so far had many 'heads' and it has been difficult to know who is the primary representative of the Union: the council's High Representative for the Common Foreign and Security Policy, the president of the commission, or the head of state of the member-state currently holding the presidency? An effort to reduce this confusion is shown in the Lisbon Treaty through the creation of one post that at the same time is the High Representative of the Union for Foreign Affairs and Security Policy and vice president of the commission. It also introduces an External Action Service, and a semi-permanent council presidency.

The treaty further introduces a solidarity clause (that exists since 2004 as a political declaration) covering the cases of terrorism and natural disasters, a common defence clause (for state aggression against a member country), and broadens the Petersberg tasks to include joint disarmament operations, military advice and assistance, conflict prevention and post-conflict stabilization. It sets out the principles of permanent structured cooperation whereby smaller groups of member-states can undertake more demanding tasks in crisis management, and it establishes the military rapid reaction capability of the battle groups, as well as a European Defence Agency. The battle groups have in effect been in place since 2006, and the political decision to establish the European Defence Agency was taken in 2003. The quick development of crisis management operations has also brought about new structures, notably the Military Staff and the Military Committee (Lisbon Treaty 2007; Howorth 2007: 74–75, 111).

Perception of security and security threats

The UN

The creation of the UN rests on the perception that states are the main threat to each other. The UN's important effort to regulate this was to create the principle that it is up to the UN Security Council to 'determine the existence of any threat to the peace, breach of the peace, or act of aggression' (UN Charter chapter vii, article 39) and then make recommendations or decide what measures need to be taken. Following from this, the UN has a function in legitimizing threats and sanctioning which threats are to be followed by state action. This is an important aspect of the organization, which it has brought with it when adjusting to a changed security environment after the end of the Cold War.

The new security thinking outlined by the former UN Secretary-General Kofi Annan in the report 'In Larger Freedom' emphasizes the fact that no common, shared, security can exist without a reciprocal recognition of threats. In the report, Annan compared security thinking to development thinking. In his opinion, an unprecedented consensus exists on how to advance global economic and social progress. Security, however, is another matter: the problem is that threats are not uniformly agreed on and, therefore, common ground on the obligations of how to counter them cannot be found. The report points out that today's security threats do not only include terrorism, weapons of mass destruction, war and organized crime (as stated in the European Security Strategy) but, also, poverty, fatal infectious diseases and the destruction of the environment. Therefore, collective security today depends on accepting that the threats which each region of the world perceives as most urgent are, in fact, equally so for all. Development, security and human rights reinforce each other, threats are interconnected. All of them need to be taken seriously and all of them need to be efficiently countered. Furthermore, it is understood that no state can protect itself by acting entirely alone and that all states need an equitable, efficient and effective collective security system ('In Larger Freedom' 2005: 7, 24–25, 57). In addition, the UN has increasingly started to emphasize the importance of Human Security, which is a widening of threat perceptions from threats to states to threats to individuals.

The EU

The EU's threat perception is semi-traditional in nature. Territorial integrity is mentioned in the basic treaties. The European Security Strategy states one of the EU's strategic objectives as being to address what are perceived as the main threats: terrorism, the proliferation of weapons of mass destruction, regional conflicts, state failure and organized crime. As pointed out by Kirchner (2007a) only one of these threats – proliferation of weapons of mass destruction – can be characterized as a traditional hard security threat. The pointing out of state failure and organized crime means that the EU's role as an explicit actor in security governance also encompasses what has previously been thought of as domestic policy: internal security. One example of this is its growing role in disaster management where, placed at the EU Commission, the Union has a Civil Protection Mechanism through which both EU member-states and non-member-states can ask for assistance in emergencies. This assistance can be in the form of both personnel and equipment and the mechanism has mainly been used in relation to natural disasters such as earthquakes and floods, but could potentially be used in the case of man-made disasters such as a terrorist attacks (Ekengren *et al.* 2006a).

In December 2007, the European Council decided to review the implementation of the Security Strategy, particularly in the light of lessons learned from ESDP missions, and possibly propose elements to complement it. In the ensuing discussions, threats linked to climate change, energy security and immigration have been prominent.[5] Energy and migration-related security concerns are very different from one member country to another. Increased emphasis on solidarity between the member-states might be discernible, and, with this, the mutual recognition of threats (see above), rather than the more traditional thinking whereby cooperation can only be based on an identical threat perception.

Spectrum of the means used

The UN

Except for its role as a provider of regulation of state behaviour with the purpose of creating global security, the UN also has a number of means to participate in more practical security creating activities, one of these being peacekeeping operations. It was during the Cold War that the activity of 'peacekeeping' (never mentioned in the charter) was developed. Peacekeeping has meant the prevention, containment, and moderation of hostilities using multinational forces (soldiers, police, civilians) in an effort to keep the great powers out of these situations (Karns and Mingst 2004: 127). If juxtaposing UN peace operations before and after the end of the Cold War, they can be characterized as follows:

Findlay (2002: 3–7) distinguishes between peacekeeping (traditional and extended), peace enforcement and enforcement. Traditional peacekeeping then

Table 1.1 UN peace operations

UN peace operations during the Cold War	*UN peace operations after the Cold War*
Peace between two parties in an international conflict already existed	Peace not always present and the conflict was more often intra-state than inter-state
The parties consented to UN peacekeeping	Consent to UN presence may be absent
UN peacekeepers maintained a high degree of impartiality	Impartiality of the UN undermined due to lack of peace agreement and consent
UN peacekeeping forces were unarmed or carrying a minimum of arms for self defence, operations established under chapter vi of the charter	UN forces more heavily armed than before. Some operations undertaken under chapter vii of the charter
Troops mainly contributed by middle and small states, not by great power or permanent members of the Security Council	Great powers contributed with troops

Source: Smith 1994: 201–206.

refers to the use of the military for compliance with peace agreements (e.g. cease fires, buffer zones), whereas expanded peacekeeping refers to a multifunctional operation linked to the entire peace process. Peace enforcement refers to peace operations with the mandate of the Security Council to induce one or more parties to adhere to a peace arrangement using military force if necessary. Enforcement operations are operations mandated by the Security Council (implicitly or explicitly) under chapter vii 'to impose the will of the international community on a single errant state or sub-state party' (2002: 7). Even though these different kinds of peace operations exist simultaneously, there has over time been a shift from traditional peacekeeping towards expanded peacekeeping and peace enforcement.

After the end of the Cold War the changed security situation meant increased calls for the UN to engage not only in peacekeeping, but also in organizing and monitoring elections, monitoring human rights violations, overseeing humanitarian relief and using its enforcement powers. The first optimism of an increased role for the UN diminished by the mid-1990s, partially due to failures in Somalia and Rwanda, and to a financial crisis due to the US unwillingness at that point to pay its contributions. In addition, the importance of other organizations such as the World Bank, the IMF, the WTO, and the G-7 grew with increased economic globalization. This meant that the importance of the UN seemed to be decreasing, even though some of its specialized agencies such as the ILO and WHO became involved. This development has also been part of pressures from within the UN to undertake summits and conferences on areas not traditionally related to security policy such as the environment, human rights, health issues (e.g. HIV/AIDS) and women (Karns and Mingst 2004: 129–131, 277–279).

In fact, the UN has also engaged practically (and not only through summits and conferences) in softer security issues such as humanitarian assistance. This role has grown as more and more conflicts are intra-state rather than inter-state ones. Since 1991 it is OCHA (the Office for the Coordination of Humanitarian Affairs) that is responsible for UN activities in the area of complex emergencies and natural disasters (OCHA 2008a). Its stated mission is to

> Mobilize and coordinate effective and principled humanitarian action in partnership with national and international actors in order to: alleviate human suffering in disasters and emergencies; advocate for the rights of people in need; promote preparedness and prevention; and facilitate sustainable solutions.
>
> (OCHA 2008b: 3)

This office thus works both with co-ordination and relief in emergencies and with more long-term projects aimed at creating safer societies. In this way, it works with the transition from humanitarian aid to development policy.

While a crucial means for the UN in its role in ensuring peace are the peacekeeping forces assigned to its operations by the member-states. Another important means for the UN are other organizations. This could be described as security governance through network or by proxy. The main idea in improving the status of regional organizations is that they should complement the activities of the UN.

'Regional arrangements' are already mentioned in the UN Charter (chapter viii). However, the virtue of regional organizations as an asset for the UN has not been undisputed. Already among the founders of the UN there was a tension between those in favour of globalism and those in favour of regionalism, the British favoured regional spheres of influence, whereas the US advocated global organization (Karns and Mingst 2004: 142–143). The status of regional organizations is defined in the Charter, where they are stated to play an autonomous role in the peaceful settlement of conflicts, but they have to report to the Security Council on their activities (article 53). However, without Security Council authorization they are not allowed to use force independently (Graham and Felício 2005: 8–19; Petman 2000: 47).[6]

Today, the discussion about the role of regional organizations is ongoing and the number of regional actors has significantly grown (to over 20), and their status has gradually improved. Regionalism is considered to support the global order and often to add marked value to the UN (Boutros-Ghali 1992, 1995; Petman 2000). Secretary-General Kofi Annan's report, 'In Larger Freedom', draws partic- ular attention to the African Union's ten-year development plan, but the goal is to sign separate Memoranda of Understanding with several different regional organi- zations. It is intended that those organizations possessing conflict prevention or peacekeeping capabilities would place such capacities in the framework of the United Nations Standby Arrangements System[7] (Petman 2000: 45). Interestingly, the EU and NATO do not consider themselves as regional organizations in this sense of being potentially placed under the authority or control of the UN. Yet, they would obviously be the most effective ones when it comes to the capacities that the UN needs (Ojanen 2005).

The EU

As stated above, the EU was not an explicit security actor from the start; it used other policy means, such as economic policy, to create security among its member- states. This means that many of the means for security governance that the Union has are of a non-military character (cf. Kirchner and Sperling 2007). Some of these means are part of the EU Commission's activities. One actor here is the EU Com- mission's humanitarian aid department DG ECHO, which was set up in 1992 and has since then offered assistance in crises all over the world. Its activities include both acute assistance, where it co-operates with the UN and NGO's in delivering, for example, food and equipment such as field hospitals, as well as long-term assist- ance, for example mine clearance expertise. There exist a number of long-term EU policies that have security governance consequences, notably enlargement and the European Neighbourhood Policy. These policies build on the tradition of economic and structural integration that traditionally have been part of the EU enlargement process. Enlargement of the Union has been strategically used to create stability and security (Ekengren 2007) and therefore such measures can be seen as more indirect means of security governance.

Direct security governance by the EU is undertaken under the name of European Security and Defence Policy (ESDP). As mentioned above, the European Union started, in 2003, to engage in what in the UN system is called peace operations, but what in the EU called civilian and military crisis management. Some five years after the missions started, the Union has been engaged in just over 20 missions, out of which eight have been military or have had military components. Civilian operations include rule of law missions, monitoring missions and security sector reform missions. In the rule of law missions, police officers are an important category of personnel that have been sent out (Kirchner and Sperling 2007; Howorth 2007).[8]

As shown in this brief overview of the EU's means in security governance, the Union indeed has a broad spectrum of means and resembles the UN. However, this often-cited unique capability equally often brings problems of coherence to the surface. Many of the novelties that will be introduced if the Lisbon Treaty comes into effect are efforts to relieve some of the problems of coherence. The EU is in no way a unitary actor in security governance and sometimes a number of different EU actors are present in the same country, but without necessarily working together.

Security-linked norm-creation

The UN

The UN's character as a regulative security organization is shown in a wide variety of basic rules about states and their behaviour in international society; from self-determination to the creation of the International Criminal Court. The most important norm to be considered here is that both the use of force and the threat of force are forbidden in international relations. However, there are two notable exceptions: self-defence and force mandated by the UN Security Council. Article 51 of the Charter guarantees the right to self-defence. Self-defence has become the most often used and the most flexibly interpreted justification for the use of military force over the past five decades. According to Graham and Felício, this was not the intention of the Charter; nor does it strengthen the collective security system. Self-defence is not very transparent and it does not always end when the Security Council has decided to take action. Some view that self-defence can now be global in nature and that it also includes pre-emptive strikes (Graham and Felício 2005: 26–28). Preventive, pre-emptive and protective use of force are new concepts by which one justifies resorting to the use of force. They are, however, not fully established concepts and have therefore caused much discord.

The principles of use of force are continuously being discussed in the UN. The Draft Outcome Document of the High-Level Plenary Meeting of the General Assembly, 14–16 September 2005, for example stated that discussion on the principles of the use of force must continue.[9] In the Secretary-General's report 'In Larger Freedom' from 2005 it was stated that the Security Council should adopt a Resolution on the principles it follows when it decides on authorizing the use of force. Force should be sufficient yet reasonable. Specifically, it was stated that one should weigh the seriousness of the threat; evaluate whether means short of the use of force might plausibly succeed in stopping the threat; whether the military option is proportional to the threat at hand; and whether there is a reasonable chance of success ('In Larger Freedom' 2005: 33, 58; Ojanen 2007).

If one thinks that the UN has a monopoly on the legitimate use of force in international affairs as, according to Weber, the state does in society, one could think that the UN also has an obligation to use force whenever it is needed. The Secretary-General has earlier on emphasized that the Security Council indeed has the necessary capability and the full authority to use military force, also preventively ('In Larger Freedom' 2005*)*. This has led to a discussion of humanitarian interventions where some legal realists have used an extensive interpretation of article 39 to legitimize interventions (Holzgrefe 2003).

There has also been a discussion about interventions with military means that do not necessarily need the authorization of the Security Council, sometimes referred to as the 'responsibility to protect' (Holzgrefe and Keohane 2003; Engdahl and Hellman 2007; ICISS 2001). This could be seen as a reaction both to the weaknesses of the present organizational structure, the lameness of the Security Council referred to above, and, as mentioned above, to a widened threat perception. Important statements by the UN high level panel has emphasized the responsibility to protect, moving the focus away from the security of the state in international relations towards the safety of the individual, including the individual's status in relation to the state (Prins 2005: 387). Such a threat perception affects the view on states' internal policies, also indicating a changed view on state sovereignty.

The EU

The European Security Strategy (ESS) might be seen as implying EU responsibility not only for security, but also for existing international norms. The EU almost assumes the role of a watchdog that sees to it that all obey international norms: 'We ... must therefore be ready to act when their rules are broken' (ESS; see also Ojanen 2006.). This means that the EU as an organization puts itself in a global security governance system and it thus becomes logical to speak in favour of 'effective multilateralism' as is done in the Security Strategy. In addition, so far the use of force has been closely knit to the UN and undertaken under its mandate or at its request. In this way, multilateralism becomes part of security governance – a means to pursue that goal. There is an ongoing discussion in the literature on whether a European strategic culture exists and what it is or should be like (see, for example, Engelbrekt and Hallenberg (eds) 2008; Biscop 2005). Howorth (2007) sees signs of a new and different strategic culture being put together in the EU – at least when compared to that of its member-states. The EU policy of intervention, or as Howorth puts it, the EU's overseas missions, would obviously be a case in which this strategy becomes visible.

Even though the strategic nature of the EU can and has been debated, the Union has developed what Charillon (2004: 261) calls an 'interventionism *à la européenne'*. It is a policy of non-military intervention in the near abroad that helps it pursue its interests, exert power and shape new political surroundings, even without any well-defined doctrines. Students of EU foreign, security and defence policy have found signs of an emerging EU profile analysed as mainly 'civilian', 'normative' or 'positive' (Sjursen 2004; Manners 2002; Biscop 2005). These categorizations all focus on civilian means that the Union has that were discussed in the previous section.

In addition, the EU influences ideas of what constitutes a modern state and how such a state should behave. These ideas are fundamental for security governance. As pointed out by Rosamond (2005: 470–472), many of the EU's external relations shape conceptions of the 'normal' in international politics. The EU is not an actor in the conventional sense, but 'seeks to wrestle for a form of agency, bound by prevailing ideational structures that dictate what an actor should be'. One example here is the power to oppose the death penalty, shown by Manners (2002). Its fields of activity have also seen good possibilities for promoting human security rather than traditional state security, strengthening the position of the individual and of human rights. That the EU explicitly should have such a human security doctrine has been proposed by a group of researchers led by Mary Kaldor in a report to the High Representative of the Common Foreign and Security Policy (*A Human Security Doctrine for Europe*, see also *A European Way of Security*). As pointed out by Sjursen (2004: 67), for an entity like the European Union, the answer to the question of *whose* security one is talking about is no longer self-evidently the state.

The EU's normative power and influence in such a setting as the UN is, however, coming under increasing criticism. The EU's influence is diminishing instead of growing, and it is losing political credibility in the changed international context. European positions are less followed in, for example, human rights, and the EU, in order to regain influence, should invest considerably more in constructing broad shifting coalitions (Gowan and Brantner 2008).

Inclusion and exclusion

The UN

Starting off with 51 members in 1945, the membership has gradually expanded and since 2006 the organization has 192 members. According to the UN Charter, (article 4, chapter 2) membership is open to all 'peace-loving states' accepting the obligations of the charter and being judged as being able and willing to carry out the obligations. New members are recommended by the Security Council and decided by the General Assembly. As stated in the introduction, becoming a member of the UN is an important part of becoming a state. One example of this is the UN Charter's endorsement of the principle of self-determination for colonial peoples and its member-states' support to former colonies in their liberation process (Karns and Mingst 2004: 128–129).

As an organization, the UN thus aims at universal membership even though this sometimes creates difficulties because of the heterogeneity among its member-states. This heterogeneity seems to have increased when the general security situation has changed (for example after the end of the Cold War) and the organization has taken on more activities beyond creating peace between states. Bailes has identified an 'agenda gap' (Bailes 2005) between (poorer) southern and (richer) northern member countries of the UN. The South has been hit by armed conflict and other forms of physical force, as well as human security challenges such as poverty, hunger, disease and natural disasters; while the North has been concentrating on its own issues (the wars and conflicts in the Balkans), and later on terrorism and asymmetrical threats. Bailes states that this development widens the gap: smaller players (and failed states) are sometimes no longer seen as people to be helped, but as a source of deadly threat. In this way different threat perceptions within the UN might create dynamics of exclusion even though the organization itself rests on an inclusive dynamic. This divisive legacy needs, in her view, to be overcome (Bailes 2005: 17, 19).

The EU

The EU on the other hand is built on a divisive legacy: some states are members and some are not. Becoming an EU member includes a thorough revision of domestic laws and political systems related to EU policies, especially those regarding the EU's internal market. Exclusion through specific and wide-ranging membership criteria implies more homogeneity among the members. However, the difference between EU members and non-members does not mean that non-EU members are excluded from EU security governance. Except for the direct governance efforts in the form of crisis management missions mentioned above, the EU has also started to develop direct management of its borders. Especially organized crime and terrorism, two problems that make the control of the external border a common task for the EU given that the Schengen *aquis* eliminates the control of borders between EU member-states (Kirchner and Sperling 2007: 130, 135). The 'European model of integrated border management' is a model based on the idea that border management does not start or end at the border, but that measures also need to be taken elsewhere (Laitinen 2008). The EU established an agency in 2004, Frontex (The European Agency for the Management of Operational Cooperation at the External Borders of the Member-states of the European Union), this agency is one of the actors supposed to implement the model of managing the borders. One task of the EU agency is to co-ordinate rapid frontier intervention groups that the member-states in 2007 agreed on committing to the EU in case a member-state has an urgent crisis at the external border of the Union. In addition, 'governance' extends beyond the organization's members through neighbourhood policy, enlargement policy, and through normative power. Rosamond (2005) observes that the EU's external activity is highly discursive, aspirational, declaratory, and full of positioning statements. In this way, EU policy is inclusive of non-member-states. Here, candidate countries have a special situation because they are expected to abide by a large amount of EU hard and soft law. This means that candidate countries are included in rules and norm systems of the Union before becoming official members.

The EU, being exclusive, appeals to the excluded. It is attractive to neighbouring states that apply for candidacy. It has also been attractive within the UN system as a model for a group of countries that would usually vote with it (the 'liberal internationalists', as Gowan and Brantner 2008 call them), which also shows its power of norm creation.

Supranational character

The UN

The UN has no supranational character but rests on traditional intergovernmental relations where the only step away from the norm of 'one state – one vote' is the special status of the permanent members of the Security Council, who have been given a stronger influence on the organization than other member-states. In this way, the UN rests on old world structures that do not change the nature of the state. This also means that the organization and its activities are relatively difficult to change, and some states and groups of states (for example India and the EU) that are more influential in world politics now than at the end of the Second World War, have difficulties in acting according to their liking in the organization. As mentioned above, there is an ongoing discussion of reforming the UN including the composition of the Security Council. An important aspect of this debate, alongside the enlargement of the Council, is the status of possible new permanent members and the question of whether they, or any member, should have the right of veto in the Security Council (Karns and Mingst 2004: 139–142).

The EU

Despite the fact that policy areas that are part of 'traditional' EU policy are not directly related to security, there are peculiar features of the integration process, of its participants and of outcomes that make the EU fundamentally different from other international organizations. These include supranational features such as hard lawmaking, the supranational European Commission, the supra- (or trans) national European Parliament and European interest groups. According to Ortega (2007: 95), these internal factors and structural processes, together with the enlargement process, shape the Union's ability to contribute to global order. In particular, however, the EU makes the 'state' different, not only in the sense that it reduces its autonomy in economic and trade policy, but also in the sense that its development as a direct actor in security governance means that policy areas such as foreign and security policy, which traditionally have been very state-centred, are no longer a concern for the states independently. The obvious question that has followed is whether the EU should have a seat of its own in the Security Council, replacing or complementing that of two of its member-states.

Conclusion: interconnecting multilateralisms

An important factor when it comes to the two organizations' perception of security and security threats is their different history of relating to security. Whereas the UN builds on explicitly increasing security between all states in the world, the EU builds on implicitly increasing security between its member-states. This has also had consequences for the organizations' threat perceptions. The threat perceptions partially overlap: terrorism, weapons of mass destruction, war, organized crime and environmental issues are stated by both organizations. In addition, the UN has a more heterogeneous membership, with the resulting emphasis on, for example, poverty and fatal infectious diseases. The EU's engagement in security in states other than its own member-states, is mirrored in the organization's mentioning of state failure and regional conflicts as threats.

When it comes to the means used to create security governance, the two organizations have moved towards each other since the end of the Cold War. As has been shown here, the EU has developed its ability in security governance in two ways: both by becoming a direct actor in security governance internally among the Union's member-states, and by becoming a direct and indirect actor in security governance externally of the Union. In this way, it can be said to have moved from being a structure indirectly enabling security governance towards an actor explicitly exercising security governance. The UN, on the other hand, has developed from being a direct actor in external security governance and moved towards exercising both indirect and direct internal security governance. In terms of policy development this means that the EU has started to develop policies that are directly related to security, whereas the UN has started to develop policies that are more indirectly related to security. This is illustrated in Figure 1.1 below.

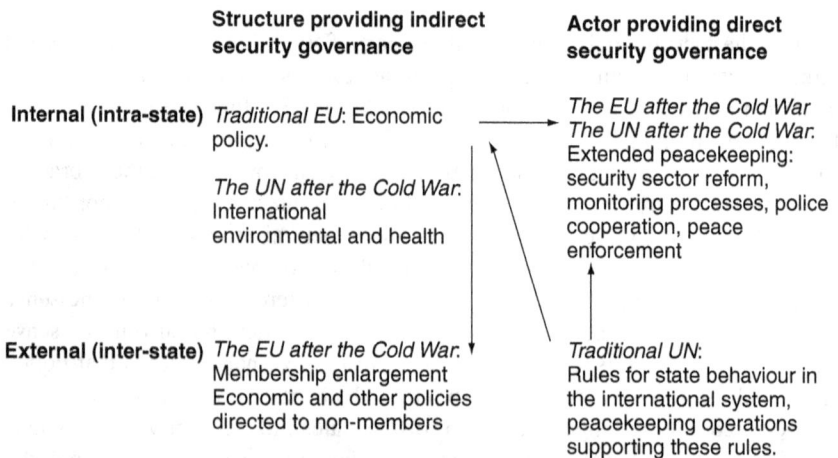

Figure 1.1 Essential characteristics of UN and EU security governance.

In this way, while UN operations were initially dominated by the military profession, EU operations were initially dominated by the police profession; and whereas the EU has increased its capacity to undertake military operations, the UN has increased its capacity to undertake civilian operations. Going back to Sperling's different policies of governance, it therefore becomes possible to conclude that both organizations these days have institution-building and conflict resolution functions, and that their instruments are persuasive in both these contexts, but only coercive when it comes to conflict resolution. This means that their main instruments are prevention and assurance, while EU emphasis originally was on the former and UN emphasis originally on the latter. In addition, even though both organizations have the capacity to exercise compellence, the EU has so far only done so mandated by the UN.

Looking at the security-linked norm creation of the two organizations, the UN is a strong provider of norms for state behaviour in the international system. However, as has been shown here it does not always manage to influence states to adhere to the rules of the organization. It seems that EU's normative power is strongest when it comes to norms of what constitutes a state and what the state–citizenship relationship should look like. In addition, the security-linked norms are one aspect of governance where the two organizations complement each other, and their governance systems are closely interconnected. When it comes to the security-linked norms, the historical time-line between the two organizations become evident. In this respect the EU rests its activities upon the norms already created by the UN, and it is very clear in stating its support of the UN's norms. This influence on both member-states and non-member-states is due to its character as a political union and its possibilities to offer membership and special policies to neighbouring countries. This possibility is obviously related to the next two points of comparison: that of inclusion and exclusion and the supranational character. Because of the fact that the EU is smaller and more homogenous than the UN, and its member-states are more tightly knit together, the issue of (non-) membership is more important and affects members and non-members more in the EU than in the UN. This is also related to the EU's supranational character where it not only means that member-states in the EU have less autonomy in international politics, but also that the organization has a greater possibility (i.e. more means) of pursuing its own policy towards non-members.

Finally, what are the modes of governance of these two organizations? Are they part of one system of security governance or of two? On the level of statements, there is one system, the UN system, to which the EU contributes but the EU also wants a certain degree of autonomy. This may create tension and there are significant complexities in the comparison between the two organizations. The EU's mode of governance could thus be characterized as ensuring peace internally between its member-states and regionally through influence on nearby outsiders, but also globally through interventions of different kinds. The UN's mode of governance is universal, based on its exclusive authority to decide on the use of force. Both organizations consist of and constitute their member-states: both make a state a state (albeit a different kind of a state).

Yet, there are also differences between the organizations – not only the obvious one between regional and global membership. One difference is that the EU changes constantly (both its inner constitution and enlargement), while the UN does not. Another is that, whereas the UN sets the structure for the international system, the EU seems to be able to govern more as a structure that affects members' internal policy, which can have a more indirect effect on security. As has been shown here, the two organizations in their practice of security governance seem to have become closer to each other, and this raises the issue of the relationship between these organizations. The EU and the UN increasingly interact as international agents (Ojanen 2006). The relationship between the two is not new, but their links have been intensifying since the early 2000s as a result of the EU's development and its active role in strengthening its links to the UN (Tardy 2005: 54). In general terms, one can say that the UN serves as a legality or legitimacy provider for the EU, particularly when operating outside Europe. The EU needs the UN as both the main partner and the main arena for fostering global governance. Thus, the EU needs the UN, but the need is mutual: also the UN needs the EU. The EU becomes a burden-sharing partner (particularly in crisis management in demanding conditions), and has also sometimes been seen to help the UN to manage or counterbalance American power (Novosseloff 2004: 7, 15; Eide 2004: 3).

What they can do together is to influence security-related thinking in a more profound way. As both can be seen to aim at a threat perception that is mutual rather than shared, this may also be the most important task of both organizations: to create communality of interpretation in what is meant by security and what is allowable in the name of security (Ojanen 2006: 40). One example of this is a common problem for the two organizations: the defence of the status of non-state actors. The UN and the EU act together in the same manner as sovereign states act in concert against non-state actors. A shared security requires that states are both bypassed and engaged. The need for cooperation in the world of non-state (individuals, MNC or NGO) and state actors is accentuated (Ortega 2007).

In the end, the interlinked modes of governance of the two organizations analysed illustrate a phenomenon that can be characterized as interconnected multilateralism. Building on the idea of mutual recognition of threats as a mode of governance, these two organizations may be seen as representing an alternative to traditional security actors, notably states and military alliances. Yet, this particular mode of governance might be under considerable strain if the new emerging powers in the world are in favour of other, more traditional, modes and are sceptical of the virtues of multilateralism as such.

Notes

1 Having lost its traditional threat or enemy at the end of the Cold War, NATO has worked to find a new role, discussing, for instance, whether combating drug trafficking or piracy is an essential task of the alliance.

2 As a minimum, the citizens' security and health in cases of natural disasters, pandemia and the like, but eventually the understanding may be extended to the security of citizens, territorial integrity, energy supplies, and similar issues.

3 The Petersberg tasks comprise humanitarian and rescue tasks, peacekeeping tasks and tasks of combat forces in crisis management, including peacemaking.

4 *A Secure Europe in a Better World.* European Security Strategy. Brussels, 12 December 2003.

5 A document that 'updates' the strategy in this sense is due in December 2008.

6 Article 51 is applied to the defence alliances (NATO and the WEU). In other words, they have no reporting obligation and the Security Council does not control them (Petman 2000: 43).

7 UNSAS, United Nations Standby Arrangements System. Online, available at: www.un.org/ Depts/dpko/milad/fgs2/unsas_files/sba.htm (accessed 1 December 2008).

8 These missions are 'civilian' as opposed to 'military', but the personnel sometimes still have uniform and arms, which is not necessarily conceived as 'civilian' by other civilian actors such as NGOs, or, for that matter, police officers themselves.

9 The Draft Outcome Document of the High-Level Plenary Meeting of the General Assembly, 14–16 September 2005, states that discussion on the principles of the use of force must continue. Draft Outcome Document of 3 June 2005. Online, available at: www.un.org (p. 12).

2 NATO's institutional decline in post-Cold War security governance

Rafael Biermann[1]

Since 9/11 and the Iraq war, the post-Cold War debate on the future of NATO has taken a turn.[2] The first debate, until the mid-1990s, was dominated by a forceful constructivist and neoliberal assault on neorealism's premature claim that NATO, lacking its former opponent, would dissolve.[3] Alliance theory obviously needed considerable refinement. There was an inconsistent twist in this debate, though. Realists who during the Cold War had unduly privileged system stability and were thus rightfully criticized for having missed the ideational, normative and domestic level indicators of change as the Soviet Empire began to crumble (Lebow and Risse-Kappen 1995) now themselves became the heralds of change, forecasting NATO's demise. Conversely, constructivists who were so adroit (at least in hindsight) in explaining the change of 1989–90 now began to privilege continuity, namely the "surprising persistence" of NATO (Duffield 1994–5: 764). Their basic guiding question was: Why did NATO survive?

By the mid-1990s, NATO had embarked on Eastern enlargement, new partnership arrangements and what was then called out-of-area operations. The alliance was proactively embracing multiple new *raisons d'être* that seemed to belie all doomsday scenarios. Constructivists and neoliberals forwarded a plethora of explanations for NATO's persistence: the adaptability of the general assets of this multipurpose alliance (Wallander 2000); the transformation into an inclusive, risk-oriented security management organization (Wallander and Keohane 1999); the organizational self-interest of NATO's bureaucracy; the high transaction costs of creating a new institution and the broad domestic support for the alliance (McCalla 1996); and the growth of a Deutschian community of liberal democratic norms and values (Risse-Kappen 1995a). The latter explanation's focus on socialization, collective bonds and a sense of common history is still prevalent in theory-driven analyses after Iraq (Gheciu 2005; Risse 2004; Sjursen 2004).

Valid as these arguments were, they were overstated. Indicators of change were underrated; the status quo was too easily projected into the future. In hindsight, the entire thrust of the first debate seems questionable. Indeed, the remaining skeptics who anticipated increasing policy disagreements, warning of a challenge to "the stability of the entire NATO edifice" (Duke 1994: 188), proved themselves right less than a decade later when the Iraq war split the alliance. Most observers agree that NATO is no longer "vibrant…, robust and healthy" (McCalla 1996: 446, 454). The alliance has slid into the "gravest crisis of its history" (Dembinski 2005b: 1).

It is, however, the future projection of current trends that is in dispute. Is this crisis a temporary one, like so many NATO has mastered in its history, or does it have a different quality? Some argue that NATO has already crossed the "Rubicon" and is "more or less irrelevant" (Cox 2005: 208, 224). Others insist that the transatlantic security community is still "alive and well" (Pouliot 2006: 119). The polling data can be interpreted both ways.[4] Those seeing the glass half full argue that NATO's declining support is still along the lines of former alliance crises. After each crisis, European attitudes rebounded. Optimists might also argue that appreciation of NATO was always a function of overall transatlantic relations, and that prospects for NATO might improve after the Bush presidency.[5]

Skeptics can argue that after the Iraq war public opinion did not rebound. Those who assumed that a "new transatlantic consensus could swiftly be re-established" proved too optimistic (Moravcsik 2003: 89). Overall, only 53 percent of Europeans see NATO still as "essential" (Transatlantic Trends 2007: 16). Skeptics might also point to quite dramatic downturns in public opinion of traditional NATO advocates. In 2007 only 56 percent of Britons perceived NATO still as "essential," compared to 76 percent in 2002; previously the historic low was 65 percent (Ziegler 1998: 17). In the US, likewise, 56 percent still see NATO as "essential," 30 percent not (2002 figures, Worldviews 2002: 28). In Germany the drop was from 74 percent to 55 percent – also a historic low (Sinnott 1997: 11). In Italy support for NATO fell from 68 percent to 52 percent and in Poland from 64 percent to 48 percent, both in 2006 (Transatlantic Trends 2006: 7). In Turkey the decline was even down to 35 percent (Transatlantic Trends 2007: 22).

Uncertainty is widespread. For many, the alliance is increasingly obsolete, appearing to some as a relic from a period gladly overcome, to others as a military instrument of negligible value in today's security environment. Will we finally observe the demise of the alliance, as forecast by Stephen Walt and others? Was it just the staying power accumulated during four decades of socialization which prevented NATO from falling apart sooner? How relevant is NATO in the new security environment?

This chapter explores the advantages of applying a security governance lens to answer these questions. It aspires to complement rather than to substitute for other lenses which have been applied to analyze the changes in Euro-Atlantic security following the end of the Cold War, including organizational and network theory (Biermann 2008a; Krahmann 2005a). Security governance is still at an early stage of theory building. Findings are quite disparate because concep-tualizations differ strongly (Kirchner and Sperling 2007; Krahmann 2003; Webber *et al.* 2004; Webber 2007). This chapter highlights those aspects that are of specific explanatory value for one single actor, NATO, in the web of actors constituting Euro–Atlantic security governance today.

I build on the theoretical framework James A. Sperling has presented in the introduction to this volume. My starting-point is a conceptualization of institutional relevance as perceived by major member-states. This relevance is determined by exogenous (external environment) and endogenous variables (within the institution). The charm of Sperling's approach is that it does not only focus on the exogenous variables the governance literature usually discusses, but also includes domestic-level variables which impact on intra-institutional affairs.

The main argument of this chapter is that NATO is experiencing a period of relative institutional decline. Short-term effects like the Bush presidency or Iraq should not obscure the *structural* nature of this decline. It is caused by the fall of the Berlin Wall (11/9) and accelerated by 9/11. Even though NATO managed to gain new legitimacy by shifting its institutional purpose to conflict resolution, enlargement and partnership, four tectonic shifts decrease the relevance of the alliance for its core members: first, a process of transatlantic decoupling since the Soviet threat dissipated; second, the rise of European actorness in security and defense, challenging NATO's primacy in its new core competences; third, the multiplication of security providers which turned NATO into an instrument of choice for regional and global security governance; and fourth, America's gradual de-prioritization of the alliance as security cultures on both sides of the Atlantic move apart. These shifts had already unfolded in the 1990s. The Bush presidency both epitomized these shifts in the extreme and deflected attention from their structural quality. The shifts cumulate to reduce the relevance of NATO both for the US and for European governments, though to varying degrees. Reversing this vector is exceedingly difficult.

The chapter has three sections: the first introduces a concept of institutional relevance and inserts a security governance perspective into this framework. The second section analyzes NATO's relevance in post-Cold War security governance, discussing the four tectonic shifts outlined above. The third section draws conclusions for the security governance concept in general and NATO's relevance in particular.

Institutional relevance

It is a myth that institutions "never die." After all, their mortality rate is "surprisingly high" – one third of all international organizations were dissolved between 1981 and 1992 alone, the Warsaw Pact and Comecon being the most prominent ones (Shanks *et al.* 1996: 594). Indeed, the number of "dissolved or apparently inactive" intergovernmental organizations worldwide has been rising dramatically since the late 1970s, up to 671 in 2005 (*Yearbook of International Organizations 2006/07*: 33, 37, 39). However, not all institutions are dissolved or deactivated. Reducing the analysis to the extreme poles of "prosper or die," as the first debate on NATO's survival after the Cold War did, is simplistic and misleading; there is much in-between. This is where NATO comes in today.

We actually know very little as to why and how institutions decline. Dying or marginalized institutions are not very attractive objects of study. Creation and change of institutions has received far more attention (McCalla 1996: 461). Still, identifying indicators, i.e. early signals of decline might help us to determine where institutions "stand" in their life cycle and, policy-wise, what to do about it. Dissolution or deactivation is mostly preceded by a period of decline.

I argue that the life cycle of an institution is determined by its relevance. So far, institutional relevance has not been conceptualized to my knowledge. This chapter starts from four assumptions derived from institutionalism. First, institutional relevance is one of degree, ranging from low to high, and it is task-related, varying across issues. For NATO, we have to look at "old" functions (such as collective defense) and new ones (such as crisis management). We have to determine its relevance both in European and global governance. Also, we consider the totality of security tasks NATO members face today: which ones are assigned to NATO, which ones are not?

Second, relevance is perceptional (Hurd 1999: 381). Member-states, representatives of international bureaucracies and populations often disagree as to the relevance of an organization. Because of the primary delegation authority of member-states, we actually look at NATO from the standpoint of its major members, focusing particularly on the American and the (as much as possible aggregate) European perspective. It is the cost–benefit calculus of these members which drives the delegation of mandates, tasks and resources to NATO (Hawkins *et al.* 2006).

Third, institutional relevance fluctuates over time. The UN Security Council lost relevance in 1947–8 when the emerging Cold War posed "West" and "East" against one another; its paralysis was temporarily overcome after 1989. Decline can be reversed; the "revitalization" of the Western European Union in 1984 is an example (Rees 1998). Thus, signals of decline should not be easily projected into the future. We should not underestimate the "adaptability" of institutions (Wallander *et al.* 1999: 12).

Fourth, more important than snapshots are trends, especially if they are sustained by long-term structural factors that resist political control. In the timeframe we are looking at, the system shocks of 11/9 and 9/11 triggered structural change in security cultures and security governance, which deeply impacted on NATO's relevance. However, determining trends requires fixing a point of reference in time to allow for comparison. The reference point here is NATO's "centrality" in European security up to 1989 (Wallander *et al.* 1999: 13).

What are meaningful indicators of decline? Some can be derived from the history of dissolved or deactivated institutions so far. First, major members leaving an organization; this happened when Britain and Denmark (1973), Portugal (1986), Austria, Sweden and Finland (all 1995) joined the EU and left the European Free Trade Association (EFTA). Second, institutional preferences shifting to other institutions; this occurred when the democratizing countries of Central Eastern Europe since 1989 turned towards the EU and NATO and away from Comecon and the Warsaw Pact. Third, the willingness of member-states to sideline an institution by duplicating some of its major institutional functions; this took place when NATO was created and effectively replaced the Brussels Treaty Organization. Fourth, the non-use of a focal organization for purposes it is designed for, such as of the UN Security Council for mandating both NATO's air campaign in Kosovo 1999 and the Iraq war 2003.

Institutional decline is motivated by three major factors: the loss of legitimacy, utility, and cohesiveness. International organizations lose relevance if their legitimacy wanes, if their usefulness as instruments to further member-state interests is in doubt and if the unity of purpose among member-states erodes. As a consequence, institutional loyalty wanes and preferences shift to other security providers.

For our purposes, it is most important to determine which variables produce declining institutional legitimacy, utility, and cohesiveness. We need to consider exogenous and endogenous variables. Both changes in the environment of institutions and changes within the member-states impact on intra-organizational affairs (Wallander and Keohane 1999: 29). I do not argue that the following variables are exhaustive. However, they are pivotal determinants of the relevance of security institutions and can help to measure NATO's post-Cold War relevance.

Exogenous variables: embeddedness and threat perceptions

The security governance lens is particularly helpful to approach the exogenous variables. Taking primarily a system perspective, it looks at the interaction of the plethora of security providers we find today, ranging from international governmental to non-governmental organizations and private security companies (see the definition in Webber *et al.* 2004: 8). NATO's relevance in this multi-actor setting is relative. Its network position is defined by its embeddedness (Gulati and Gargiulo 1999: 1448). This relational profile has become part of its corporate identity and shapes its policy output (Biermann 2008a). We have to assess NATO's relevance from this system perspective, for example by looking at the rise of rival institutions such as the European Security and Defense Policy (ESDP) and their impact on NATO.

Sperling's (Introduction, this volume) primary system-level variable is threat perceptions. Shifting sources and targets of threat over time strongly shape the relevance of actors such as NATO, particularly their legitimacy and utility. As threat perceptions evolve, security agendas shift. Some tasks assume prominence, others recede. Since individual security providers are designed to meet specific threats, their relative relevance varies accordingly. Adaptation is the means to remain relevant.

Endogenous variables: "Westphalianness"

Traditionally, the security governance literature hardly considers domestic-level variables. Sperling's approach is different. He takes a bottom-up approach, arguing that security governance systems are largely determined by state preferences which are derived from their security cultures, particularly their degree of "Westphalianness." Actors with Westphalian identities tend to cling to Westphalian security systems, whereas actors turning post-Westphalian favor post-Westphalian security systems. This explains much of the difference we see today in regional security governance, for example comparing Western Europe and the Balkans, the Caucasus or the Middle East.

Thus, in order to understand security governance systems, we need to look at the Westphalian profile of their constituent parts (Biersteker 2005; Higgott 2005; Wallace 1999). The "Westphalianness" of states and institutions can be measured along several dimensions: in how far actors have moved from exclusive to inclusive images of Self and Other; in how far they have moved from a focus on territorial integrity, borders and sovereignty to positively identifying with pooled sovereignty, interdependence and integration, including the primacy of international law; in how far they have moved from a preoccupation with national security to the idea of an "international society" (Bull 1995); and in how far norms have shifted from coercive, hard-power to persuasive, soft power approaches. These are ideal-types. In reality, we find a "continuum bounded by the Westphalian and post-Westphalian forms" (Sperling, Introduction, this volume). Actors can be located on this continuum. Sperling introduced three types: Westphalian, late-Westphalian, and post-Westphalian.[6]

Security institutions are composite actors. The "Westphalianness" of each member may vary along the entire spectrum from Westphalian to post-Westphalian. When basic identities are in harmony, security communities form and thrive. When they diverge, cohesiveness suffers, as security communities rest on the "we-feeling" (Anderson 2006) among their members. To a large extent, this depends on like-mindedness in terms of identities and interests. The amount to which members of a security institution adhere to the classical attributes of the Westphalian state is one crucial indicator of their like-mindedness. Thus, this domestic-level variable strongly shapes member-state interaction on the intra-organizational level.

Based on this analytical framework, we will now identify the major causal factors impacting on NATO's relevance in the post-Cold War era. Five structural shifts will be assessed: NATO's shift to conflict resolution and partnership; transatlantic decoupling; European "emancipation" via the ESDP; the multiplication of security providers; and the US de-prioritization of NATO.

NATO's post-Cold War relevance

The shift to conflict resolution and partnership

NATO was the lynchpin organization of the collective defense system which dominated the Cold War. According to Sperling (Introduction, this volume), this is one form of security governance, besides collective security, Westphalian security community, and post-Westphalian security community systems.[7] In collective defense systems, the security referent is an identifiable enemy outside the group; the mechanisms for conflict management are defense, deterrence and balancing, and the strong security dilemma motivates in-group amity and out-group enmity.

This obviously captures NATO's Cold War reality. NATO started out as an exclusive alliance. The external security dilemma triggered its very existence.

Threat perceptions were intense and NATO was perceived as irreplaceable. However, threat perceptions oscillated during the Cold War. Since the Harmel Report of 1967, NATO began to adopt a more persuasive approach based on détente, arms control and confidence-building. This intensified once the "Gorbachev factor" unfolded. European security governance became more inclusive, NATO increasingly hybrid.

1989–90 was a system shock whose impact unfolded only over time. System shocks have an epicenter where change is most profound and they send shock-waves of decreasing intensity across the international system. The Soviet Union was the epicenter of 1989–90; the shock waves overturned the regimes in Central Eastern Europe, made German unification possible and transformed bipolarity into unipolarity. The effect on well-established Western institutions like NATO, however, was uncertain. After all, the "West" witnessed the "triumph of liberal capitalism"[8] – and it seemed that "hanging tough paid off" (Gaddis 1989). George H. W. Bush had reason to "dance on the Wall." Why should NATO change? 1989–90 was a "rectifying revolution" (Habermas); a "long and tragic digression that was the Communist illusion"[9] finally came to an end. "Back to Europe" (Havel) was its leitmotiv, and those advocating a "third path" were marginalized.

However, most obviously NATO's core article 5 lost its immediate relevance. The basic rationale for NATO's creation in 1949 vanished. European security governance was moving from collective defense to a new, far more inclusive and cooperative form of governance. The joint American–Soviet effort to drive Iraqi forces out of Kuwait in January 1991 nurtured hopes for the realization of the "four policemen" concept of collective security that Roosevelt had envisioned in 1945. NATO appeared obsolete, particularly among Germans. In spring 1990, only 16 percent of them still favored NATO's continuing existence, 54 percent favored the creation of a new European security system, 20 percent opted for neutrality and 49 percent advocated a US troop withdrawal from Germany (Biermann 1997: 483–484).[10] The need to re-legitimize NATO was obvious.

The alliance reacted in three consecutive steps, corresponding to organizational theory: first, denial of a need to change; then affirmation of that need as the legitimacy crisis unfolded; finally adaptation "to expand the base of support" (McCalla 1996: 458). The attainment of NATO membership for united Germany consolidated NATO at a critical juncture. Equally as important was the fact that the strong aspirations of all the Central European countries to join NATO pointed to its continuing attractiveness. Perceptions in Western and Eastern Europe on NATO's relevance sharply diverged, due to different geopolitics and historical experience. Ironically, it was NATO's collective defense function that drew countries like Poland or the Baltic states into NATO. The agonizing and prolonged debates on the pros and cons of enlargement and NATO's "out-of-area" role in Bosnia, coupled with a lack of US leadership until 1994, demonstrated how much NATO's entire *raison d'être* was in doubt.

NATO's hybrid nature increased in the process of transformation. Two new institutional purposes moved up front: conflict resolution and partnership. As to conflict resolution, the shift was strongly motivated by Senator R. Lugar's warning that the alliance would either go "out of area or out of business." After much wavering and bickering, it was the alliance which ended "ethnic cleansing" both in Bosnia and in Kosovo. The instruments were both compellence (the NATO air campaigns in Bosnia 1995 and in Kosovo 1999) and assurance (post-conflict peace building in Bosnia and Kosovo, later also in Macedonia).

The "new NATO," or NATO III in Helga Haftendorn's (2002) count, began to pursue broader milieu goals. The alliance multiplied its network of cooperation. NATO staff became deeply involved in all kinds of partnership activities, centering on a continuously expanded Partnership of Peace program. The rationale was, first, to prepare Central Eastern Europe for membership through a process of norm diffusion which focused on civil control of the military; second, to stabilize those in the neighborhood not willing or able to join NATO; and third, to build up the capacities of partners and future members to effectively contribute to NATO's peace operations. Thus, the alliance assumed security management functions of an inclusive, risk-oriented nature (Keohane and Wallander 1999: 45).

With this new *raison d'être*, the first post-Cold War debate on NATO's relevance subsided. Opinion polls reflected this shift. In 1996, 69 percent of Germans, 71 percent of Britons and 54 percent of the French recognized NATO as "essential" again (Ziegler 1998: 16). Persisting doubts in Washington, which increasingly pressed to make NATO available for its global agenda, were dispelled once NATO moved into Afghanistan after 9/11. Today, the alliance has assumed global security governance tasks: training security forces in Iraq and African Union peacekeepers in Darfur, providing airlift for the latter, patrolling in the Mediterranean and being engaged in disaster relief work such as in Pakistan. Thus, NATO reinvented itself as a major actor both in European and global security governance. Where is the problem then, Atlanticists might ask?

Transatlantic decoupling

The alliance was built on two pillars: collective defense and the transatlantic link. After 1989, attention was concentrated on how to re-legitimize NATO by substituting collective defense. What went largely unnoticed was how much 11/9 impacted on the transatlantic link.

Throughout the Cold War, "coupling" was the formula linking the American ally as closely as possible to the European "theater." Europe was the focal point of a global confrontation. For the Americans, control of Western Europe, legitimized through benign hegemony, was pivotal; for the Europeans, the US "umbrella" was indispensable. It was, though, "an unnatural – even aberrant – situation" (Howorth 2007: 52), dictated by an existential threat which drew the partners together.

Once that threat faded, mutual dependence came to an end. For American global design, Europe lost its geostrategic prominence. The decline of its world power status dates back to 1945 and now the consequences had to be faced. The reduction of American forces in Europe (from 315,000 in 1989 to 98,000 in 2005[11]) and their redeployment elsewhere signaled this decline, as did the early US disengagement from the Balkan wars, following Secretary of State Baker's

1991 dictum "We don't have a dog in this fight" (Silber and Little 1995: 201). Such disengagement in a major European crisis was unthinkable a few years before. Obviously, the Europeans had to prepare for contingencies where the US and thus NATO were not prepared to act (Howorth 2007: 53).

The disengagement was accelerated by 9/11 and the shifting US focus towards the Middle East and China. The US Quadrennial Defense Review which appeared just after 9/11 argued that "Asia is gradually emerging as a region susceptible to large-scale military competition" (three paragraphs devoted to this issue), whereas Europe is "largely at peace" (one paragraph devoted to this issue).[12] Admiral Dennis C. Blair, Commander-in-Chief, US Pacific Command commented: "In the past ... the 'Big Three' regions have always been Europe, Southwest Asia and East Asia, and in that order ... Now you find that East Asia comes first, Southwest Asia second and Europe third."[13]

For the Europeans, "coupling" also lost urgency. During the Cold War, any move to seriously undercut the US presence was taboo, even for France. The threat of a US troop withdrawal limited European "free riding." Without the Soviet threat, "extended deterrence," "first use" and the forward deployment of US forces on European soil lost relevance. The ease with which NATO downplayed its nuclear deterrent and the US withdrew its nuclear weapons and troops demonstrate how much transatlantic coupling eroded.

Instead of falling back into the coupling rhetoric, the Europeans began to pursue their own policy preferences. Sometimes they now assumed a leadership role themselves, such as when they encouraged American abstention from the Yugoslav theater, asserting "Washington is being kept informed but it is not being consulted."[14] On occasions they acted against explicit American preferences, for example when they recognized Croatia and Slovenia in 1991 and when they dismissed Clinton's "lift and strike" initiative. Throughout the Balkan wars American and European mediation efforts competed up to blatant obstruction as in the case of the Vance-Owen plan (Biermann 2006).

Thus, the transatlantic partnership lost its preeminence once the external security referent disappeared and NATO's cohesiveness suffered. The more the Cold War relaxed its mental hold, the more this ideational shift unfolded. Since it occurred gradually, its implications were overlooked. The statement of German Chancellor Gerhard Schröder in 2005 that the American presence "is no longer the security policy priority that it used to be"[15] reflected a widely accepted reality. US–European relations returned to the pre-1945 patterns of cooperation and rivalry. The Cold War had just been an intermezzo. The wider public took notice only when the allies clashed over Iraq in 2003.

European "emancipation"

NATO spans across the Atlantic and into Central Asia, including three non-European members with quite distinct security cultures (Canada, Turkey, and the US). It was originally conceived with a Westphalian logic, corresponding to the basic outlook of all its member-states. However, since the 1950s Europe began to turn towards pooled sovereignty, establishing supranational institutions, introducing qualified majority voting, striving to overcome the separating qualities of borders, cultivating the image of a civilian power and moving into a coordination even of foreign policy.

It is for this reason that Europe serves as the template for much of the security governance literature today. Most authors assume that the "logic of anarchy and power ... drives the international system outside the narrow ambit of Europe" (Sperling 2007: 282). It is in Europe that a post-Westphalian security community has emerged with a unique "prevalence of peace and cooperation" (Webber 2007: 51). Major norms of this converging European security culture, such as an inclination to multilateralism or to the restrained use of force, emerged already during the Cold War (Meyer 2006).

NATO's lead nation did not follow this liberal internationalist turn of governance (Krahmann 2005b). Indeed, the EU disposition for pooled sovereignty was quite "incomprehensible to US foreign policy makers" (Higgott 2005: 581). The US remained a "late-Westphalian state" (Sperling 2007: 283). As a consequence, NATO was already during the Cold War more diverse internally than the EU, despite much heterogeneity also within the EU (Hyde-Price 2004). Sperling (Introduction, this volume) tags the EU a post-Westphalian, and NATO a Westphalian security community.

The consequences of Europe's turn towards pooled sovereignty for NATO's security community character were hardly discussed during the Cold War. The more Europe moved toward a distinct, postmodern identity and America remained late-Westphalian, the more intra-alliance tensions on the very basics of NATO's *raison d'être* had to emerge. As European identities shifted, strains within the organization increased: while the US clung much more to traditional strategies and instruments of statecraft, the Europeans began to prefer new strategies and instruments. NATO was the primary arena where these differences in "Westphalianness" clashed.

These differences were aggravated by the structural imbalance within the alliance. From the beginning, the alliance was strongly asymmetric. "Hegemony [was] mirrored by dependence" (Howorth 2007: 52). Issues of burden-sharing and leadership style were on the agenda at an early stage. In 1949, the Europeans had dragged a reluctant America into the assistance pledge for Europe (Wiebes and Zeeman 1983). The far-sighted argument of the "third force" advocates in Washington that NATO will only endure if Europe is a strong independent pole in world politics with equal "voice opportunities" (Hirschman 1970) within the alliance was not seized by the Europeans. They were just interested in quick fixes such as a maximum of US aid (Weber 1992: 641–643). Still, the US agreed to an alliance that was strongly multilateral in character based on the "one member – one vote" principle and the consensus rule.

However, there was a countervailing US interest in unrestrained leadership (Council on Foreign Relations 2004: 14). It began to dominate alliance politics once Kennedy turned towards "flexible response" in the early 1960s, which required "unity of planning, concentration of executive authority, and central direction" (Weber 1992: 673). Nuclear strategy triumphed over alliance politics. Reflecting on the subsequent years, the former British Foreign Secretary Geoffrey Howe remarked, "More and more Europeans were coming to feel that ... the governments had no real influence on America's strategic thinking and that established NATO mechanisms for consultation risked becoming uni-directional" (quoted in Rees 1998: 24).

This increasingly collided with the post-war rise of Europe. The "entire American–West European relationship had to be redefined" (Lundestad 1986: 275). However, beyond rhetoric, this did not take place within NATO. The result was cumulating tensions, ranging from Suez to MLF, Yom Kippur and SDI. The Europeans began to experiment with institutional alternatives. The revitalization of the WEU since 1984 as a Europe-only security caucus signaled their growing discontent with NATO. They wanted to coordinate security policy without Washington at the table (Rees 1998: 22–56). Still, the external security dilemma constrained them.

When the Soviet threat disappeared, this constraint was removed. Transatlantic decoupling opened the door to conceptualize European security beyond NATO. The Europeans began to call louder for a "new transatlantic bargain." But what should it look like? Atlanticist and Europeanist views were diametrically opposed. The split ran right through Europe. The rivaling Franco-German and British–Italian proposals in Maastricht of October 1991 (which were basically re-tabled in Amsterdam) revealed how much both differed on NATO's future relevance relative to the EU and the WEU (Menon *et al.* 1992: 109–111). The Europeanists around France, which was increasingly joined by Germany, Belgium, Luxembourg and Spain, revived Kennedy's two-pillar idea and called for equal voice opportunities in a re-balanced alliance. They became more willing to articulate their grievances, pursue national agendas within NATO and probe alternative forums of defense. Public opinion shifted accordingly. After the 1991 Gulf War, 75 percent of EU citizens favored adopting a common foreign policy to deal with such crises, 61 percent even supported establishing a European military intervention force (Eurobarometer 35 1991: 28).

The new Common Foreign and Security Policy (CFSP) of the EU, which was initiated in Maastricht and deepened in Amsterdam, moved the EU gradually into NATO's domain. The Atlanticists (Britain, Denmark, Netherlands, Portugal), supported by the neutrals, were able to limit the impact on NATO. Still, an EU defense option was on the horizon once the Maastricht treaty formulated the perspective of a "progressive framing of a common defence policy, which might lead to a common defence" (article 2). NATO and the EU were increasingly perceived as "two competing forms of European security governance" (Sperling, Introduction, this volume).

Thus, the "correlation of forces" (Cox 2005: 226–227) was shifting. The reasons were both exogenous and endogenous. Without the Soviet threat, European dependence on the US declined. Also, with European integration moving into Economic, Monetary and Political Union, the post-Westphalian EU was increasingly perceived by many as the primary and, indeed, superior

European reference point even in foreign and security affairs. Indeed, the logic of European integration implied a spill-over to the defense realm at some point in time. Institutional preferences thus began to shift towards the EU – first in France, then in Germany, at last also in Britain (Howorth 2007: 146–160).

In contrast, the US position moved towards a more imperial exercise of leadership. From a "Westphalian" point of view America had attained global hegemony. The central realist parameter to measure relative power, military capabilities, did not suggest rebalancing the alliance; indeed, the "capabilities gap" was dramatically widening. Once crisis management became the centerpiece of NATO's *raison d'être*, force projection counted most. Thus, Washington was hardly inclined to attenuate US primacy. Already the Bush administration issued stiff warnings not to duplicate the alliance (Duke 1994: 172–173). Although the Clinton administration in a profound policy turn began to advocate a European Security and Defense Identity (ESDI) *within* NATO in 1994, not least to ward off any European initiative outside NATO, European ambitions soon met US resistance, especially in the arduous NATO–WEU negotiations on European-led operations using NATO assets and capabilities (Dembinski 2005a: 69–72).

The US-dominated Dayton negotiations in 1995 and particularly the air campaign against Serbia in 1999 dramatically revealed the magnitude of European dependence (Brenner 2005: 9–12, 29–32). Much as the Suez experience in 1956 inspired Britain and France to acquire their independent nuclear forces and de Gaulle to demand a redistribution of power within the alliance, the experience with US unilateralism now inspired European "emancipation" (Cogan 2001). The dispute regarding the allocation of command posts in a reformed command structure, particularly Allied Forces in Southern Europe (AFSOUTH) in Naples, revealed how much the European call for re-balancing was frustrated.

Thus, NATO was increasingly perceived as insufficient to meet distinct European interests. Even if the historic turnaround of Tony Blair in Saint Malo was motivated primarily by the quest "to save NATO" by "silencing the voices of isolationism" in Washington (Howorth 2000: 34), it also testified to transatlantic decoupling and a new willingness in London to build a European autonomous defense capacity outside NATO. The impasse among "Atlanticists" and "Europeanists," which had protected NATO's primacy since the 1960s and prevented any alternative venue from rising, was overcome.

The ESDP was the result of shifting institutional preferences. This shift has continued since and inspired the growth of the ESDP. Atlanticists have discovered the added value of the ESDP. This now includes even Central Eastern European countries such as Poland. The ESDP is increasingly duplicating NATO – in terms of scope, institutions, capabilities and missions. Its focus on civilian missions and peace-building, however, also reflects European post-Westphalian preferences. Gerhard Schröder asserted in 2005, "We are formulating it [German foreign and security policy] in Europe, for Europe and from Europe."[16] This is backed by public opinion. In 2001, 43 percent of Europeans argued that decisions on European defense should be taken by the EU, 17 percent by NATO, 24 percent by the national governments. This attitude was most pronounced in Italy and France, least in the UK (Special Eurobarometer 146 2001: 11–15). At the height of the Iraq campaign, two years later, 67 percent of the French, 63 percent of Italians, 52 percent of Germans and 48 percent of Britons (but only 29 percent of Americans) wanted US–European ties to be "more independent" (Pew Research Center 2003: 2).

Summing up, the creation of the ESDP was triggered both by an exogenous factor, the demise of the Soviet threat which allowed for more European "emancipation," and an endogenous factor, the rise of the post-Westphalian security community within the EU. The price, though, was not only an estrangement of the alliance leader, but also a decline of NATO's relevance, both in terms of its utility for the Europeans and of its internal cohesion. The increasing calls for making direct EU–US consultation the dominant forum for the transatlantic security dialogue demonstrates how much loyalties have shifted. These changes were imposed on the US and NATO, and both are still adapting to the new fait accompli in European security governance.

The multiplication of security providers in Europe

The creation of the ESDP was the culmination of a process of actor multiplication in European security governance. Already during the Cold War, the number of institutions with a security dimension continuously increased. The Western Union, founded one year before NATO, and its successor organization, the WEU, had an even more binding collective defense clause than NATO. The European Community restricted itself to a loose foreign policy coordination since 1969; however, European Political Cooperation successively moved into the non-military dimensions of security, several times explicitly challenging US leadership, such as on Afghanistan and SDI (Nuttall 1998). Also, the CSCE, founded in 1975, became an instrument for inter-bloc confidence-building, arms control and norm setting. Thus, potential rival organizations of NATO were in place when the wall fell.

In the 1990s, the definition of what security is constantly expanded. NATO is acting today in a reframed ideational milieu with a broadened understanding of security, and this far more in Europe (and Canada) than in the United States. Some threats – such as global terrorism – have newly emerged; others – such as proliferation, failing states and trafficking of humans, drugs and small arms – have re-surfaced; and still others – such as migration, energy supply, environmental degradation or pandemics – have been "securitized." Most of these threats stem from non-state actors, are transnational in nature and target society at large (Kirchner 2007b: 5). States are neither the source nor the target of most threats. This put into question "the utility of traditional forms of governance, including a collective defence arrangement like NATO, in meeting the challenges of the contemporary threat environment" (Sperling Introduction, this volume).

NATO was the evident first choice to deal with these post-Cold War security risks. Whether it would be assigned the new tasks became a litmus test for NATO's utility in the new security environment. Given its post-Westphalian turn, "civilian power" Europe perceived the new risks as primarily non-military, pre-ferring civilian means to deal with them (Manners 2002). The US elite neither shared nor fully grasped this new post-Westphalian reality in Western Europe (Berenskoetter 2004; Brenner 2002; Kagan 2004). Security concepts increasingly diverged on both sides of the Atlantic. Indeed, while the European Security Strategy of 2003 argues that "no single country is able to tackle today's complex problems on its own" (European Union 2003: 3), the US is capable and determined to disregard institutional solutions and international law if necessary.

Thus, the delegation of mandates, tasks and resources to deal with the new security risks proved highly controversial. Washington preferred to concentrate authority within NATO. However, the Europeans often favor other venues, some of which, such as ESDP missions, do not need US approval. As a consequence, European security governance has moved from single-actor dominance (NATO) to a multi-actor setting of horizontal networking. Governments can select from a broad menu of options to respond to security threats. Mandates, tasks and resources are dispersed among actors.

NATO's relevance is most challenged by the ESDP. Its core competence, collective defense, is still officially reserved for NATO; yet if the Lisbon Treaty enters into force, its solidarity clause on terrorism and particularly its mutual assis-tance clause will give the EU a nascent collective defense dimension (Howorth 2007: 117–124). In military crisis management, NATO is first choice for high-intensity operations, such as Afghanistan, and will remain so for quite some time. However, NATO already handed the Bosnian mission over to the EU and will do the same in Kosovo. The more the EU acquires capabilities such as the battle-groups to tackle the more robust "Petersberg tasks," the less the EU needs NATO, i.e. US assets and capabilities for military crisis management, and the more NATO becomes an instrument of choice. Only two out of 24 EU operations so far ("Concordia" in Macedonia and "Althea" in Bosnia) were based on the "Berlin plus agreements." Many Europeans are no longer willing to yield to NATO's primacy, essentially claiming a right to forum shop pragmatically between NATO, the EU, the OSCE and other security providers (Reichard 2006: 147–170).

There is a widespread image in Europe of NATO as a still basically military alliance which should not be entrusted to deal with risks of a political dimension. This is not only true for global warming and energy dependence (dealt with mainly on the UN, G8 and EU levels). It is also true for civil crisis management, the sig-nificance of which NATO has acknowledged in its 2006 "Comprehensive Political Guidance" (Yost 2007: 21–23). NATO's headquarters and the US are eager to take over major responsibilities in this realm, too, with the Provincial Reconstruction Teams in Afghanistan serving as blueprints. Many Europeans have reservations (Yost 2007: 26, 150, 155–156). The OSCE already has major civilian crisis man-agement capacities, e.g. its long-term missions. Also, since 2000, the EU has rapidly taken the lead in this field, building on its unique comparative advantage to integrate its broad range of instruments into one comprehensive, "inter-pillar" approach, thus reflecting its dominant post-Westphalian understanding of security today (Nowak 2006).

If we move on to the "terrorism–tyrants–WMD" triangle, the interconnected threats of terrorism, failing states, and proliferation that dominated the Bush administration's agenda, even here NATO is just one actor among others and not the primary one. All these threats are primarily met by a combination of national US endeavors and varying "coalitions" (such as the Six-Party Talks on North Korea or Operation Enduring Freedom on terrorism), supported by different international organizations (such as the IAEA on Iran). Most of these threats are of a global nature, and NATO has to share responsibility with other major players.

Summing up, multiple security providers compete today for mandates, tasks and resources, both in Europe and globally. At first sight, the cause is shifting threat perceptions: different providers capable of meeting specific threats. Many of these, being non-military, did not meet NATO's traditional profile, and so providers multiplied. However, the choice of security providers is an institutional selection process. Security providers can be adapted to perform new tasks. This depends on the willingness of member-states to do so. They decided on the amount of transformation of NATO. Beyond doubt, they delegated substantial new mandates and resources to NATO to make it relevant for the new security environment. However, whereas the US elite preferred to hand over most responsibility for post-Cold War security governance to NATO, the Europeans limited NATO's transformation and entrusted major security tasks to other organizations. They did so either unilaterally within European-only institutions or by blocking US initiatives within a consensus-ruled NATO.

The result is mixed for NATO. It lost exclusiveness in European security, but moved into global security governance; however, here it is just one, and not the primary security provider among many. It retained the leadership on collective defense, but the ESDP is increasingly encroaching in this domain. It gained a new core competence in military crisis management, but is increasingly challenged by a rivaling ESDP-autonomous capability in and beyond Europe. It tries to increase its role in civilian crisis management and cooperative activities, yet is confined to a secondary role in this field which gained most prominence in post-Cold War security governance.

America's de-prioritization of NATO

Throughout NATO history, US administrations were the engines of alliance transformation. This is still true today – be it "global partnerships," the next enlargement round or the NATO Response Force. However, this "persistent US prodding" (Schmidt 2006–7: 98) is motivated by a growing sentiment in Washington that NATO is of decreasing utility as a tool of US grand design.

The American capability-oriented Westphalian perspective is at the heart of the matter. Whereas many Europeans deeply doubt the usefulness of military means to achieve political ends, US administrations still privilege those parameters of hard power that America dominates. They point to the fact that the US spends more than the next (in order of military expenditure) 15 countries together on defense, two and a half times more than the EU defense budgets combined in 2006. Also, the American R&D budget on defense exceeds the European Union aggregate almost six times (European Defence Agency 2007). Still, only 15,000 to 20,000 European troops out of 1.7 million are at any time available for "serious military missions" (Howorth 2007: 104).

American impatience with its NATO allies increased throughout the 1990s. At that time, it was the Euro-centric focus and the slow shift to force projection which reduced NATO's relevance for Washington. The introspective European agenda clashed with the US ambition to make NATO relevant for the American global agenda and the slow transformation of major European forces, which were rarely deployed beyond Europe before, contrasted with the American focus on force projection.

The shock of the Gulf War of 1991, when only 15,000 out of 289,000 French forces could be deployed abroad, triggered the Defense Review processes both in France and Great Britain (Howorth 2007: 96). Yet, in the Kosovo air campaign, the combination of the striking US air power dominance and European "softness" in terms of targeting and collateral damage in a consensus-ruled NATO led the Clinton administration to blatantly sideline the North Atlantic Council by establishing purely national channels of communication to the American SACEUR. Still, what was perceived as European foot-dragging afterwards motivated calls in Washington to either change the consensus rule within NATO (Michel 2003) or to avoid this kind of coalition warfare in the future altogether (Brenner 2002: 26–33). The notorious statement of Secretary of Defense Donald Rumsfeld well reflected the American frustration: Wars "should not be fought by committee. The mission must determine the coalition, and the coalition must not determine the mission. If it does, the mission will be dumbed down to the lowest common denominator, and we can't afford that."[17]

The attacks of 9/11, the first major system shock after 11/9, first appeared to offer NATO a new sense of mission. However, Gerhard Schröder's call for "unconditional solidarity" and *Le Monde*'s declaration that "we are all Americans" revolved into the deepest crisis NATO experienced so far (Pond 2004). The 9/11 attacks had, much more than 11/9, a deeply asymmetric ideational impact on the allies. This time the epicenter of the system shock was in the US. Whereas Europe declined "to be defined" (Ash 2001: 68), America experienced "the most sweeping reorientation of US grand strategy in over half a century" (Council on Foreign Relations 2004: 2). It "shattered the [American] sense of physical invulnerability" and defined US policy "in every conceivable dimension" (Daalder 2003: 158).

The US strategic agenda became distinctly more Westphalian: exclusive in the sense of dividing strictly between those for and those against "us" in the "global war on terrorism"; preoccupied with the territorial integrity of the "homeland"; subordinating multilateral approaches and international law to national security; and privileging coercive, hard power instruments. US threat perceptions today fundamentally diverge from those in Europe, with America declaring war and the EU responding that "Europe has never been so prosperous, so secure nor so free" (European Union 2003: 1). Assessments about the root causes and the appropriate instruments for fighting terrorism strongly diverge (Berenskoetter and Giegerich 2006b, versus Shepherd 2006). Europe is hardly an attractive partner for the new US security agenda. Decision-making within NATO has become even more arduous.

Thus, NATO's first-time invocation of article 5 after 9/11 and its far-reaching offer of assistance were met with indifference in Washington. When the Bush administration designed Operation Enduring Freedom (OEF), it "did not give any thought to acting through NATO," according to a former official (Schmidt 2006–7: 104). NATO took over major responsibility in Afghanistan (ISAF), yet the US still relies on OEF to fight the Taliban. The refusal of major European allies to expand the ISAF mandate and the multitude of national caveats seriously reduces NATO's effectiveness in American eyes (Kaim 2006). Even more so, NATO is hardly present in the theater, which, during the Bush presidency, commanded almost exclusive US domestic attention, namely Iraq. NATO thus became one of the "victims of 9/11" (Haftendorn 2002).

Imperial inclinations towards the European allies were always present in American politics. They were never fully shared. However, they gained considerable ground for three reasons. First, the "unipolar moment" (Krauthammer) of 1989 allows American diplomacy to opt for non-institutional, i.e. non-NATO approaches to an extent not conceivable before. Second, the long-standing transatlantic security culture gap has widened significantly since 9/11. The more Americans and Europeans diverge in their "Westphalianness," the more their fundamental choices as to ends and means of security governance differ. This stimulates mutual frustration and a temptation to act unilaterally. Third, the US has resorted to an ad hoc coalition approach many times before – yet only in recent years did the alliance turn global and thus available for global tasks. *Not* using NATO today implies sidelining it. America engineered the globalization of NATO, yet in global security governance its *relative* relevance has become most obvious.

Conclusions

Let us step back and take a macro view of today's security governance and NATO's place within. Is the security governance lens helpful to assess the relevance of individual security providers within such a governance system? How was NATO's relevance affected by 11/9 and 9/11? Is NATO's relative decline that we observed permanent or reversible?

The security governance approach has both added value and limits when approaching the empirical question posed here. Research on security governance is still in an embryonic stage. Conceptualizations strongly differ, inspiring cherry-picking approaches. This investigation followed Sperling's conceptualization in the introduction to this volume. It privileges, itself, some features of security governance while marginalizing others. This might be unavoidable for an emerging research program. In the longer run, a core of accepted propositions on security governance is indispensable if we aim at cumulative research.

The relevance of one actor within a governance system can only be investigated by combining an exogenous and an endogenous perspective. The security governance approach is most helpful in investigating the exogenous perspective. I have demonstrated that two variables have strong explanatory power: the embeddedness of individual security providers which allows assessing their *relative* relevance within a multi-actor network of governance, and threat perceptions which condition the utility of individual providers to meet those threats over time.

Endogenous variables constantly figured in Sperling's bottom-up approach, explaining different types of security governance systems with different degrees of "Westphalianness" of its constituent parts, proved useful in complementing the system perspective usually predominant in security governance research. Without a close look at domestic-level factors, especially security cultures and their impact on policy, the relevance of individual security providers could hardly be assessed. This is particularly true for organizations composed of states with diverging preferences.

Distinguishing types of security governance over time and across regions, as Sperling recommends, is the key for any security governance research in the future that aspires to compare governance systems across time and space. We need conceptualizations which are not confined to post-Cold War Europe. Also, we need to think more about how transitions from one governance system to another take place, especially in times of rapid change. For cross-regional comparisons threat perceptions and degrees of "Westphalianness" appear to be good starting-points.

System shocks provoke tectonic shifts, setting security governance on a markedly different path. They affect governance in several ways. First, they give rise to new threats and downplay old ones. They thus shift security agendas, trigger the transformation of existing security providers and stimulate the emergence of new providers. Second, system shocks might impact security cultures quite differently; some change more radically in terms of "Westphalianness" than others. As a consequence, discord as to the strategies and instruments to meet the new threats might increase. Individual security providers are such instruments.

How was NATO's relevance affected by 11/9 and 9/11? This chapter has privileged the 1990s, because analysts during those years strongly misperceived how much NATO's legitimacy, utility and cohesiveness eroded once the "overlay" (Buzan and Wæver 2003: 61) of bipolarity was lifted. Focusing on NATO's new functions in crisis management, partnership and integration was short-sighted. Indeed, NATO compensated the demise of collective defense by expanding its functional and geographical scope. Transformation brought about re-legitimization. However, the "taken for grantedness" that this imparted was premature. Transformation averted dissolution, but not decline. It was the ideational effect of 11/9 on threat perceptions and the transatlantic partnership, including NATO–EU relations, which proved most erosive. The "magnitude" of this tectonic shift was grasped late, and only by some (Andrews 2004: 4).

NATO's second crisis of legitimacy after 9/11 was predetermined by its first one. Unfortunately, the reaction to 9/11 not only revealed the extent of this shift but hastened it. Again, the effect was mainly ideational, as security cultures diverged. Since the crisis of the 1990s has only been resolved on the surface, its disintegrating potential could unfold unchecked. Again, there was a time-lag until the effect of 9/11 was translated into policy. Today, a fundamental debate on NATO's very purpose is in full swing. All allies have shifted allegiances away from NATO. Most consequential is the preference shift of the alliance leader.

NATO's decline is an entirely logical consequence of the end of the Cold War. Most obvious is the decreasing *cohesiveness* of the alliance, which goes along with a loss of *utility* for most member-states. We can discern four major causes. First, intra-alliance conflicts escalate more easily since the external security referent waned and Europe and America lost the geopolitical exclusiveness they had for one another. Second, European frustration about the categorical American refusal to allow them equal voice opportunities combines with deep-rooted American disillusionment about the European unwillingness to follow its more Westphalian approach to world politics. Cynicism, stereotyping and even expressions of arrogance spread. Third, the frequent use of alternatives to NATO – be it the ESDP or ad hoc coalitions and unilateral action – stimulates not only sustained inter-, but also intra-institutional conflicts within NATO and the EU, particularly on the division of mandates, tasks and resources (Biermann 2008b). The creation and cultivation of these alternatives testifies to the fact that NATO has become an instrument of choice, both in European and even more in global security governance. Few, primarily the Britons, try hard to keep the menu of choices limited and NATO's primacy intact.

Fourth, the transatlantic discourse on the future of the alliance is fundamentally split: in America it is basically task- and capabilities-oriented, in Europe norm- and institution-oriented. The proper balance of coercion and persuasion, unilateralism and multilateralism, national prerogatives and international law is constantly disputed. For most Americans NATO's utility, meanwhile, is restricted to collective defense and peace building; for many Europeans, NATO is a fall-back institution for those tasks where autonomous European action is not feasible. The revision of NATO's Strategic Concept of 1999, which is outdated on major counts, will expose fundamental disagreements about the entire *raison d'être* of the alliance.

NATO's institutional decline is not temporary, attributable to an imperial Bush presidency. Threat perceptions, security cultures and structural asymmetries are resistant to political engineering. The five shifts outlined above will outlast the Bush presidency – systems of governance remain as heads of state and government come and go. However, NATO's institutional decline is reversible. NATO has mastered many ups and downs throughout history. New system shocks will come. Transatlantic relations will change in style and substance under the Obama presidency Also, NATO's decline is relative. It is more perceived among Europeanists than Atlanticists, and more in continental Europe than in the US and Britain. Three of the four indicators of decline elaborated above apply: a shift of institutional preferences (primarily to the EU), the creation and use of alternative frameworks of action (the ESDP, coalitions, unilateralism) and the non-use of NATO for purposes it is designed for. However, no member-state is considering leaving or dissolving the alliance; indeed, it is still expanding, and its attractiveness among countries such as Georgia or Ukraine is high. It remains true that "no countries are more likely to agree on basic policy, and to have the power to do something about it" (Moravcsik 2003). Europe and America remain pivotal partners for a healthy world economy, for fighting terrorism, and for advancing democracy. Although only 36 percent of Europeans today view US leadership as desirable (down from 64 percent in 2002), still a majority (54 percent) wants to address threats "in partnership" with the US (Transatlantic Trends 2007: 5, 12, 16). Whether or not the allies learn to cope with divergence and re-frame their partnership according to post-Cold War realities will, to a significant degree, determine the future not only of the Atlantic alliance but of governance worldwide.

Notes

1 The views expressed in this text are solely the author's and do not reflect the stance of any of the institutions he is affiliated with.
2 I would like to thank the editors of this volume for their valuable guidance as well as David M. Andrews, Felix Berenskoetter, Matthias Dembinski and especially David Yost for commenting on earlier drafts of this chapter.
3 For the realist argument, see Mearsheimer (1990), Waltz (1993) and Walt (1997); for the constructivist and neoliberal argument see Wallander (2000), and McCalla (1996). Both arguments are confronted in Hellmann and Wolf (1993).
4 See the graph averaging the British, French and German responses between 1969 and 2006 to the question "Is NATO still essential?" Testimony for John K. Glenn, Director of Foreign Policy, German Marshall Fund of the United States, US House of Representatives, Committee on Foreign Affairs, Subcommittee on International Organizations, Human Rights, and Oversight, 23 March 2007. Online, available at: www.globalsecurity.org/military/library/congress/2007_hr/070322-glenn.htm (accessed 20 May 2008).
5 Risse: "It is domestic politics, stupid!, rather than structural changes in the international system that has made the Atlantic a wider ocean" (2004: 233).
6 Note that this typology implies a notion of progress, i.e. a teleological dimension, which is as yet not empirically tested.
7 Sperling diverges here considerably from the literature, which implies that security governance is a new term for a new phenomenon, which arose in the post-Cold War context. He effectively argues that different types of security governance have existed before 1989 and still exist today. This allows the analysis of NATO's evolution over time from one coherent analytical framework, and it permits the comparison of forms of governance across regions.
8 G. S. Jones cited in Kumar (1992: 315).
9 F. Furet cited in Kumar (1992: 318).
10 When asked whether NATO is still essential, 53 percent still agreed in 1990 (Ziegler 1998).
11 The 2005 figures include US troops in Bosnia, Kosovo and Central Eastern Europe. Online, available at: www.heritage.org/Research/NationalSecurity/troopMarch2005.xls (DoD data, accessed 14 November 2007).
12 The Review of 30 September 2001 is online, available at www.defenselink.mil/pubs/pdfs/qdr2001.pdf.
13 Quoted in R. Halloran, "Eastern Threat: The Bush Administration's Major Review of Defence Policy Sees the Focus Shift to East Asia," *Far Eastern Economic Review*, 18 October 2001.

14 Gianni de Michelis, on behalf of the EC Presidency, quoted in *New York Times*, 4 July 1991, A7.
15 Speech on the 41st Munich Conference on Security Policy, 12 February 2005. Online, available at: www.securityconference.de/konferenzen/rede.php?menu_2005=&id=143&sprache=en& (accessed 25 November 2007).
16 Speech at the 41st Munich Conference, 2005. Online, available at: www.security conference.de (accessed 24 April 2008).
17 Remarks at the National Defense University, Washington, DC, 31 January 2002. Online, available at: www.defenselink.mil/speeches/speech.aspx?speechid=183.

3 The EU in global security governance

Lessons for conceptual development

Arita Eriksson[1]

Introduction: the concept of governance in relation to security and the global context[1]

In developing the concept of security governance, one research task is to elaborate on characteristics and to fill the concept with content based on empirical studies (as argued by, for example, Sperling 2007). As the concept is comparatively young, its theoretical development needs feedback from empirical studies. Analysing the European Union (EU) civil and military operations in the Democratic Republic of Congo (DRC) is a way of capturing security governance in a global context, compared to a regional one. These operations provide good illustrations of different forms of security governance that allow the researcher to capture a great deal of various interaction patterns. It also makes further theorizing concerning global security governance possible, for example through identifying whether or not the components of security governance spelled out by Webber *et al.* (2004) are present. As this definition is often used as something of a starting point for an analysis of security governance, it is interesting to analyse its applicability in various contexts. Does security governance have important components that are still unexplored? What different forms may security governance take? How can security governance shed light on universal security efforts? Keohane (2001) has identified five main *functions* of institutions of global governance. The first is to limit the use of violence, the second is to manage problems that spill over from the different parts of the system to other parts, the third is to "provide *focal points* in coordination games" (Keohane 2001: 3), the fourth is to handle major disturbances and the fifth is to "provide a guarantee against the worst forms of abuse" (Keohane 2001: 3). Though Keohane's argument is not limited to security policy, these functions may well fit the discussion concerning security governance as defined by Webber *et al.*, even though we are not speaking of a particular physical institution here, but rather of a cooperation network engaged in security efforts within the framework of international law. We will return to the issue of functions in the conclusion, and also relate these to the categories of governance identified by Sperling in the introduction to this volume.

Security politics at the global level at the beginning of the twenty-first century are torn between traditional state centrist perspectives which represent the fundamental building blocks of the study of international relations, and post-modern structures of global governance – the conceptualizations of which are more immature. Since the end of the Cold War, the international community has, in various formations, engaged in security efforts on a global scale. The term *security governance* is, in this chapter, used as a way of conceptualizing the analysis of this trend. Recently, researchers have begun to speak of *security* governance at the international or global level (Krahmann 2003; Webber *et al.* 2004; Kirchner and Sperling 2007b).[2] The concept of security governance is valuable, as many of the traditional theories of international relations are unsuitable for an analysis of modern global security efforts. They often focus on cooperation within a particular organization or the like. This study leaves the internal problematique of international organizations behind and takes a broader view on how security governance materializes in a particular setting. The objective is not, however, to evaluate the *effects* of security governance.

The purpose of this chapter is to increase and develop the theoretical and empirical understanding of the concept of security governance through the analysis of EU security governance. The role of the EU in global security governance more generally is also discussed. The EU interacts with many different actors in its external actions, and its efforts usually cross several policy areas as it pursues its comprehensive approach to security. Many studies consider the role of the EU in international affairs (Ginsberg 2001; Bretherton and Vogler 2006; Teló 2006). These studies mainly focus on the EU's role as a kind of normative power, strengthened by its attractiveness as a partner and by membership aspirations in the countries dealt with (Whitman 1998; Manners 2002; Sjursen (ed.) 2006). Recent studies have highlighted the EU's civil and military crisis management capability – a relatively new dimension of EU actorness (Ekengren *et al.* 2006b; Kirchner 2006; Engelbrekt and Hallenberg (eds) 2007; Kirchner and Sperling 2007a). Kirchner and Sperling (2007a) analysed different EU policies in relation to civil and military crisis management as a form of EU security governance. Indeed, the EU, when it acts at a global level, practises a form of security governance in the sense of Webber *et al.* (2004). The characteristics of the global security governance in which the EU takes part need, however, further research. In line with Karen Smith (2005), this author also argues that it is time to direct attention to what the EU does in practice on a global scale – not only on what it achieves with the help of its attractiveness in the near neighbourhood. One interesting issue that we will return to in the conclusion is how this post-Westphalian actor functions together with actors situated at other ends of the Westphalian/post-Westphalian continuum suggested by Sperling in the introduction to this volume.

The EU in the Democratic Republic of Congo: a case of security governance

The focus of the empirical analysis in this chapter is the five EU operations in the Democratic Republic of Congo that took place from 2003 to 2007 in the framework of the European Security and Defence Policy. The operations are; the

2003 EU military operation Artemis, the 2004–7 police mission to Kinshasa, EUPOL Kinshasa, the 2007–8 police mission EUPOL RD Congo, the 2005–6 EU advisory and assistance mission for DRC security reform EUSEC – RD Congo and the 2006 (April–November) EU military operation in support of the United Nations Organization Mission in the Democratic Republic of Congo (MONUC) during the election process, EUFOR RD Congo.[3] The DRC is situated in central Africa. During the 1990s it was haunted by cruel wars. In the spring of 2003, a peace process had been under way for a couple of years – monitored by MONUC. In 2005 a constitution was ratified and elections were held the following year. A government was formed in 2007.[4] However, this enormous country still faces serious challenges – as was shown in the autumn of 2008 when the situation worsened in Eastern DRC (UNHCR 2008).

One way to approach global security governance empirically as it has been enacted by the EU in its external relations is to carry out a policy analysis. Previous research has shown that the categorization of a policy process into the dimensions of problems, solutions and participants has been useful in high-lighting various important factors at play as a policy process evolves (Kingdon 1995).[5] Here, these dimensions are used to analyse how global security govern-ance materializes and universal security efforts are pursued. The effects of security governance are, however, not evaluated. Three organizational levels are introduced; the macro level concerns the system's broader institutions as well as the national and international/global level, the meso level concerns organizations in subsectors and the micro level concern actors/individuals within an organi-zation. The dimensions (problems, solutions and participants) apply to these levels in different ways.

The analytical focus on *problems* illuminates what Keohane calls the *func-tions* of institutions of global governance (see above). By "problems" are meant issues that need to be addressed by the EU/and or the participants involved in the operation. Theoretically, there are two aspects that are of interest in relation to problems; what types of problems become the focus of security governance and the level of unity concerning the problem at hand. With respect to types of problems, we could expect to find different forms of security governance efforts in relation to different problems. The severity of a problem could also be of relevance. Regarding unity, we could assume that the more common problems that the participants involved have; the more likely it is that a global security governance effort is pursued. However, it could also be that the participants involved function well together holding diverse problem definitions.

Solutions are understood as ideas or sets of ideas for managing problems. Solutions constitute the essence of governance; policy materialized in various forms of concrete security governance efforts at different organizational levels. It is also a key to knowledge of who is engaged and who the participants are. An analysis of solutions highlights the presence or lack of presence of institutionali-zation, heterarchy and the involvement of norms. These components shed light on the form of security governance pursued. Drawing on Kooiman (2000) a typology is used in order to conceptualize various forms of governance at each organizational level.[6] Global security governance as understood in this chapter is most likely to be characterized as some form of co-governing. Co-governing is conceptualized in terms of co-ordination, co-operation and collaboration, characterized by different degrees of intentional action and structure at different organizational levels (Kooiman 2000: 147–154).

The analytical category *participants* answers to questions such as who are the multiple actors involved in security governance? For whom is global governance supposed to provide a focal point? It thus sheds light on essential questions raised by Keohane and Webber *et al.* Participants are understood as those actors that are actively involved in the operation or the process surrounding it, including in some cases the counterpart – the host state – and international organizations such as the UN. A number of questions could be posed in relation to participants of security governance. At what level of organization do different actors become engaged? How does the number of actors involved affect security governance? How does the character of the involved actors matter?

Problems, solutions and participants in EU security governance in the Democratic Republic of Congo

The results of the empirical study are illustrated in three tables which highlight the results for the analytical categories of problems, solutions and participants, respectively. Below each table, the empirical findings are analysed.[7] The analysis of security governance in the EU operations studied is sorted in terms of the organizational levels macro, meso and micro. With respect to *solutions*, the organizational levels imply different forms of governance.

Problems in security governance

The focus on problems illuminates issues that need to be addressed by the EU and/or the participants involved in the operation. Problems capture the purpose and, in some cases, the functions behind the security governance effort studied. It is possible to identify two main sets of problems in the empirical material; those that are of a "high risk" character and involve military means, and those that are of a more "low risk" character and focus on, for example, assistance in a transition process. Problems are mainly identified at the macro level of organization; in some cases, however, it is possible to detect different or more specified problems at lower levels.

The "high risk" category of problems is represented by the EU military operation Artemis and to some extent by the EU military operation EUFOR RD Congo. With respect to Artemis, the Council Joint Action (2003) and the Council Decision (2003) provide only little reference to the problem at hand (compare Eriksson 2008 on problem definition in the European Security and Defence Policy). However, the EU's Secretary General/ High Representative (SG/HR) Javier Solana has elaborated on the problems to be dealt with (Brussels 2003b; Solana 2003). The problem analysis in the official texts in relation to EUFOR

Table 3.1 Problems in security governance

Operation	Macro level	Meso level	Micro level
Artemis	Peace process at risk, peace and security in the wider region	Risk of humanitarian crisis, people and logistic functions need protection	Risk of humanitarian crisis, people and logistic functions need protection
EUPOL Kinshasa	Deteriorating security situation, transitional process and regional and international security at risk		
EUPOL RD Congo	Advise and assist on SSR, play a role in reform and restructuring of the police		
EUSEC RD Congo	Security of the Congolese people, national reconciliation, stability in the region		Integrate former belligerents
EUFOR RD Congo	Ensure stable transition process and the conduct of elections	Ensure ability of international community to uphold responsibilities	Protection of civilians and logistic functions

RD Congo is also minimal. Through an analysis of the solutions, problems may, however, be reconstructed. In both these military operations the problem is related to peace and security during a limited period of time and that civilians are to be protected. Security concerns are expressed also in relation to the civilian operations, but in these cases the concern does not appear to be as pressing.

The "low risk" set of problems is represented by the police mission EUPOL Kinshasa, the advisory and assistance mission for security reform EUSEC RD Congo and the police/justice/SSR[8] mission EUPOL RD Congo. Here, the fragile security situation and possible negative consequences upon the transition process are highlighted (Council Joint Action 2004: paragraph 13; Council Joint Action 2005: paragraph 9). A key problem to be dealt with during EUSEC RD Congo was to integrate former belligerents and create a national army (Council Joint Action 2005; Information Document 2007: 2). EUPOL RD Congo is one of the most specific when it comes to problem definition. This mission is directed towards the interface between the police and the juridical system. Its aim is to advise and assist on security sector reform – in particular to play a role in the process of reform and the restructuring of the National Congolese Police (PNC) (Council Joint Action 2007c). As is shown in Table 3.1, a problem definition at the macro level appears to be sufficient for security governance to start; it can be assumed that if no other problems have been identified at lower levels, the macro level problem definition goes for all the levels of organization.

What can be said about problems that have a bearing on security governance? The problems identified in the empirical analysis concern many of the functions of *institutions* of global governance acknowledged by Keohane above; to limit the use of violence, manage major disturbances and provide a form of guarantee against severe abuse. Some of the operations related to "low risk" problems aim at integration and coordination, through which the operation manages problems related to different parts of the system (the effects of a failed state). We need, however to connect the results concerning problems with the results concerning solutions and participants in order to receive a better picture of the patterns of security governance at work in the DRC.

Solutions in security governance

Solutions are ideas or sets of ideas for managing problems which materialize in policy and security governance efforts at various organizational levels. Solutions allow us to further analyse how security governance emerges in the different operations. There are differences in how developed the solutions are at the various organizational levels. This suggests that there are differences in the depth of security governance, or maybe in what form of security the effort is aimed at creating. The empirical material provides most detailed information on the solutions established when the operation is characterized by a "low risk" problem. The solutions related to the high risk operations Artemis and EUFOR RD Congo are thus not very developed.

At an overall level, the Artemis operation was to function as an emergency mission in order to stabilize the region of Ituri during the time it took to strengthen MONUC (Brussels 2003b: 2). Problems should be dealt with through assistance to the UN, through stabilizing the security conditions and through creating secure conditions for people and logistic functions (the airport) (Brussels 2003b: 2). These solutions stretch over the meso and micro levels of organization and can be characterized as both co-operation and collaboration.

The main idea behind EUFOR RD Congo was also to support MONUC during the election process in DRC (Council Joint Action 2006b). A background note develops the details of the tasks involved.

- To support MONUC to stabilise a situation, in case MONUC faces serious difficulties in fulfilling its mandate within its existing capabilities,
- to contribute to the protection of civilians under imminent threat of physical violence in the areas of its deployment, and without prejudice to the responsibility of the Government of the DRC,
- to contribute to airport protection in Kinshasa,
- to ensure the security and freedom of movement of the personnel as well as the protection of the installations of EUFOR RD Congo,
- to execute operations of limited character in order to extract individuals in danger.

(Background 2006: 3)

Table 3.2 Solutions in security governance

Operation	Macro: coordination	Meso: co-operation	Micro: collaboration
Artemis	EU operation to provide stabilization as temporary support for MONUC	Assist the UN; stabilize security conditions, secure people and logistic functions	Assist the UN; stabilize security conditions, secure people and logistic functions
EUPOL Kinshasa	Complement Commission project, monitor, mentor, and advise the Integrated Police Unit (IPU), reinforcement during election period	Enhance management capability of IPU, monitor, mentor and advise operational units in the execution of their tasks, support integration to PNC, advise in relation to SSR	Monitor, mentor and advise the operational units in the execution of their tasks, training programme, reform of the PNC, coordination in relation to election period
EUPOL RD Congo	Advice and assistance	Interaction with Congolese authorities, various committees, promoting certain policies, work to create a professional multiethnic police force, improving contacts between police and juridical system	Mentor the police
EUSEC RD Congo	Reform of the security sector, advice and assistance, integration, reconstruction and restructuring of the Congolese army	Promote policies compatible with human rights, international humanitarian law, democratic standards, principles of good public management, transparency and observance of the rule of law; provide advice, support and assistance on the development of plans and policies regarding the Congolese army	Projects related to payment of wages, administrative and financial regulations, and technical and logistical support for the biometric census of troops
EUFOR RD Congo	Support for MONUC during the election process	Support MONUC to stabilize a situation, protect civilians, airport protection in Kinshasa	Support MONUC to stabilise a situation, protect civilians, airport protection

The EU was also engaged through the first pillar in different projects in support of the election process, including an EU election observation mission (Background 2006).

More detailed information is provided on the operation EUPOL Kinshasa. It followed a Commission funded project initiated in 2003–4. A police mission was launched in April 2005 with the task to:

> Monitor, mentor, and advise the setting up and the initial running of the [Integrated Police Unit] IPU in order to ensure that the IPU acts following the training received in the Academy centre and according to international best practices in the field. These actions shall be focused on the IPU chain of command to enhance the management capability of the IPU and to monitor, mentor and advise the operational Units in the execution of its tasks.
>
> (Council Joint Action 2004: article 3)

The tasks of the mission came to involve further activities, including a training programme, activities related to the reform of the Congolese national police[9] and coordination activities in relation to the election period. The training programme included Human Rights information provided by the International Committee of the Red Cross (ICRC) (Press document 2006). In late December 2006, an amendment was introduced implying that the operation assisted the Integrated Police Unit to integrate into the National Congolese Police and to strengthen focus on security sector reform (Council Joint Action 2006c). EUPOL Kinshasa thus moved closer to EUSEC RD Congo (see below). EUPOL RD Congo was to take over after EUPOL Kinshasa. The aim of the mission was to be fulfilled through advice and assistance at the meso and micro levels, through direct interaction with the Congolese authorities and various committees (Council Joint Action 2007c). The police was to be supported through work directed at creating a professional and multiethnic police force and improving contacts between the police and the juridical system (Council Joint Action 2007c: article 2).

In the case of EUSEC RD Congo, the problems identified were to be solved by a reform of the security sector; through advice and assistance to the DRC authorities (Council Joint Action 2005; Information Document 2007). The mission was extended and amended several times to enable a particular project, to allow the head of mission to implement additional projects supported by certain member-states and directed towards the authorities in the DRC. The task of integration, reconstruction and restructuring of the Congolese Army was highlighted in 2007 (Council Joint Action 2006a; Council Joint Action 2007a; Council Joint Action 2007b; Information Document 2007: 2). The two missions EUSEC RD Congo and EUPOL RD Congo were to work closely in order to promote possible synergies. The possibility of them becoming a single mission was announced (Council Joint Action 2007b).

In most operations it is possible to identify solutions at all different levels of organization although the extent to which they are developed differ. Only in the case of Artemis and EUFOR RD Congo was the solution at the meso level transferred also to the micro level. In those operations that concern advice and assistance we find, however, more developed ideas on how the security effort materializes in terms of solutions, in particular at the meso and micro levels – when it comes to co-operation and collaboration. In the case of "high risk" operations, where the problem and solution can be seen as an effort to produce immediate security, solutions are less developed – in the case of "low risk" operations, problems and solutions can be seen as an effort to contribute to the evolvement of security and solutions are more developed. This suggests differences in the intentionality and structure of governance, as suggested by Kooiman. The more developed form of security governance appears to involve more of norm spreading and institutionalization. Thus, at least two types of security governance can be said to have been identified in the operations studied. During the time period studied, these different types of security governance work along a time span, sometimes by themselves, such as in the case of Artemis, sometimes together in a complementary fashion such as in the case of EUPOL Kinshasa, EUSEC RD Congo and EUFOR RD Congo.

Participants in security governance

The analytical category "participants" sheds light on who is engaged in security governance. Participants are those actors that are actively involved in the operation or the process surrounding it. The empirical study resulted in interesting findings concerning relations among participants in security governance and shows who is engaged and at what level of organization different actors appear.

The UN is a main player at the macro level, and in several cases also at lower organizational levels. In operation Artemis, relations with the UN crossed organizational levels. The EU thus seldom appears to act in an isolated way. This is usually explicitly recognized. For example, in the case of EUSEC RD Congo, the EU mission was to take place in cooperation and coordination with the international community (Council Joint Action 2005: paragraph 7, article 2). The EU stated in 2006 that it wanted to take a coordinating role in the field of security sector reform (in cooperation with the UN).

In several of the operations analysed, synchronization is explicitly sought with other EU missions, in particular at the meso and micro levels. Harmonization also takes place with the activities of individual EU member-states. For example, EUSEC RD Congo received a unit responsible for specific projects involving member-states (Council Joint Action 2007a). The Commission is a participant mentioned at the macro and meso levels. It is clear that multiple actors are considered necessary. In the case of EUFOR RD Congo, the Council called upon various actors to contribute to the conduct of successful elections; the transition authorities, the political forces, the Congolese security forces, all parties and candidates as well as regional actors (Council of the European Union 2006a). Here, in particular, the role of local participants for the success of security governance is being highlighted. It is clear that all cases of security governance analysed involve a multilevel interaction of participants. The EU documents

Table 3.3 Participants in security governance

Operation	Macro	Meso	Micro
Artemis	EU presidency, SG/HR, EUSR, EU operation commander, EU member-states, UN (Secretary General)	SG/HR, EUSR, UN, DRC authorities, neighbouring countries	EU force Commander, MONUC, local authorities, NGOs
EUPOL Kinshasa	Commission, UN, DRC, SG/HR, EUSR	EUSR, Head of mission, IPU (PNC)	Head of mission, IPU (PNC), ICRC
EUPOL RD Congo	EUSR, Congolese authorities, head of mission, Commission	Head of mission, police advisors, legal advisors, experts in Police Reform Monitoring Committee, DRC authorities, MONUC, third states involved in SSR	Head of mission, police advisors, legal advisors, experts to the PNC
EUSEC RD Congo	UN, EU actors including the Commission, DRC government	Head of mission, experts, Congolese administration, EUPOL Kinshasa/EUPOL RD Congo, Commission, member-states, other international actors (incl. MONUC, third states)	Experts involved in Congolese administration at central and regional level
EUFOR RD Congo	UN, EU actors (SG/HR, EUSR, presidency), DRC authorities	EU operation commander, SG/HR, Department of Peacekeeping Operations (DPKO), MONUC, Gabon	EU force commander, EUSR, head of mission EUPOL Kinshasa/ EUSEC RD Congo, MONUC, local authorities, international actors

provide relatively rich information on the participants thought to be involved in the operation and the process surrounding it, as for example in the case of Artemis. It has, however, not been possible to verify through the material used in this study exactly how these contacts unfolded as the operation started.

The type of participants involved is varied, including both civilian and military actors. In operations Artemis and EUFOR RD Congo military units are involved. The other operations consist of civilian participants. For example, EUPOL RD Congo consisted of police and legal advisors at both the strategic and the operational levels, including experts taking part in certain committees and in the PNC (Council Joint Action 2007c). Local participants and neighbouring states are also active participants. Local participants appear particularly involved in the advice and assistance missions. In the course of the Artemis operation, Solana visited both the president of the DRC and the presidents of neighbouring countries – an indication that neighbouring countries were considered as being participants in the process surrounding the operation, whose cooperation was crucial to the success of security governance (Brussels 2003c). During EUFOR RD Congo, neighbouring state Gabon played a role as it hosted EU over-the-horizon forces (Solana 2007).

Non governmental organizations (NGOs) were part of the process surrounding the operations and thus also participants in security governance. For instance, during Artemis Solana met with NGOs involved in humanitarian support (Brussels 2003c). In EUFOR RD Congo, civilian international actors such as the Independent Electoral Commission (IEC) and the International Committee in Support of the Transition (CIAT) appear to have played an important role in the elections (Council of the European Union 2006b). It appears from this study that NGOs are important participants mainly at the meso and micro levels of organization. What is interesting is that they appear not only in relation to civilian missions, but also in connection to military operations.

In relation to the different types of problems and solutions identified above, it is interesting to ask whether there are also differences with respect to participants. It is not easy to detect such differences. As suggested above, NGOs are present to some extent also in the military operations – something which would perhaps not be expected. The Commission is, however, one participant which is engaged in those operations dealing with advice and assistance. Though the number of participants has not been quantified, there appear to be more participants engaged in the more comprehensive operations dealing with advice and assistance.

Conclusions

This study has produced several key findings of relevance for further analysis and understanding of the concept of security governance. The findings are related in various ways. First, two different types of security governance were found. This observation is of relevance for the further development of the concept and should contribute to increased understanding in future empirical analysis. The second key finding relates to the theoretical question regarding how security is created. Does security governance produce security or contribute to the evolvement of rules of security? A third key finding relates to the functions which security governance fulfils and the role of the EU in a universal system of security efforts. The fourth key finding concerns the relationship between different security efforts, an empirical finding which may be of use in various strategic considerations and have conceptual value in relation to a more overall long-term view of security governance as part of a universal system of security efforts. Below, each key finding is further developed and linked to some main issues introduced by Sperling in the introduction to this volume.

Regarding the first key finding, the analysis of the empirical material suggests that two types of security governance may be at work in the operations studied. The first may be labelled limited security governance, the second comprehensive. Limited security governance appears in relation to strategies where the production of security is achieved through short-term efforts and comprehensive security governance in relation to strategies where the evolvement of rules of security is central. These two types of security governance each relate to one of the two types of problems and corresponding solutions identified. The empirical study highlights one "high risk" category and one "low risk" category of problems, which fits in with limited security governance and comprehensive security governance, respectively. This distinction corresponds in principle with the two forms of functions Sperling set out in the introduction to this volume; institution-building and conflict resolution. There appears to be a mix of both persuasive and coercive instruments at work in the empirical cases studied here.

According to Kooiman (2000), the different levels of co-governing are characterized by different levels of intentionality. This is difficult to measure, but it appears that it is easier to identify the lower levels of governance (co-operation and collaboration) in what is called comprehensive security governance. This may have to do with the security environment surrounding the operation, which allows for governance to function and reach deeper into the state. Judging from the findings above, the difference between the two forms of security governance thus seems to concern extension, both with respect to time and ambition, and "organizational" depth. The analysis of participants does not, however, fit easily into this scheme. Both forms of security governance are characterized by multi-level involvement of different participants. The role of various participants deserves further research.

A second key finding is related to how security is created in security governance. Short-term efforts in order to produce security are often contrasted to long-term efforts that contribute to the evolvement of rules of security. In the context of "high risk" problems which are solved through short-term military interventions security is produced from the top downwards. This form of security governance does not necessarily contribute to the evolvement of long-term rules of security, at least if it is not followed by other measures. The aim of security governance efforts in relation to "low risk" problems takes the form of solutions that contribute to the evolvement of rules of security; for example through the introduction of Western policies and standards regarding the security sector. This is more of a bottom-up effort. In the EU missions of this character it is very clear that what is being transferred through security governance is largely of an ideational character. Norms are being transferred concerning, for example, the appropriate conduct of the police and the juridical system. The work is structured according to polices highly related to Western values concerning human rights, the rule of law and what characterizes democratic and good governance. However, at the same time, the spread of these norms and the correct pattern of conduct produce security. This suggests that the evolvement of rules of security and the spread of norms which produce security are hardly separable on empirical grounds. These processes reinforce each other. Relations of an ideational character, which Webber *et al.* consider a central feature of security governance, are mainly found in relation to comprehensive security governance – at least there is a difference in the depth of the relations established during the two types of security governance. The same observation can be made regarding formal and informal institutionalization. To a varying degree, the missions aim at supporting and participating in the build-up of both institutions and practices related to security.

A third key finding concerns the different functions of security governance. In various ways, and at different levels of organization, both civilian and military missions fulfil several if not all of the functions of institutions of global governance identified by Keohane (2001), reiterated below. Problems indicate what functions security governance fulfils. For example, military operations clearly aim at limiting the use of violence. They, and to some extent the civilian operations as well, also manage major disturbances. Indeed the very presence of EU engagement and security governance functions as a form of "guarantee against the worst forms of abuse" (Keohane 2001: 3), although the guarantee is not full in the sense that the EU or the security governance effort neither aims at ensuring nor is mandated to ensure the security of the entire DRC or its inhabitants. Indeed, the state is formally still a central provider of security and the EU efforts are limited both in time and scope. The security sector reform/civilian operations aim at integration and coordination, something which manages problems related to different parts of the system (or, rather, it manages the effects of the system's disintegration). Functions or problems constitute a form of "collective purpose" in the cases of global security governance that have been studied; it is quite visible that the concerns of several actors, the UN, the EU and the DRC, are taken into account in outlining various efforts. The problems dealt with are diverse; from traditional writings on regional and international security to the protection of civilians and logistic functions. It is also clear that the competence or reputation of the international community, in particular the UN, is at stake at some points – when the EU enters in order to support MONUC. Judging from the empirical analysis in this study, categories of security governance are issue–area specific rather than actor specific and contrary to what is often claimed, the EU engages in both civil and military forms of security governance.

A fourth key finding that may be of empirical and strategic value is that it appears that there are rather smooth passages between various types of security governance efforts, between civilian and military missions, between the EU and the UN. It is interesting to note that the different missions complement each other in various ways. The observation could be made thanks to the time perspective and the focus on efforts in one specific country. This could be an indication that the overall approach to security efforts in relation to the DRC is indeed characterized by political determination. Thus, it may serve as an example of a universal security system at work – though recent developments in the DRC indicate that the efforts haven't prevented the violence from continuing. What is the character of the actors involved in this universal security system, considering the discussion pursued by Sperling concerning the possibilities for interaction between actors along the Westphalian and post-Westphalian continuum? The EU missions analysed show the involvement of a large number of actors at various levels, both public and private. The EU takes into account the interests of the international community both with respect to problems and solutions. However, all participants involved need not necessarily share all problem definitions made by the EU – it is likely that security governance may take place in spite of different agendas. Still, the EU does provide an important focal point for universal security efforts, a link between the involvement of the international community and the local authorities. What is interesting in the case studied here is that the DRC could be considered a pre-Westphalian actor, involved in security governance efforts with post-Westphalian actors. In the case of the limited security governance pursued, the goal is to transform the situation from chaos (a pre-Westphalian environment) to something characterizing a stable Westphalian actor (the ambition is to help the state control its territory and protect its citizens in certain limited situations). In the comprehensive security governance efforts many post-Westphalian actors are engaged together with the pre-Westphalian or newly established Westphalian state in order to build a stable Westphalian actor. This suggests that interaction across the continuum is indeed possible, also when there is no immediate "attraction" such as EU membership. It could, however, be considered strange that post-Westphalian actors contribute to creating Westphalian actors. Perhaps it is in the interest of all actors to achieve a positive development along the continuum. The role of non-state actors in security governance, which have not been characterized along this continuum, should also not be forgotten. Indeed, post-Westphalian state actors may be highly dependent upon the experience of non-state actors of working in pre-Westphalian settings. More information is needed on the interaction of participants in global security governance.

The concept of security governance has potential value in future research endeavours concerning many of the questions central to security, development and international cooperation today. As shown in this chapter, it is possible to analyse challenges of governance at every arena of conflict through this lens; state, society and a regional/global milieu. Although the theoretical development of the concept is still ongoing, security governance provides a new analytical framework that can incorporate security efforts at multiple levels, involving various actors and methods. Thus, it provides a fresh and inspiring alternative to work with as compared to many state centrist and intergovernmental perspectives on international cooperation.

Notes

1 The author wishes to thank the editors of the volume for valuable comments on draft versions of this chapter.
2 The uses of the concept of governance have increased since the 1990s. During the last decades there has been an erosion of the state's political power base, which is challenged both from within and from external developments beyond its control. According to many researchers, the concept of governance should be understood against this background (Pierre 2000a: 1f.; Rosenau 2000; Kjaer 2004: 6–7). Globalization implies that a new post-national conceptual framework is needed, and that political actions need to be legitimized differently than they were before. Many authors argue that the concept of (global) governance seeks specifically to confront these issues (Müller and Lederer 2005: 1; Pierre 2000b; Rosenau 2000; Kjaer 2004: 65).

3 The main empirical material upon which the analysis builds is the EU decisions concerning an operation within the framework of the European Security and Defence Policy, the Council joint actions and related documents such as press releases. The empirical material is limited, however, to the second pillar of the EU. Thus, it should be recognized that a broader picture would have been provided, had the activities of the first pillar been taken into account. This was, however, not possible within the framework of this chapter. The focus in the empirical analysis is on problems, solutions and participants. The details on internal EU decision-making structures and command structures, financial arrangements, contacts with third states, access to restricted material, mission status, etc. in relation to each of the missions analysed are largely left out of this study. The study involves empirical material up and until December 2007.

4 Council Common Position 2003; Brussels 2003a; Council Joint Action 2007b.

5 The dimensions have also been used in order to analyse the embeddedness of policy processes at multiple levels (Eriksson 2006).

6 Kooiman identifies three main characters of governing interaction: self-governing, co-governing and hierarchical governing. Drawing on Kooiman (2000: 146–147), the different modes of governance are understood in the following way; self-governing means that the parts of the system mainly govern themselves. This can be seen as sovereign states acting mainly autonomously. Co-governing consists of autonomous parts interacting in multilevel settings, though many relations are horizontal. Heterarchy is a central feature of this form of governance – the autonomous parts may partly give up their autonomy under certain conditions. Hierarchical governing implies a hierarchically organized, formalized type of interaction set in an environment of political and juridical guarantees. It often takes the form of policy or legal intervention in a corporatist setting. In a security policy framework it could, for example, be illustrated by an occupation. Various forms of mixed governing are also possible.

7 The list of references at the end of the chapter contains the full references upon which the results summarized in the tables are built. In the following text, however, only parts of the references are used.

8 At the Organization for Economic Cooperation and Development (OECD) homepage a commonly used understanding of Security Sector reform (SSR) can be found. It says that "SSR seeks to increase the ability of [partner] countries to meet the range of security needs within their societies in a manner consistent with democratic norms and sound principles of governance, transparency and the rule of law." Online, available at: www.oecd.org/dac/conflict/ssr (accessed 2 August 2008).

9 Several participants were involved in this particular endeavour; MONUC, France, Great Britain, Angola, South Africa, the EU Delegation of the Commission in Kinshasa and the police mission EUPOL (Press document 2006).

Part II

Barriers and opportunities to security governance

Recalcitrant hegemon and sectoral resistance

4 Global governance, security governance, and an imperious United States

Andrew L. Ross[1]

Introduction

Global governance and security governance remain incomplete and under construction. Despite the evident need for global and security governance and the opportunities for broadening and deepening the project provided by the Cold War's end, its future remains uncertain. Governance has been undermined of late, put at risk by a United States long considered one of its foremost champions. Its future and the prospects for a post-realist, post-Westphalian world depend in no small part on the future grand strategic choices made by this erstwhile champion. If a longer term governance crisis is to be averted, the system hegemon must be made safe for the global and security governance project. A distinctly institutional approach to global and security governance is employed here. Institutional arrangements, both formal and informal, are the infrastructure of governance. Without institutions, governance cannot be sustained. In the absence of a legitimate institutional framework, problems will not be addressed, managed, or solved collectively and cooperatively. The oft-noted distinction between government and governance thus should not be overdrawn. Global governance and security governance entail the development and the broadening and deepening of effective governmental-like functions and capabilities that can mitigate the effects of systemic anarchy and the security dilemma.

This exercise in theoretical exploration and reflection, theory and practice, and protest proceeds in five parts. First, the concept of security governance is situated – as it must be – in the broader context of global governance; an attempt is made to convey the conceptual and, briefly, empirical essence of both. Second, the nature of the relationship between domestic and international governance is explored; questions are raised about the implications of departures from the practice of good governance at home and the embrace of global and security governance abroad. Third, America's recent break with its previous support for the global and security governance projects[2] are addressed and, as it cannot but be, lamented. Fourth, the European Union's embrace of governance is contrasted with America's retreat from it. And fifth, the prospects that the governance projects will be restored to a prominent position in US grand strategy are considered.

Much like governance itself, this piece is a multidimensional analytical exercise. First, it is an exercise in theoretical exploration and reflection, if not theory development.[3] Second, it is an exercise rooted in the relationship between theory and practice;[4] more specifically it is a theoretically informed critique of practice – the practices of the system hegemon. Third, it is an exercise in protest – the exercise of Hirschman's "voice" (Hirschman 1970). The United States lost its way after 11 September 2001. That deserves, and requires, the attention of not only international and national leaders and citizens but scholars. Students of public affairs, whether domestic or international, must not remain silent in the face of demonstrably illiberal, illicit policy choices.

Security governance: a component of global governance

Conceptually, ideationally, and empirically, security governance is a component of, and subordinate to, global governance. The concept of global governance is itself analytically anchored in liberalism, particularly neoliberal institutionalism.[5] In a discussion of the relationship between global governance and power, Barnett and Duvall (2005) declared that that "the very language of global governance conjures up the possibility and desirability of effecting progressive political change in global life through the establishment of a normative consensus – a collective purpose – usually around fundamental liberal values."[6] Incorporated as well are constructivism's contra-realist and late-, if not post-, Westphalian emphasis on ideas and norms (Wendt 1999). The idea (as well as the ideal) and reality of global (and security) governance and a post-Westphalian world remain under construction. All may still be regarded as in a state of "becoming," even if that becoming cannot be regarded as inevitable.

Robert Keohane's work on global governance is central here.[7] Over time he has quite consciously and explicitly proceeded "from interdependence and institutions to globalization and governance" (Keohane 2002). For Keohane (2001: 2), institutions – "persistent and connected sets of formal and informal rules within which attempts at influence take place" – are at the heart of governance, global or otherwise.[8] Conceding that "global governance will have to be limited and somewhat shallow if it is to be sustainable," he depicted what can be fairly characterized as realistic, even modest, global governance, despite – or perhaps because of – his focus on institutions (Keohane 2001: 2). In a comprehensive and instructive approach that is as much prescriptive as theoretical and analytical, Keohane argued that global governance's consequences, functions, and procedures be informed by liberal democratic principles and practices. Its consequences, or outcomes, should be "security, liberty, welfare, and justice" for *individuals*. Its "five key functions" are to: check the resort to war; curb "beggar thy neighbor" policies and other "negative externalities of decentralized action"; provide "focal points" for cooperation; cope with "system disruptions"; and obviate "the worst forms of abuse." And its procedural criteria are to be accountability, participation, and persuasion (Keohane 2001: 2–3).

As suggested by the functions, procedures, and outcomes emphasized by Keohane, global governance can be conceived of as multilevel and multidimensional. Of the three levels of the governmental component of governance – supranational, national, and local – identified by Keohane and Nye (2002), however, only one is located on the international level.[9] Yet, in its international manifestations, whether global or regional, governance may be not only supranational but transnational and intergovernmental. All three levels are evident in the European Union, the most prominent example of regional governance.

In an important contribution, Higgott (2005: 577) initially conceived of global governance broadly as "the way in which actors – both public and private – attempt to accommodate conflicting interests through processes of collective-action decision making beyond state borders." He went on, however, to define global governance rather more narrowly as "those arrangements ... that actors attempt to put in place to advance, retard or regulate market globalization" (Higgott 2005: 577).[10] Globalization, economic or otherwise, indeed "depends on effective governance," as Keohane (2001: 1) emphasized. While the economic governance necessitated by globalization is critical, even for Keohane, global governance encompasses not only trade and monetary governance in the economic realm but also, in other realms, security, environmental, and legal governance (Hurrell 2007). In not a few of these realms, global governance is about "governing the commons" (Ostrom 1990).

The global governance project is aimed squarely at escaping international anarchy, which is postulated by realists, particularly neo- or structural realists, to be the defining feature of the Westphalian system. For global governance's conceptualists, ideationalists, proponents, and agents, international anarchy need not be all it has been made out to be by realists. It can be and has been (and should be) reigned in and constrained. Order – consisting of rules, institutions, governance – can be constructed where there is little or none. Even if anarchy will not be displaced totally by order, anarchy can be ordered; interstate relations can be domesticated, even if as yet only incompletely and imperfectly.

The potential for global or, more accurately, regional governance to mitigate anarchy is evident in the construction of what has become the European Union (EU). In an explicit and quite deliberate cooperative, collective search for an alternative to the practices that led to the disastrous world wars of the twentieth century, its members have sought to shed Europe's past (Eilstrup-Sangiovanni and Verdier 2005; Sheehan 2008). For the EU, "governance" is the watchword; it is the means by which systemic anarchy is to be tamed (Sandholtz and Stone Sweet 1998). The EU is an exceptional experiment in the construction of supranational, transnational, and intergovernmental governance arrangements (Ross 2008). A complex institutional and legal infrastructure complete with executive, legislative, and judicial bodies has been built (Stone Sweet *et al.* 2001). Common policies have been developed and adopted across a diverse array of issue areas. Keohane's normative standards, functions, procedures, and outcomes figure prominently in its institutions. As an experiment in the constitutionalization, and domestication, of interstate relations, the EU is arguably an instance of increasingly "hard" governance rather than the "soft," modest governance that Keohane believed to be the most that might be achieved. Its members have pooled their sovereignty, investing it in a supranational polity (Gerven 2005). Within its boundaries, the distinction between domestic and international has been blurred, rendered increasingly meaningless. The EU represents the state of the art in global governance. While it remains in the process of becoming, it has sufficiently become to give the lie to contemporary realism's dismissal of the prospects for and significance of collective, institutionalized cooperation and action.[11] Whether regarded as late- or post-Westphalian, the EU is an increasingly formidable international actor, particularly in the economic realm. Its market power and an ascendant Euro continue to confound diehard Euroskeptics, whether those found on the western shores of the English Channel or the North Atlantic.

Security governance

Security governance, arguably, is global governance's "hard case." In the security realm, global governance's conceptualists, ideationalists, proponents, and agents confront realism on what is presumed to be its home turf. If global governance takes aim at international anarchy, security governance puts the security dilemma thought to be inherent in an anarchical international system in the bull's eye. The security dilemma can be mitigated, if not eliminated; a game postulated to be zero-sum can be made safe for positive-sum gains.

Building on Webber *et al.* (2004) – as does James A. Sperling in this volume – Kirchner (2007: 3) defined security governance as "an intentional system of rule that involves the coordination, management and regulation of issues by multiple and separate authorities, interventions by both public and private actors, formal and informal arrangements, and purposefully directed towards particular policy outcomes." The concept is captured well in the five features of security governance identified by Webber *et al.* (2004: 8): heterarchy; "the interaction of a large number of actors, both public and private"; "institutionalisation that is both formal and informal"; "relations between actors that are ideational in nature, structured by norms and understandings as much as by formal regulations"; and "collective purpose." Pervasive throughout the conceptual explorations of security governance provided by Webber (2002, 2007), Webber *et al.* (2004), Kirchner (2007), Krahmann (2003), Sperling (2003) and others is Keohane's emphasis on norms and values, outcomes, functions, and procedures or processes.

Security governance is of course grounded in work on governance and global governance. As is evident in Sperling's contribution to this volume, however, the conceptualists, ideationalists, proponents, and agents of security governance have also incorporated and built upon analytical and theoretical work on the role of ideas[12] – particularly ideas about security (Buzan 1983; Buzan *et al.* 1998; Kolodziej 2005; Krause and Williams 2005) and soft power (Nye 1990, 2002, 2004) – and the concepts of concerts (Jervis 1985), collective security (Kupchan and Kupchan 1991, 1995; Weiss 1993), security institutions (Haftendorn *et al.* 1999), security regimes (Jervis 1983; Young 1999), security communities, (Adler and Barnett 1998b), and cooperative security (Carter *et al.* 1992; Nolan 1994). Ideally, security governance is collective, collaborative, institutionalized, and founded on "principles, norms, rules, and decision-making procedures around which actor expectations converge" (Krasner 1983: 1). In its most advanced, if not quite paradigmatic, form it is the democratic, pluralistic security community that spans the North Atlantic and features cooperative security's "overlapping, mutually reinforcing arrangements" (Carter *et al.* 1992: 8) embodied in institutions such as the OSCE, the EU and NATO and the complex interdependencies among them and their members. Even though this community has undeniably Westphalian roots and includes Westphalian, late-Westphalian, and post-Westphalian elements, the makings of a late- if not post-Westphalian order are evident. The proposed concert of democracies also exhibits late- and perhaps even post-Westphalian potential (Daalder and Lindsay 2007; Daalder and Kagan 2007; Diehl 2008; Carothers 2008).

Security governance, like global governance more generally, is multilevel and multidimensional. Most broadly, it can be said to operate at the global and regional levels. Globally, it is seen as manifest – and manifestly underdeveloped – in the work of the United Nations, whether the Security Council, the General Assembly or other organs such as the Disarmament Commission and the Geneva Conference on Disarmament, and in peacemaking, peace-building, peacekeeping, and peace-enforcement operations. The proposed concert of democracies has the potential to be global if not universal. At this broad global level, security governance, though encompassing both "hard" and "soft" security, is at its weakest.

It is at the regional level that the security governance project has exhibited the greatest potential. Although the emergent regional security governance capabilities of institutions such as the African Union, the Economic Community of West African States, the Caribbean Community, the Commonwealth of Independent States, the Shanghai Cooperation Organization, and Association for Southeast Asian Nations have merited mention (Sperling *et al.* 2003), it is the European, or transatlantic, project that has been highlighted. And within the European context, it is the EU that has been featured. The EU, with its embrace of instruments and functions that privilege the persuasive, particularly prevention and assurance, rather than the coercive, represents the state of the art for global governance and security governance alike. With the European Security and Defense Identity, Common Foreign and Security Policy, European Security and Defense Policy and the European Security Strategy, security governance within the EU has exhibited not only late- but post-Westphalian potential at the supranational, transnational, and intergovernmental levels (Mérand 2008). To the EU's multilevel governance – Union, societal, national and human – must be added multidimensional – common, comprehensive, and cooperative (Evans 1994) – security.

Governance: the domestic–international nexus and "good governance"

The relationship between domestic and international – or national and supranational, transnational or intergovernmental – governance has not yet been fully and systematically explored, much less definitively established. Analytically, the relationship may be depicted as "inside–out," "outside–in," or reciprocal. National principles and practices could shape, even determine, international principles and practices; international principles and practices could shape, even determine, national principles and practices; or the relationship between national and international principles and practices of governance could be interactive or reciprocal, both shaping the other.

At issue here, in yet another instance of an as yet unresolved (and perhaps irresolvable) debate among international relations theorists, is the primacy of systemic or unit-level explanations. With their emphasis on the implications of anarchy for state behavior, realists, whether of the structural/neorealist or other persuasions, have long insisted on the primacy of systemic over unit-level explanations, and on how systemic forces shape unit-level behavior and even characteristics. Unit-level explanations of international behavior and system characteristics are dismissed as "reductionist" (Waltz 1979). Systemic forces may well necessitate changes in national governance principles and practices; and what constitutes "good governance" may change in response to systemic, even structural, pressures. Yet – as realists themselves are wont to remind us – the principles and practices of international governance are less developed and institutionalized (and of less import) than those in place at the national level; the outside–in effect thus far is unlikely to be pronounced, much less profound. As, or if, the principles and practices of international governance are further developed and institutionalized (or entrenched), an interactive, reciprocal relationship may well become more evident. The focus here, consequently (and, arguably, necessarily), is on inside–out dynamics rather than on the reverse or on interactive, reciprocal dynamics. After all, the global governance enterprise is an effort to domesticate interstate relationships, including security relationships, by extending "good governance" from the domestic arena to the international arena.

The principles and practices of domestic good governance are well established and widely accepted (if not widely practiced). They are the near-universal standards to which the internal behavior of regimes are held. According to an oft-cited and authoritative United Nations Economic and Social Commission for Asia and the Pacific (undated) primer, good governance "assures that corruption is minimized, the views of minorities are taken into account and that the voices of the most vulnerable in society are heard in decision-making. It is also responsive to the present and future needs of society." A total of eight central characteristics of good governance were identified: participation; consensus; accountability; transparency; responsiveness; equity and inclusiveness; effectiveness and efficiency; and rule of law.

Two central points emerge from consideration of the nexus between domestic and global governance. First, the standards of good governance are applicable internationally as well as domestically. They apply to global (and security) governance practices no less than to domestic governance practices. Good governance need not – indeed must not – admit of a distinction between domestic and international. Second, the extent, effectiveness, and credibility of state support for global (and security) governance can be expected to reflect domestic (good) governance practices. The inside–out presumption here is that state attitudes toward global governance and, ultimately, security governance, are in no small part a reflection of, and are shaped by, domestic governance principles, or norms, and practices. Regimes that fail to practice good governance and fall short of its standards cannot be expected to embrace global governance. While domestic liberalism may not necessarily directly beget international liberalism, domestic illiberalism will not yield international liberalism. An absence or deficit of domestic liberalism and good governance is unlikely to fuel state support for international liberalism and global governance. Consequently, the expectation here is that states within which good governance principles and practices are observed will be the states most favorably disposed to champion global governance. Conversely, states with a good governance deficit or – importantly for the purposes of this argument – states within which good governance has been compromised or eroded can be expected to be less favorably disposed to global governance.[13] Indeed, states perceived as suffering from a good governance deficit are unlikely to be effective and credible proponents of any global and security governance project; they may do more to undermine than advance the project.

From a good governance perspective, whether global or domestic, consistency matters. Can good governance be promoted abroad when it is not fully evident at home? Is collaborative governance likely to be pursued abroad when the commitment to it at home is less than it could be? How can legitimacy not but lose stature as an international standard when it is perceived as insufficiently valued at home? Will oversight and accountability be promoted abroad when they are not always the gold standard at home?[14] Can transparency be embraced abroad when it is compromised at home? How can inclusion be held up as a standard abroad when it is not steadfastly ensured at home? Are the most vulnerable likely to be safeguarded abroad when they are not adequately protected at home? Will a regime that prefers not to engage its political opponents at home constructively engage those with whom it disagrees abroad? Is the centralization of power at home conducive to the sharing of power and sovereignty abroad? Will imperious behavior abroad be foresworn if an imperial executive is being created at home? Is it possible to be an effective voice for the rule of law abroad when it is less than faithfully adhered to at home? How can human rights be credibly promoted abroad when long-established civil liberties have been eroded at home? Can leadership in the construction and maintenance of a liberal order be exercised abroad when liberalism at home is at risk?

Governance and the system hegemon

"Governance" has fallen on hard times in the Unites States.[15] In the wake of presidential election of the November 2000, good governance and collaborative governance gave way to dysfunctional governance. Neither global nor security governance have been held in terribly high regard by the assertive nationalist and neoconservative denizens of the regime that held sway for two terms after January 2001. Instead of the principles and practices of global and security governance, the spirit animating US dealings with the rest of the world, particularly since 11 September 2001, has been a Manichean "either you are with us or you are against us."[16]

Despite valiant attempts to discern the continuities in pre- and post-11 September US behavior,[17] it was not always thus. The history of US grand strategy during the second half of the twentieth century is a history of US leadership in the construction of the institutions now regarded as integral to global and security governance. As John Ruggie (2007: 17) correctly observed: "More than any other country, the United States was responsible for creating the post-World War II system of global governance."

Indeed, as hegemonic stability theorists and neoliberal institutionalists alike have recognized, US hegemonic leadership played a necessary, if not sufficient, role in the establishment and development of a post-World War II order that featured a liberal, open economy and collaborative, institutionalized governance.[18] Ruggie (2007: 17) succinctly and evocatively captured the vision informing the US effort to construct the post-World War II world order as: "A modest form of constitutionalism embodying rules and institutions promoting human betterment through American-led collective security, free trade and stable money, human rights and decolonization, as well as active international involvement by the private and voluntary sectors."[19]

That US power, including military power, was deployed in pursuit of national interests as well as in the construction of an open, liberal order complete with institutionalized mechanisms of collaborative governance (Kupchan and Trubowitz 2007) does not diminish the centrality and force of the vision that inspired US policy and strategy in the wake of World War II. American power was harnessed to a vision that incorporated a broad, enlightened conception of its interests, one that admitted the interests of others, acknowledged the futility of pursuing narrow, short-term national interests at the expense of broad, long-term mutual interests, and generally, despite evident departures, emphasized absolute rather than relative gains.

The foundations of the "liberal democratic order" that emerged in the aftermath of the Great Depression and World War II featured, as John Ikenberry (1996: 81) has noted, "economic openness, political reciprocity, and multilateral management of an American-led liberal political system."[20] This American-led but increasingly "domesticated" order, as Ikenberry (1996: 84–87) pointed out, was built on a set of four central principles: economic openness – "a system of nondiscriminatory trade and investment"; collaborative governance; support for economic and social welfare; and "constitutionalism" – a joint commitment to "principled and binding institutional mechanisms." Open markets, transparency, free trade, nondiscrimination, shared economic and social welfare – collaboratively pursued and arrived at – served to ensure economic prosperity and a geopolitically circumscribed democratic peace. The grand result was globalization and the prospect of a late- if not post-Westphalian world. Thus the global governance project for which the United States bears no small responsibility both yielded globalization and is required to manage and sustain it.

Through the 1990s, the US maintained its commitment to liberal internationalism and global governance. And the United States in the early twenty-first century has continued to give voice to "the [liberal] ideas that conquered the world" – peace, democracy, and free markets (Mandelbaum 2002). In the wake of 11 September, however, the liberal rhetoric of the nation's forty-third administration failed to translate into liberal practice. US goals were cast as broad, collective milieu goals, but remained essentially particularistic in content and purpose. The principles, norms, rules, conventions, institutions, and processes of the global and security governance projects that served to ensure that the governance allegedly provided by the US Goliath was liberal rather than illiberal were no longer accorded the support that they received in the past (Mandelbaum 2005). Instead, the sinews of global and security governance were assaulted, put at risk by their former champion. The post-World War II US embrace of strategic restraint, the "binding effects of international institutions" and "increasing returns to institutions," and the open, accessible domestic political order emphasized by Ikenberry was little in evidence (Ikenberry 1998–9, 2001). In effect, the United States was perceived as having withdrawn from the "constitutional bargain" in which it agreed "to operate within mutually acceptable institutions, thereby muting the implications of power asymmetries, and other countries ... agree[d] to be willing participants" (Ikenberry 1998–9: 77).[21] The distinctly liberal hegemony of old gave way to an illiberal hegemony that took on the cast of a hierarchical, imperial order long regarded as alien to the American way (Ikenberry 2004; Rhodes 2003). Contra Mandelbaum, "strategic restraint" and "reassurance" appeared to have been dropped from the US strategic lexicon. It was no longer clear that multilateralism and institutions mattered. The Kantian tripod of democracy, economic interdependence, and international law and institutions was a distinctly less prominent feature of US policy and strategy than it was during the 1990s and earlier. A blatantly and imperiously hegemonic Westphalian mode of behavior was embraced; the coercive was privileged at the expense of the persuasive.

Tragically, the record of US departures from liberal internationalism and global governance's principles and practices after 2001 became all too familiar. Global governance was largely cast aside. When expedient, or merely convenient, the United States sought to exempt itself from the principles and norms of global and security governance and the body of international law in which they are embedded. The Geneva Conventions were held to be quaint and obsolete. What had previously been judged to constitute torture was recast as "enhanced" interrogation or "special methods." Secret legal opinions condoned the use of interrogation practices formerly regarded as illicit (Shane *et al.* 2007; Eggen and White 2008; Warrick 2008). Executive branch officials were routinely obliged to deny that the United States employed torture; an attorney general refused to confirm or deny that waterboarding constitutes torture. Instead of a commitment to due process and the rule of law, extraordinary rendition, secret prisons ("black sites") and military tribunals were employed, habeas corpus was compromised, and civil liberties were circumscribed (Mayer 2008; Holmes 2007). A nascent International Criminal Court was undermined at every turn. Preventive war was practiced under the guise of preemption; preemption, in turn, was enshrined as a strategic cornerstone. Openness and transparency gave way to secrecy, the preferred modus operandi. The steadfast refusal to be held accountable was compromised neither at home nor abroad. Reciprocity fared no better than accountability. American statecraft fell into what appeared to be a terminal state of disrepair.[22]

The strategic multilateralism and tactical unilateralism of old, particularly the 1990s, was displaced by strategic unilateralism and tactical multilateralism. What has been labeled "the multilateralist imperative" was regarded with scorn (Krauthammer 2002–3: 12; see also Bolton 2007). Multilateralism became inherently suspect. In its institutionalized form, multilateralism was regarded more as an effectual constraint on action – particularly US freedom of action – than as an effectual form of action. Institutions such as the UN and the UN Security Council were thought to be most useful when they followed the US lead; America's rulers did not think that a sole superpower needed a permission slip to defend its security.[23] Sovereignty rather than international legitimacy was held dear and near. American sovereignty was not to be sacrificed at the altar of global and security governance; neither was it to be regarded as "perforated." International obligations were shunned. The costs of dismissing conventions such as the Kyoto Protocol were adjudged to be low, even negligible. Soft power was viewed as just that – soft, much like the states and institutions attracted to it. Soft power and international institutions were seen as the refuge of the weak. Hard power ruled; soft power, for what it was worth, was derived from and subordinate to hard power.

The message from Washington after 2001 was quite clear: Governance requires rule, ruler, and ruled; security requires a security provider and "decider." If it is governing and security that are needed, the United States would be happy to oblige, but on American terms and with American methods. It would be US ideas, principles, norms, rules, conventions, institutions, processes, and outcomes that would prevail. Cooperation and collaboration meant following the US lead. Traditional alliances and coalitions of the willing were favored over collective or cooperative security institutions. Freedom and democracy – American style – were to prevail. Soft power gave way to hard power. Imperious nationalists and neoconservatives reigned.

During the early twenty-first century, "torture memos," Guantánamo, Abu Graib, Haditha, and Blackwater rather than the Declaration of Independence, the US Constitution's Bill of Rights, and the Statue of Liberty came to symbolize that for which America stood. The moment seized by the United States early in the twenty-first century was not the 12 September 2001 *Le Monde* moment – "We Are All Americans" – but an imperious, if not imperial, unipolar moment.

Governance: the EU–US divergence

The EU member-states and the United States have been portrayed as joined in common cause in a transatlantic democratic security community that features "collective identities and shared values; transnational economic and societal interdependence; and governance structures that channel and resolve political conflict" (Ikenberry 2004: 617). During the early years of the twenty-first century, however, their levels of commitment to the normative standards, functions, procedures, and outcomes of global and security governance diverged markedly (Schori 2005). Today it is not the United States but the EU rather that is governance's foremost champion.

Although the EU is a regional rather than a global manifestation of supranational, intergovernmental, and transnational governance that remains in the process of becoming, it is nonetheless the most fully realized manifestation of governance. The EU, as Russett and Oneal (2001) have pointed out, embodies the liberal, Kantian tripod of democracy, economic interdependence, and international law and institutions. Yet the EU is more than that. If the normative standards, functions, procedures, and outcomes of global governance are embedded anywhere, they are embedded in the EU. As a testbed for the constitutionalization, and thereby domestication, of interstate relations, governance is at the heart of the EU polity. On display is not merely the broadening and deepening of a complex, strategic interdependence within an international institutional framework, but the forging of a late- or even post-Westphalian political union among states that once guarded their sovereignty no less jealously than did the United States after 2001.

Unlike the United States of late, the EU and its members continue to hold dear the precepts of liberal internationalism and governance. While the principles, norms, rules, conventions (informal as well as formal), institutionalism, and processes that underlie global and security governance have been undermined by the United States, they are embodied – embedded even – in the EU. Having come together in no small measure in search of an antidote to the corrosive nationalism and militarism that once animated Europe's major powers (particularly during the late nineteenth century and the first half of the twentieth century), the EU member-states recognize – as is evident in the 2003 *European Security Strategy* – that tackling contemporary security challenges requires nonmilitary as well as military ways and means and a recognition that the resort to force should indeed be a last resort. Unlike the post-2001 United States, the EU is little inclined to hit every nail with a military hammer (Bacevich 2005). For the EU and its members, the instruments of choice are persuasive rather than coercive; state sovereignty and national interests have given way to collective authority and collective interests; the rule of law has triumphed over the rule of war; security cooperation has displaced the security dilemma.

The commitment to strategic multilateralism exhibited by the EU contrasts starkly with the strategic unilateralism and, at best, tactical multilateralism practiced by the United States after 2001. For the EU, multilateralism and institutionalism is the answer; for the United States, they have been the problem. Multilateral, institutional procedures and processes celebrated by the EU have for the United States been merely barriers to action that need be circumvented. The EU's high regard of the legitimacy thought to be conferred by global governance's normative standards, functions, and procedures, particularly when the use of military force is contemplated, has been looked upon askance by an incredulous United States. America's sovereignty and freedom of action are not to be sacrificed upon the altar of international legitimacy. The EU's veneration of international law and the well-advanced erosion of the distinctions among national, European, and international law left the United States nonplussed; after all, the depredations of international law – "lawfare" – must be resisted rather than embraced. For the post-2001 United States, the instruments of choice have been coercive rather than persuasive; state sovereignty and particularistic, national interests have trumped notions of collective authority and shared interests; the rule of law has given way to the rule of war; and security dilemmas have been little affected by security cooperation. Not only did the United States demonstrate its lack of appetite for any transition to a post-Westphalian security community, it put the existing Westphalian transatlantic security community at risk. In short, for the EU, there is a deficit of global governance; for the United States, there has been a surfeit of governance. Little wonder that the EU has displaced the United States as the leading proponent and exemplar of global and security governance.

Prospects

What are the prospects for a US return to constructive engagement in the global and security governance project? Progressivism's decisive victory on 4 November 2008 bodes well for good (and, at the least, competent) governance at home and global and security governance abroad. The regime change represented by the January 2009 advent of the Obama administration was a precondition for restoring the global and security governance project to its former grand strategic prominence. Yet its predecessor's combination of liberal, Wilsonian rhetoric and imperious behavior served to undermine the liberal world order and the global governance project long championed by the United States. The liberal project, even the promotion of democracy, has been rendered suspect at home as well as abroad by the illiberal (and inept) pursuit of liberal ends. Its predecessor's profoundly, and tragically, counterproductive record will long haunt the Obama administration and the country.

Realists were generally quicker than liberals – analytical or political – to point to the potentially disastrous consequences of America's imperious practices, particularly during the run-up to the March 2003 invasion of Iraq. Many liberals were too inclined to bandwagon behind a regime that, despite its evident rejection of liberal processes, indicated a willingness to pursue liberal, Wilsonian goals – to not just talk but act – particularly during the buildup to the Iraq War.[24] Before March 2003, the French and the Germans recognized that liberal ends may be undermined by illiberal ways and means. Too few of America's liberals – and Democrats – did, or at least too few who were willing to stand up and be counted. The illiberal American imperium that emerged in the early twenty-first century was not made possible simply by the post-cold war absence of external constraints on the exercise of American power; it was made possible as well by the absence of effective internal checks on the exercise of that power.

This early twenty-first century imperious legacy will not be easily or quickly overcome. From the start, the Obama administration has been burdened with a strategic salvage operation of enormous proportions. Overcoming the strategic legacy of its predecessor is no small task. Strategic triage cannot but be the order of the day. The new administration also confronts the no less challenging longer term grand strategic task of realigning the country's ends, means, and ways. There can be no guarantee that strategic realignment will yield a sustainable commitment to the restoration of the global and security governance project. The apparent erosion of the domestic political coalition that enabled the United States to embrace liberal internationalism during the post-World War II period places a formidable internal obstacle on the path to a realignment that features a restoration of the governance project (Kupchan and Trubowitz 2007).

None of the clearly realist alternatives in the continuing US grand strategy debate feature such a restoration.[25] Neo-isolationists and off-shore balancers would leave the global and security governance project to its own devices, bereft of superpower support and engagement. Selective engagement's proponents would have the United States take a more discriminating approach to global and security governance; a commitment to global economic governance is more likely to be in the offing than a serious commitment to security governance. Scarce resources are best not devoted to an enterprise the costs of which are likely to exceed its benefits, particularly in the near term. Primacy's realist advocates would seek a more efficient and effective exercise of US hegemony, one stripped of the overweening liberal, Wilsonian pretensions of the recent past. The neoconservative champions of empire – an analytical and political hybrid that amounts to primacy on steroids – agree with the realist advocates of primacy that America's empire must be run more efficiently and effectively than it was from 2001–8; yet they are little troubled by the liberal rhetoric and illiberal ways of the recent past.[26]

Liberal internationalists alone are attuned to the "made in the USA" crisis in global governance. They alone would move promptly and decisively to restore the US commitment to constructing a world order that features global and security governance. It is not global and security governance that must be made safe for the world and the United States; it is, instead, the United States that must be made safe for the global and security governance project. America must return to the fold. Even a sole superpower is not in a position to long go it alone; unilateralism is not sustainable.[27] The nontraditional, transnational challenges that beset global, regional, national, societal, and human security are best met with nontraditional, transnational strategic responses. Traditional Westphalian policies and strategies will continue to fall short. The United States can most effectively enhance its security by investing with others in institutionalized governance arrangements that impart legitimacy to the multilateral use of soft and hard power alike. A return to the broadening and deepening (and reform[28]) of existing institutional arrangements and the construction of new ones will provide the framework both for the pursuit of liberal ends in liberal rather than illiberal ways and for the legitimate, multilateral, collective exercise of hard and soft power.

Despite the tension between its progressive and realist impulses, the Obama administration is far more likely than a McCain administration would have been to return to the liberal internationalist program. Yet that return will be hamstrung by not only the grave economic turmoil that propelled now-President Barack Obama into office but the blowback prompted by its predecessor's imperious pairing of liberal ends and illiberal ways. The legitimacy of even liberal ends is undermined when, as was the case from 2001–8, they appear to be little more than cover for US hegemony and they are pursued in an illiberal manner. Means are no less consequential than ends. Even as the United States moves to find its way back to the fold, recovery – for both the United States and the global and security governance project – will be prolonged.

Notes

1 The author thanks Arita Eriksson, Jan Hallenberg, Maria Hellman, Mary Hilderbrand, Bertil Nygren, James A. Sperling, and Charlotte Wagnsson for their comments, suggestions, and insights; John Dyrcz and Yury Bosin for their research assistance; and Faith Brandt for her administrative support.

2 That global (and security) governance is not only an analytical or theoretical construct but a project is evidenced by the work of the Commission on Global Governance (1995), which was established in 1992 and produced a report published as *Our Global Neighborhood*. Michael Barnett and Raymond Duvall (2005: 1) have pointed out that global governance is "one of the central orienting themes in the practice and study of international affairs of the post-Cold War period.... For policymakers and scholars, global governance is one of the defining characteristics of the current international moment."

3 It is recognized that what some may regard as rather heroic – or, alternatively, foolhardy – analytical leaps are incorporated here. Rest assured that the author did look before leaping, though leap he did. However, while analytical leaps are countenanced, leaps of faith are not.

4 The global governance and security governance literatures are not only descriptive and explanatory but prescriptive – they are not merely about what is, and why, but about what should be, and how it can be.

5 For useful discussions of the concept of governance see Kahler and Lake (2003) and Pierre (2000b). An ontological perspective is provided by Hewson and Sinclair (1999).

6 Barnett and Duvall (2005: 5–6) go on to note the "liberal undertones" of conceptualizations of global governance.

7 Despite Higgott's (2005: 576) call for "European scholars of global governance ... to be 'theory makers' not simply 'theory takers,'" Keohane's work is central to Higgott as well.

8 Keohane (2001: 1, 11–12) here emphasizes the obligation of theorists to contribute to the improvement of political practice.

9 See also Nye and Donahue (2000). It is curious that the editors of *Transnational Relations in World Politics*, (Keohane and Nye 1970, 1971) detected only one level of governance in the international arena.

10 Higgott (2005: 577) went on to argue that "interest in the theory and practice of global governance reflect growing despair over the mismatch between the over-development of a global economy and what we might call the 'underdevelopment' of a global polity." Here again global governance is limited to the governance of globalization. Higgott is quite correct in noting the disparate levels of development of the global

economy and the global polity; why the global economy should be viewed as over developed is not clear, however.

11 For an example of contemporary realism's disregard – disdain even – for collective, institutionalized cooperation and action see Mearsheimer (1994–5).

12 Thus the prominence of constructivist thought.

13 This is a significant empirical issue that deserves greater analytical attention.

14 The Bush administration's embrace of the notion of the "unitary executive" and disregard for oversight and accountability were evident in its September 2008 "Legislative Proposal for Treasury Authority to Purchase Mortgage-Related Assets," which stipulated that "Decisions by the Secretary pursuant to the authority of this Act are non-reviewable and committed to agency discretion, and may not be reviewed by any court of law or any administrative agency." "Text of Draft Proposal for Bailout Plan," *New York Times*, 21 September 2008.

15 As Paul Krugman (2007) put it,

> Sometimes it seems that the only way to make sense of the Bush administration is to imagine that it's a vast experiment concocted by mad political scientists who want to see what happens if a nation systematically ignores everything we've learned over the past few centuries about how to make a modern government work.

Good riddance to good governance.

16 As President George W. Bush put it in his "Address to a Joint Session of Congress and the American People" on 20 September 2001, "Either you are with us, or you are with the terrorists."

17 For one such apologia see Gaddis 2004.

18 Hegemonic stability theorists and neo-liberal institutionalists disagree, however, on the extent to which hegemonic leadership has been needed to ensure the continuation of the open, liberal post-World War II order. See Gilpin 1977, 1981; and Keohane 1984.

19 See also Ruggie 1996.

20 See also Ruggie 1998.

21 As evident in the liberal interpretations provided by Ikenberry (2001, 2006), and Ruggie (1996) and the realist interpretation provided by, for instance, Leffler (1992), the history of America's post-World War II policy and strategy is a contested history. Yet even the decidedly realist interpretation advanced by Layne (2006) recognizes the centrality of liberal internationalism.

22 Necessitating works such as that by Dennis Ross (2007). Richard N. Haass (2006), a former member of the Bush administration, has also called for a revival of diplomacy.

23 President George W. Bush declared in his State of the Union Address of 20 January 2004 that "America will never seek a permission slip to defend the security of our country."

24 For one of the too few *mea culpas*, see Ignatieff (2007). For a post-mortem on liberal internationalism's role after 11 September 2001, see Smith (2007).

25 On the US grand strategy debate and the alternatives noted here, see Posen and Ross (1996–7); Ross (2005); and Dombrowski and Ross (2006, 2007). See also Posen (2007).

26 Indeed, they are responsible for it.

27 If nothing else, the United States during the early twenty-first century has demonstrated that unilateralism, even for the system hegemon, is not sustainable at an acceptable cost. Indeed, an attempt to sustain unilateralism will only serve to erode US hegemony.

28 On the need for reform, see Bradford and Linn (2007).

5 Unilateral endeavours challenging governance in the energy sector

Russia, China and the US

Bertil Nygren

Introduction: the "Great Game" in the Caspian Sea and Central Asian region

The end of the Cold War meant different things to European, American or Chinese state and private, political and economic actors, as it did to Turkey, Iran, Afghanistan, and Pakistan. To all it meant, however, 11 new states to place on the political and economic maps, with all that this suggested in the form of new opportunities as well as risks. But more generally, one might have believed that given the common (Soviet) history, common (Russian) language of communication, common (Soviet) experience with political and economic planning, common (Soviet) norms and behavioural rules, security governance would have had fertile soil in the Caspian Sea and Central Asian region (hereafter the CSCA region). One might also have believed that the end of the political, military and ideological conflict between Russia (the USSR) and China and the common road to market economy would favour security governance between these former adversaries as well. Finally, one might have believed that all of this would favour at least energy security governance. This chapter argues that post-Westphalian security governance is not evident in the CSCA region today, that both the newly independent states of the region and the major powers involved in the CSCA region are rather acting in an anarchical regional system where Westphalian state values are set high and the powers are playing out a traditional great power contest game – a "second Great Game" over the resources on the territories of the new states of the CSCA region.[1] The state actors of the region as well as the major external state actors, Russia, China and the United States basically have a zero-sum game approach even when it comes to the hydrocarbon resources, which in principle constitute readily divisible entities. The state actors very much think in terms of building alliances and creating balances of power, of continental territories and resources, and denial of "external" actors to the region. The threat typology of the states in the CSCA region, including those of Russia and China, is typical of the Westphalian state system: although new state threats to society abound in the region, the seriousness is seen in the threat to the state structure. Traditional threats to statehood and international wars are still seen as a distinct possibility, and new threats like terrorism are seen as threats to the state.

The post-Westphalian challenge to traditional state-centred thinking is thus particularly austere in the often clan-ruled CSCA states. The European norm transfer with respect to elections is particularly to the point. Here, the clash is evident: while Russian and CIS election observers (after the Orange revolution in 2004) have consistently judged in favour of the regime already in power – regimes which are nothing but dictatorships masquerading as democracies – European organizations have judged most of them as both unfree and unfair.

The coercive instruments of statecraft are invariably dominating in all fields of activities in the CSCA region and the policies of governance are basically coercive.[2] The function of conflict resolution is compellence, in Central Asia as well as in the Caucasus. In hardly any other part of the world, with the possible exception of the Middle East, is coercive conflict resolution as a strategy as common as here.

There are some obvious similarities between today's Great Game and the territorial quest of the colonial Russian and British powers of the nineteenth century over the CSCA region. There are also some significant differences. Neither the similarities nor the differences, however, point in the general direction of a pluralistic security community or of "security governance in the making". The reasons for this are spelled out more in detail below, but in general they include the fact that there are several great external powers today, most significantly China and the United States, but also regional powers like Iran and Turkey, as well as institutional actors like NATO and the EU, quite apart from the traditional great power and colonizer in the region – Russia – and the many new state actors themselves. Another reason is the fact that territory is important not only in its own right, but also because of the extent to which it contains exploitable hydrocarbon resources and/or transportation pipelines. Furthermore, while the first "Great Game" was played out with powers that were (for all practical reasons) "unitary", the second "Great Game" involved both state and private actors inside and outside of the region and only a few states of the region could be seen (even for practical purposes) as "unitary", although the persistent authoritarian features of government among the states in the region make them much more Westphalian than most other states of today's world. Furthermore, while the Russian "soft belly" of the nineteenth century still is "soft", its state actors are also very much more diversified than they were in the nineteenth century: weak and/or failed states, rogue states, de facto states as well as the five (or eight, including all of Caucasus) new *de jure* states, and also because there are private international and national companies as well as a multitude of non-state actors involved (clans, private armies, para-militaries, secessionists, freelancing peacekeepers. Therefore, today's "Great Game" might look different on the surface, and traditional great power thinking certainly does not catch the entire picture. It is a good starting-point, I argue, since the state actors involved, either in their capacity of states or in the capacity of state-owned and state-controlled companies, regard the game in very much the same way as did traditional great powers of the nineteenth and twentieth centuries. The nature of the Great Game of today is incomprehensible in any post-modern paradigm but fully understandable in a Westphalian one – the CSCA region is anarchic in nature, full of alliance shifts and emerging and falling contenders of regional powers (Kazakhstan, Uzbekistan and Turkmenistan).

One of the similarities of today's "Great Game" with that of the nineteenth century is derived from the hegemonic interests between the United States and reflected also in the CSCA region and the increasingly overt resistance to such interests by Russia and China. In a contest with three powers, the two weakest are bound to ally against the stronger. In addition, two of these – Russia and China – have an extremely evident inclination to remain Westphalian as well as authoritarian, still relying on military power boosted by economic might as the ultimate instrument of order. Another similarity between the first and second "Great Games" is the extent to which geo-political (and geo-economic) thinking is cherished and applied, inviting confrontation rather than cooperation due to the zero-sum character of the game.[3] Finally, the energy resources of the region constitute a major reason for the interest of the "external" powers in the CSCA region and, through this, are reminiscent of the colonial hunt for raw material as much as for territory itself (Karasac 2002: 18; Vinogradov and Wouters 1996: 87). The two go hand in hand, of course, and the state-centrism of the three major actors contributes to the strong link between geopolitical and geoeconomic objectives.

There are also obvious differences between the two "Great Games". First, the mix of a hunt for energy resources with a more traditional great power contest in the political and economic power vacuum following the demise of the USSR is further spiced with numerous local conflicts among groups of people not bound by state borders. Second, the CSCA region itself now contains eight new states (the former Soviet republics of Azerbaijan, Armenia, Georgia, Kazakhstan, Uzbekistan, Kyrgyzstan, Tajikistan and Turkmenistan), and the adjoining Afghanistan, Iran and Turkey. This creates several possible constellations and alliances between small and medium powers, quite apart from the constellations of the great powers.[4] Third, the emergence of a new type of actor and the interest of the EU in the CSCA region adds to the difficulty of interpreting this new "Great Game" along the same scales and dimensions as the first "Great Game". Finally, there are also other types of actors in this recent game, especially oil and gas companies some of which sometimes act out of other interests than those of any state. On the grander scale, today's "Great Game" also pinpoints the difference between the "Atlantic system of governance" and the Eurasian, more traditional, system of state conflicts (Sperling 2003).

Today's struggle over the energy resources of the CSCA region takes place in a region that for several millennia have been the battleground of different civilizations – of Turkish, Persian, Mongol and Arab origin and is also the last colonized region of the European and Russian colonization process. A shorthand review of the recent decades of the region helps us to understand today's situation and the way in which the second "Great Game" is similar/dissimilar to the first.

Recent history of the "Great Game" in the Caspian Sea and Central Asian region

After the demise of the USSR, there was a genuine geopolitical and geoeconomic vacuum in the CSCA region (Syroezhkin 2005: 113). Russia was weak and inward-looking, seeking a new identity and role. Russia did not pay much attention to the CSCA region where the many new states there were eager to consolidate their suddenly acquired independence. The United States, China and several neighbouring powers (Turkey and Iran in particular) were quite happy to watch a powerless Russia lose influence and their own opportunities grow. So did Islamic revival forces, inspired by Wahhabis and the Taliban (Syroezhkin 2002: 113).

From the mid-1990s, however, Russia began to develop a new foreign policy platform where the "near abroad" held a more prominent position – the Primakovian period had begun. Too late, one might have thought, since problems were swiftly mounting in Central Asia and the Caucasus where the influence of the Taliban in Afghanistan spilled over national borders and the drug routes almost achieved highway status: the "borders" were as easily penetrated by Islamist ideologues as by criminals.

By the turn of the millennium, Russia had recovered some of the regional influence lost to Turkey and Iran, but by then, both American, Chinese and European interests had established a foothold, partly for strategic, partly for economic interests. To maintain stability was a major security-related goal for the "outside" great powers. So was development of the rich hydrocarbon-based resources of the region. With Putin's coming to power, Russia emphatically re-entered the regional CSCA scene. The stage was now set for the second "Great Game" with one external great power, China, and the one global hegemon, the United States, a game basically over natural resources rather than territory. Old European great powers as well as the European Union itself invested both in stability and in the energy sector.

By this time, at the turn of the millennium, and when Putin entered the Kremlin stage, Russia had already been disappointed by the West. The NATO enlargement debate and NATO behaviour in the late 1990s epitomized by the Kosovo War and formalized in the new NATO doctrine of 1999 estranged Russia. Anti-US and anti-NATO feelings were thus running high in Russia. The next swing of the pendulum began in the summer of 2001 with the Putin–Bush summit in Ljubljana and became evident in Putin's unconditional support for the United States in the immediate post-September 11 period and in his acceptance of US military presence in Central Asia. In one stroke, Putin ended the post-Kosovo 1999 chill in the US–Russian relationship and in the two summits that followed (in Texas in November 2001 and in Moscow in May 2002), the former major conflict issues seemed to disappear (the resistance to the US abrogation of the ABM treaty and the further NATO enlargement to include former Warsaw Pact members). In a flash, Russia was back as an important strategic player on the world scene; second only to the hegemonic US power itself. This was probably the greatest calculated gain of letting the US into Central Asia and of supporting the "war on terror" (Syroezhkin 2005: 99).

This seemingly happy reunion with the United States did not last for very long, however. The disagreement over the Iraq invasion turned the tide once again, and within a few years demands for a timetable for US withdrawal from the Central Asian bases were heard. US policies toward Iran further distanced Russia and the United States as did the US demands for a "democratic life" in the CIS region. Since 2005, several CIS states have been more or less forced back into the bear hug, not by US design but by a failed attempt by the United States to play tunes to which the traditionally not so democracy-minded CIS leaders were unable to dance.

The Russian rapprochement and subsequently renewed disappointment with the United States and the West generally after a few years in the early 1990s was countered by a turn to China from 1994, when the official policy became one of "equal distance" to the two (Lukin 2003: 305). With the "Primakov period" starting in 1996, China seemed to come out on top. The new policy was epitomized by Yeltsin's visit to China, the first for decades, when a "strategic partnership" was announced (Lukin 2003: 309). Resisting US global influence and stabilizing Central Asia to prevent spill-overs of terrorism were obvious ingredients. Later, in June 2001, Putin raised the level of the relationship when Russia and China signed a Treaty of Good-neighbourly Friendship and Cooperation. The immediate post-September 11 Russian reaction and temporary rapprochement with the US temporarily changed the positions of the strategic triangle when Russia had let the United States into "its own space" without asking for China's reaction.

The later US finger-pointing at Iraq, Iran and North Korea as the "axis of evil" met with strong Russian and Chinese criticism and in a joint declaration in May 2003, the two condemned "unilateralism and power politics" (Wilson 2004: 38). This common opposition to the hegemonic behaviour of the United States in Iraq and elsewhere has remained the cornerstone of the Sino-Russian relationship since then. Sino-Russian relations reached an all-time high in 2005 with the final demarcation of the common border (the major issues had been resolved in the 1990s) and with the first joint Russia–China military exercises (named "Peace Mission 2005" and conducted under the aegis of the SCO) involving some 10,000 troops and some 140 vessels from the Russian Pacific Fleet. Speculations about the actual purpose of the exercise abound, especially whether they were directed against the United States or not. In August 2007, two years later, SCO joint military exercises were held in Chelyabinsk (Russia) – Peace Mission 2007 – enrolling some 6,000 soldiers the absolute majority of whom were Russian and Chinese.

This is one history of the 1990s, the other being the hunt for hydrocarbon resources, which constitutes another nexus of the new "Great Game" and lies "at the heart of this rivalry between regional and international powers" (Bahgat 2002: 314). The CSCA region is a "magnet pulling in the world's powers" and today the CSCA regional maps are on the tables of oil and gas executives as much as on the tables of governments (Fang 2006; cf. Johnson 2005: 274). The close link between energy security and traditional security concerns is evident, and competition to secure energy supplies among contestants like China and Japan, between India and Pakistan, between the East and the West, and even between the United States and Europe is increasingly desperate. At the same time, Russia is itself an important energy-producer as well as energy-consumer and has been the one major power in the CSCA region for at least one and a half centuries (retreating for a decade only in the 1990s). In addition, the major trait of Putin's foreign policy in the CSCA region is energy-related, and Putin has made a fairly successful re-integration attempt.[5] Given that boundaries are the "key in resource conflicts", the absence of good fences indeed make bad neighbours, particularly evident in the fact that the Caspian Sea has been the object of unsuccessful negotiations over how to delimit it for 15 years and is today being militarized (O'Lear 2004: 161, 163). In short, energy resources and their transit routes have become the focal point of the new "Great Game".

In conclusion, Russia has tried to balance China and the United States since the demise of the USSR. At times, Russia has had to choose between the two (especially immediately after 11 September) when Russia for little more than a year ended up clearly on the side of the United States, leaving a silent and deserted China on the sidelines. Then, the United States drove the two together again with its Iraq invasion, and the Russian–US relationship has deteriorated even further since then, and Russia and China have both been able to block UN sanctions against Iran and stand firm against Kosovo independence. Sino–Russian relations have also improved because of the eight-fold increase in trade (from US$5.7 billion in 1999 to 48.2 billion in 2007 and for 2010 amounts to US$80 billion) which has made China Russia's second largest trading partner after the EU (Lo and Rothman 2006: 14; RIA Novosti 17 January 2008). In order to see where the triangular relationship of Russia, China and the United States stands today in the CSCA region, first some security, then some energy aspects are discussed.

The nature of the new "Great Game": the contest for security in the CSCA region

The most important Russian security goal in southern Russia, the Caucasus, Central Asia and China is stability and order, especially resistance to separatist forces and to Islamic fundamentalism. Russia's problems in this respect are well-known and related to its century-long attempts to subjugate the Caucasus and the Chechens for the last one and a half decades. In Central Asia (as in the Caucasus), peoples and nationalities are mixed in fairly concentrated areas of otherwise vast lands. In the 1990s, this was spiced by an Islamist revival and spill-over effects from Afghanistan. China has its own domestic Islamist and separatism problem bordering on Central Asia – the Uighurs in Xinjiang (related to the Uzbeks in Uzbekistan, present also in Kazakhstan and Kyrgyzstan). State borders and separatism issues are obviously connected and by the mid- to late

1990s, China settled her borders with the three relevant Central Asian states (Kazakhstan, Tajikistan and Kyrgyzstan) as well as with Russia: no territorial issues as such were to hamper the goals of security and stability.

This recent "intrusion" of the United States and China since the 1990s in the typically Russia-dominated CSCA region is remarkable in many respects. First of all, Central Asia as a region has received an attention it has not enjoyed since the first "Great Game" in the nineteenth century and before that, since medieval times. Second, under Yeltsin, Russia could not do very much about the "intrusion" in its period of extreme weakness. Third, the increasingly tense energy quest of new and old great powers further elevated the interest of external actors of the region. The Russian disengagement was definitely to change with Putin and since his elevation to the Kremlin throne in 2000 there have thus been three great power contestants for influence in Central Asia and the CSCA region. The European Union has not been able to withstand the temptation to link stability and security to energy issues either, and to the extent that the EU is involved in the region it is basically for the same reasons – political stability to avoid energy disturbances.

With respect to the involvement of the West, the United States, NATO and the EU in the CSCA region, one would have to make a differentiation between Central Asia and the Caucasus. First, no Central Asian state has aspired or aspires to become a member of the EU or NATO (although all but Turkmenistan are Partnership for Peace (PfP) members), while in the Caucasus, Azerbaijan and Georgia have NATO aspirations, and all three Caucasus states have an interest in closer relations with the EU. Second, the Central Asian states have no traditions of belonging to the West and the major incentives for them to be at all interested has had to do with economics now that the Russian economy was down. Third, the economic interests of the United States, the EU and individual European states and private actors in the CSCA region have basically concerned energy resources in the Caucasus region. Here, at least two of the three Caucasus states, Georgia and Azerbaijan, have been looking to the United States and to NATO as security providers against Russia while Armenia has been a firm ally of Russia. Furthermore, all three Caucasus states have joined the European Neighbourhood Policy and look forward to economic relations with the EU as an alternative to the present economic relationships with Russia. In addition, while Azerbaijan has been one of the Caspian Sea's fortunate energy holders for an entire century, the other two Caucasus states are typical consumers in need of hydrocarbon based energy.

The United States has also engaged itself as a security provider in Central Asia, especially after 2001. While overflight rights for support of the war effort in Afghanistan were granted by several countries, Kyrgyzstan and Uzbekistan provided air fields. Putin met with strong domestic opinion (especially from the Defence Minister Sergey Ivanov), but the customary interpretation at the time was simply that it was better to have the United States in Central Asia than Islamist warriors in Moscow (Nygren 2007: 207). Kyrgyzstan, a heavily dependent ally of Russia, let the Manas airbase to US air forces and received US assistance in securing its Afghan borders. A Russian airbase was soon established in Kyrgyzstan as well, generally seen as a counter-move. Tajikistan also had to be protected from "spill-over" effects from Afghanistan and the United States and NATO have been assisting border control when Russian border guards were withdrawn from the Afghan–Tajik border in 2006. The more flagrant competition between Russia and the United States in Central Asia has been played out in Uzbekistan, which was something of a problem to Russia in the 1990s because of its attempts to become an independent leader in Central Asia. With 11 September, a US airbase was allowed on Uzbek territory and Russia for some time feared that the US would become the prime security provider in Uzbekistan (Jonson 2004: 89). Due to the row with the United States over Uzbekistan's human rights record after the Andijon events in 2005, Uzbekistan closed the US airbase and turned it over to Russia, which changed the balance of power drastically in favour of Russia.

Apart from the Afghanistan-related engagements of the United States, the US has also supported the Kazakh naval build-up and financed a Kazakh naval base in the Caspian Sea (in 2003), some aspects of which met with firm Russian protests in 2004 and 2005 (Nygren 2007: 209). Military equipment has nevertheless been provided by the United States and high-level visits by US officials in 2005 resulted in an individual partnership action plan (IPAP) with NATO being signed. Kazakhstan and the United States have also held anti-terrorist military exercises in 2005, 2006 and 2007.

The other external security provider in the CSCA region is China, which has worked mainly through the SCO (which it initiated), but China has also had some bilateral arrangements with Central Asian states. Since 2004, China and Kazakhstan developed security cooperation and the two have held annual joint military exercises since then (Alibekov 2004; Klevemann 2004: 13). Chinese anti-terrorism cooperation with Kyrgyzstan and Tajikistan has also been frequent. Furthermore, when Uzbek–US relations turned for the worse in 2004 and 2005, China's relations with Uzbekistan improved. The general issue in all security-related activities has been anti-terrorism and the reason is China's own terrorism problem – the Uighurs – a Turkish-speaking Muslim minority in northern China.

The post-Soviet history of Russia as a security provider in the CSCA region starts in the early 1990s with its involvement in the Tajik civil war, where Russian forces actively fought on the side of the Tajik government against the insurgent forces. Apart from that, inactivity and reactivity were the main traits of Russian Central Asian policies during Yeltsin's early regime. With the Taliban victory in Afghanistan in 1996 the situation changed and worsened the situation for Tajikistan, Kyrgyzstan and Uzbekistan and by the late 1990s Russia had become heavily involved in the defence of borders against Islamist forces invading from Afghanistan. The Taliban threat became all too obvious in 1999 when intrusions were seriously threatening the entire region. Russia had now become the major security provider to assist the weak regional actors in avoiding widespread influence of destructive Islamic activism. This Russian involvement had the evident character of a regional hegemon exercising a "duty" as much as a "necessity".

The major security vehicle in Central Asia today is the SCO – the Shanghai Cooperation Organization (in its earlier manifestations the "Shanghai Five" and "Shanghai Six"). The initial objective was to regulate the 7,000 km borders and reduce military forces along them (Kazakhstan, Kyrgyzstan, Tajikistan and China signed border agreements in 1996 and Russia and China signed their border agreement in 2001). The initial thrust on border issues soon changed into an "anti-terrorism" pact when, in April 2001, the Shanghai Six (Uzbekistan had joined) signed a treaty to fight "terrorism, separatism and extremism". The Shanghai Six became an international organization in 2002 and its charter holds the main objectives to be to strengthen mutual trust, friendship, and good-neighbourliness.[6] The SCO has held several anti-terrorism exercises since 2003 (in Kazakhstan and in Xinjiang in China), the most renowned exercises were the basically Russia–Chinese military exercises in summer 2005. They were followed by new exercises in Uzbekistan in March 2006 and in Russia in July 2007. From 2005, new objectives have been added, particularly on resisting Western-influenced "colour revolutions" in the member-states. China has been more eager to use the organization to keep the United States out of Central Asia than has Russia.[7]

The nature of the new "Great Game": the contest for hydrocarbon resources in the CSCA region

Energy resources and energy outlets generally have a potential to create conflicts and to reinforce existing ones, and since energy is bound to remain the most important object of resource competition in the decades to come, the CSCA region will remain the focus also of "external" powers.[8] Indeed, the gas resources of the Caspian Sea have already become the object of severe competition between the larger consumers, Europe, Russia, China and the United States (Belton 2006). Central Asia, and western Siberia, together with the Russian Far East, constitute major world hydrocarbon reserves, second only to the Persian Gulf region.[9] We should be careful not to overstate the hydrocarbon resources of the CSCA region since they are often blown up out of all proportion.[10] On the other hand, as the hunger for oil and gas continues to grow in the world, the CSCA region is important enough for the major consumers to compete over, especially if its export routes are believed to be more reliable than other outlet routes. Furthermore, the energy resources in the CSCA region are geographically close enough to be of direct interest to three of the four consumer areas, to China as well as to Europe and Russia. Even more important, Russia is not only a major consumer and a major transit route for exports of hydrocarbon resources from the CSCA region, but is itself also a major producer of hydrocarbons and is thus also competing with the Central Asian states for export both to Asian and Western markets. For this reason, Russia tries to gain control (not necessarily ownership) of all hydrocarbon resources in the CSCA region, and President

Putin himself has been an eager proponent of building a new "energy empire" (Hill 2004; Nygren 2007).

The competition for pipeline routes among the great powers is part of this energy contest. While the EU and the United States for the last decade have been involved in pipeline projects aimed at avoiding Russian territory (under the banners of "diversification of suppliers"), the real issue is access to the resources themselves. This creates a dilemma for the West. On the one hand, the West is buying hydrocarbons from Russia, and the West is also cooperating with Russia in the construction of pipelines through Russia of Russian and CSCA hydrocarbons. On the other hand, the West does not want Russia to control the routes of alternative suppliers in the CSCA region to the West. Instead it supports the construction also of alternative routes. In this pipeline competition, Russia has the upper hand since it is both a provider of hydrocarbons and a major transit route for CSCA hydrocarbons. To Russia, avoiding the construction of alternative routes makes business sense as much as it does to the West of assisting alternative routes.

We should also note that oil and gas pipelines have particular geopolitical traits quite apart from the geoeconomic ones. "Pipeline politics" is, generally speaking, a little bit of both. Since the oil and gas producing countries in the CSCA region are trapped by the pipeline geography inherited from the Soviet era, they have basically been at the mercy of the Russian transit policy. With Putin's attempt to reassert the great power role of Russia and with the soaring oil and gas prices in the first decade of the twenty-first century, Russia has tried to conclude long-term agreements with Central Asian producers on joint production, deliveries and transits. At the same time, active attempts by some Central Asian states to escape the "transit trap" have been strongly resisted by Russia. In fact, the Russian "transit weapon" (the possibility to deny transit or design the import/re-export price), especially on gas, has been a major instrument of Russian foreign policy in the CSCA region (Nygren 2008b). Geopolitics is also involved in avoiding some routes, especially the Iranian oil route resisted by the US (Karagiannis 2003: 156–157).

Many important gas pipelines have been prospected in the CSCA region – especially the underwater Trans-Caspian gas pipeline (TCGP) from Turkmenistan to Azerbaijan, the prospects of which are still slim after more than a decade of planning. This pipeline is basically aimed at bypassing Russian territory to tap directly into Turkey as an energy hub for the Middle East as well as for the CSCA region. Both the EU and the United States favour this project, which has stranded basically because of the need for consent from the other littoral powers of the Caspian Sea. All three great power contestants, Russia, China and the United States, as well as the EU, began an eager flirtation with the new Turkmen leadership in 2007 and the TCGP is still on the table, although the resistance among the other Caspian Sea states is strong, especially Russia, which has of late gone to great lengths to secure its influence over the Turkmen gas resources and transit routes (see below). To Europe, the Trans-Caspian gas pipeline might be as important as it is to Turkmenistan.[11] On the other hand, the construction of the South

Caucasus Gas Pipeline or the Baku–Tbilisi–Erzurum pipeline – BTE – from Azeri gas fields to the north Turkish hub at Erzerum began in 2004 and has been in use since late 2006. This, too, is designed to avoid Russian territory.

Much more flagrant an attempt to bypass Russia is the South Caucasus Oil Pipeline or the Baku–Tbilisi–Ceyhan (BTC) pipeline project, a 1,700 km "southern route" outlet designed to empty the Azeri oil fields in the Caspian Sea and export oil via Georgia to the south Turkish Mediterranean port of Ceyhan. The construction began in 2003 and the pipeline was finally inaugurated in its entire length in 2006. The major capital investments are American and both presidents Bill Clinton and George W. Bush openly supported the project, which has greatly irritated Russia (Kleveman 2004: 12).[12] The EU has in recent years become more and more convinced of the need for constructing a hydrocarbon transit corridor – the southern corridor – from the Middle East via Turkey to Europe: the Nabucco pipeline. This extremely expensive corridor via Turkey would receive more legitimization if it could swallow also the gas reservoirs of the CSCE region. Some new hopes were lit in the summer of 2008 when a Turkmenistan–Azerbaijan summit discussed joining Nabucco (Pannier 2008b). The Turkey hub would in a decade rival the Ukrainian route to Europe.

Russia has not been idle in renewing its oil and gas pipelines in the last decade to handle hydrocarbon exports from the CSCA region (and from Russia itself). Russia for one has built an underwater gas pipeline across the Black Sea (from Novorossiisk in Russia to the Turkish Black Sea port of Samsun and further to Ankara) – Blue Stream – in use since the early 2000s (and to be complemented by a second gas pipeline – Blue Stream II, yet to be built). The recent (early 2008) conclusion of a multilateral deal on the South Stream project whereby gas from Russia and the CSCA region will be piped to Bulgaria (and then further into central and southern Europe) is further proof of Russia's determination to also compete in the pipeline routing.

China has also been an active economic player in Central Asia since the demise of the USSR. China was quick to recognize the Central Asian states. State visits and agreements on trade and economic cooperation followed and by 2004 investments reached US$1 billion (O'Rourke 2005).[13] Economic cooperation mainly concerns energy resources. Transports are generally long and expensive (Bahgat 2005: 124, Gelb 2006). From 2003, China has assisted in building and financing a 2,400 km oil pipeline worth some US$9 billion, Kazakhstan's biggest oil pipeline project ever and the first oil pipeline from Central Asia not crossing Russian territory, inaugurated in late 2006 (Fang 2006).[14] The part of the oil pipeline that runs through Kazakhstan (960 km) is partially in operation in 2008 and will be completed by 2010 and transport 20 million tons of oil annually (Pannier 2008c). Other fields of energy cooperation include nuclear energy cooperation since 2004, and in late 2005, Kazakhstan signed a US$10 billion agreement to export electricity to China. China has made its largest investment abroad ever with respect to energy in a gas pipeline from Kazakhstan to Xinjiang, to run parallel to its oil pipeline, in an agreement signed in 2006 to which also Uzbekistan and Turkmenistan will connect. The pipeline will be

7,000 km long and run from eastern Turkmenistan through Uzbekistan and Kazakhstan; the throughput is 30 bcm (billion cubic metres) annually for 30 years (Pannier 2008c).

From 2005, China has invested some US\$600 million also into Uzbek oil and gas fields. In April 2007, it was announced that a 530 km gas pipeline would be built from Uzbekistan to China, with a capacity of some 30 bcm a year, constituting approximately half of the Uzbek gas production, to be linked up with the abovementioned gas pipeline on the Chinese side. Such a pipeline drastically decreases Uzbek export transit dependency on Russia. China's relations with Turkmenistan have been limited until very recently, and the routing of the Turkmen gas pipeline to pass Uzbekistan has hitherto prohibited Turkmen export to China, but in 2005, plans for Turkmen gas exports to China took off again, and in 2006 a 30-year Turkmen–China gas pipeline agreement was finally signed. The pipeline will largely be financed by China, with construction costs estimated at an astounding US\$10 billion. In July 2007, the new Turkmen president made a state visit to China to reaffirm Turkmen interest in the pipeline, with construction supposed to begin in 2008.

That leaves us with Russia. Energy resources and energy transits have been major instruments in Russia's dealings with the CSCA region during the Putin presidency. While Russia was distraught with domestic political and economic problems all through the 1990s, the last decade shows a very different story. Grand ideas have not been lacking. In 2002, Putin suggested creating a gas cartel (the Eurasian alliance of Gas Producers) composed of Russia, Turkmenistan, Uzbekistan and Kazakhstan, in order to implement a "single export channel policy", the basis for which could be Gazprom's pipeline network in the region (*RFE/RL Newsline* 22 January 2002). While nothing came out of this attempt to control the Central Asian export links at the time, bilateral negotiations and agreements followed later with Kazakhstan, Uzbekistan and Turkmenistan, pointing towards an idea which was ripe for the time: a "cartel". First, we will look at the three main Central Asian actors one by one, and then return to the issue of a possible gas cartel under Russian leadership.

The Turkmen gas fields have been the most locked-in and Turkmenistan has been the most difficult nation to handle for Russia, largely due to the recalcitrant Turkmen leadership until 2007. In 1999, an agreement to resume large gas export volumes via Russia was finally signed after a decade of limited Turkmen gas exports. The suspensions of deliveries due to price quarrels have been frequent since then, and only in 2003 did a major 25-year agreement on gas exports via Russia get signed that vouched for Russia as the major (some 70 per cent) buyer of Turkmen gas (most of which to be re-exported by Russia to Europe at high profits). In 2004 and 2005, delivery disturbances followed from failed gas price discussions, and a *price* agreement was reached only in late 2006. The picture would change drastically in 2007 and 2008.

Russia has also been the main export route for Kazakhstan's hydrocarbon resources, although Kazakhstan has tried to diversify its export routes. The completion of the Caspian Pipeline Consortium oil pipeline via Russia in the summer of 2001 (which complemented the old Atyrau–Samara oil pipeline) reinforced Kazakhstan's dependency on routes via Russia.[15] With respect to co-production, in 2005, Russia and Kazakhstan signed a 55-year production sharing agreement to develop a new oil field, where the total investments were estimated at more than US$30 billion. In 2007 and 2008, the "gas cartel" also solved much of Kazakh gas transit problem (see below).

Russian investments in a new gas export pipeline also from Uzbekistan to Russia have come forward in the Putin presidency. In 2004, Uzbekistan signed a 15-year production sharing agreement with Gazprom and LUKOIL signed a production sharing agreement for 35 years to develop a gas field. In 2005, several more follow-up agreements were signed, and in 2006, Gazprom announced its intention to invest US$1 billion in Uzbek gas projects. In all these deals, Putin was personally engaged. Finally, Uzbekistan was let into the "cartel" deal by connecting to the pipeline from Turkmenistan.[16]

To return to the Russia-led gas cartel (or "gas OPEC"), the idea was first floated in 2002 and re-surfaced in May 2006, when in negotiations with Europe, Gazprom threatened to establish "an alliance of gas suppliers more influential than OPEC" (Kupchinsky 2007). Russia officially denied cartel plans, but stuck to cooperation and coordination schemes with the Central Asian states. In 2007, the new Turkmen president showed an obvious interest which opened up for discussions on a possible "gas cartel". Then, in May 2007, Putin and the presidents of Kazakhstan and Turkmenistan signed an agreement on constructing a new US$1 billion gas pipeline that would drastically increase gas exports to Europe via Russia. The pipeline would run from western Turkmenistan via Kazakhstan to Russia along the east Caspian Sea coast, parallel to an existing smaller gas pipeline (the Prikaspiiski gas pipeline), then connect to the existing Russian gas pipeline network destined for Europe. This agreement was a blow to US and European efforts of finding a southern route for gas across the Caspian Sea, to Azerbaijan, and further via Georgia to Turkey and to Europe. The new pipeline reinforces Russia's role as the main exporter of gas to Europe. With this new major pipeline and with the modernizing of existing ones, Russia could import from Turkmenistan up to 80 bcm (from today's 40 bcm), to help tap the estimated (CIA estimates) 2 tcm (trillion cubic metres) available in Turkmenistan (Vershinin 2007). The gas agreement was signed in a treaty in September 2007.

In conclusion, this gas agreement basically established a "gas cartel". The new "Great Game" for Central Asian energy resources among Russia and the United States and Europe has therefore been won by Russia, since the agreement amounts to no less than a showdown in the fight over export gas pipelines from Central Asia to Europe. The agreement revamps the odds in the "Great Game" in favour of Russia where the West is the obvious loser, or even subject to a "disaster" (Blagov 2007). To China, the "gas cartel" deal created some uncertainties about its own plans for future Central Asian gas. What is left of the new "Great Game" after the "cartel deal" is in any event for Russia and China to pick up, with the United States and Europe having more the role of spectators.[17] To cement the "cartel", the major demand by Central Asian producers was met in the spring of 2008 when Russia conceded to pay to the Central Asian producers "European" prices, i.e. some USD 350–400 per 1,000 bcm of gas instead of the much lower price paid before that (Pannier 2008a). If implementation runs smoothly, the "cartel" deal will become a major piece in future history books, as proof that Russia has learnt to act also as a "soft power" (Hill 2004: 6; Nygren 2008a).

Conclusions – the new "Great Game" – results so far and what is to follow

The "second Great Game" started more than a decade ago with the entrance of the United States into the CSCA region, an uninterested EU and with Russia at its weakest. Since the early 1990s, US security and energy involvement in the CSCA region has been directed at diverting the traditional dependence of the new states from Russia. China made its overtures as a serious player in the CSCA region at least from the mid-1990s, both in the security and the energy spheres. Both the United States and China were to be contested by Russia since it began to reassert itself in the latter years of the 1990s and especially since Putin became president in 2000. After 11 September, an entirely new dimension was introduced with the "war on terror" adding to the skyrocketing prices of hydrocarbon energy resources, which in themselves acted as a magnet for consumers. The CSCA region has thus become an object, and a prey, for diverse political, military and economic forces. The United States was gradually to lose influence in both fields of activities after a boost as a security provider immediately after 2001, and later even to become a burden to some of its earlier security clients in the region because of its calls for democracy and human rights. There is today a triangular game being played out in the CSCA region, among Russia, China and the United States and where the EU is not really involved as a serious player.

On the surface of the matter, China seems to be on the same side as Russia and the United States with respect to the "war on terror", but China has kept a very low profile fearing long-term consequences. On the one hand, stability in the region increases from US involvement, although on the other, China faces serious competition for security influence and has no choice but to carefully follow the doings of Russia and the United States. In addition, China has its own interests in the anti-terrorism campaign – named Taiwan, Tibet and Xinjiang – in which a conflict with the United States is quite possible. Furthermore, as in Central Asia itself, the Chinese political leadership has learnt the downside of US support on anti-terrorism, i.e. its equal support also for democratic rule, which directly threatens the leadership of these countries.[18]

With respect to security and defence in the CSCA region, there are two types of threats to the CSCA region (and to Russia) emanating from China. First, if China grows too strong militarily, it poses a traditional security threat to Russia. Or, if China implodes, the chaos will spill over into the CSCA region (and possibly also into Russia) (Lukin 2003: 246ff). Second, the very fact that China solidifies its position as an economic power, that power will most likely also be translated into military capabilities. This is a typical Russian threat perception of China which will move against Russia as soon as it is strong enough to do so. The present Russian "hug your enemy" response to challenges from China will thus not remain for long (Lo and Rothman 2006: 20–21).

Most importantly, there are a few circumstances that would have to enter any equation of the future triangular relationship in the region, i.e. Russia's long-standing basic distrust of China and the real fear that a strong China might threaten the Russian Far East. This induces the United States to make a choice of supporting one of the two against the other. There is simply no reason to believe that the mutual Russian and Chinese distrust of the United States after the Iraq invasion is a stable foundation for Sino–Russian relationship, or that the "multi-polarity" doctrine would survive a serious test in the longer term (as the immediate post 11 September situation indicates). Second, the United States is by far the most important security and economic interlocutor to both Russia and China. In the security sphere, the United States still has a serious advantage over any of the others against a third state. Just to take one example: would Russia unequivocally stand up behind China in case of a developing conflict over Taiwan? Simply put, would Russia risk its relationship with the United States for China's ambitions with respect to Taiwan? The answer is obvious. Or, should the United States put economic pressure on China, would Russia follow suit or stand by its economic and energy commitments to China? Or, should the United States put economic pressure on Russia, would China risk its economic relations with the United States for Russia? The general uncertainty stems from the fact that both Russia and China are much more oriented towards the West than to each other, and a Moscow–Beijing axis is therefore to a significant extent illusory (Lo and Rothman 2006: 23). Russia also holds some trump cards in its close defence cooperation with some of the Central Asian states and as the prime security provider for Kazakhstan, Kyrgyzstan and Tajikistan (and possibly also for Uzbekistan). China's role as a security provider in the CSCA region is much less significant, and should the Central Asian states ever have to make a choice between Russia and China, they would all opt for Russia.

Russia is today the strongest security provider in Central Asia and it would be difficult for any other state to challenge this position. The United States is likely to continue its general security policies in the CSCA region, linked to the Afghanistan as well as Iran *problematique*. The prospects are, however, that once the US has withdrawn from Afghanistan, and provided it does not avert to military means towards Iran, the CSCA region will become even more dependent on Russia than it was before 2001 (cf. Nygren 2007; Pershin 2003; Feiser 2003). For all of this, the triangular "Great Game" is likely to continue in the security sphere and there is no reason at all to suggest that anything but a vile Westphalian-based struggle lies ahead.[19]

With respect to the energy side of the "Great Game", it is obvious that although the United States will not entirely lose interest in the region, the future "Great Game" in the CSCA region will, rather, be a struggle between Russia – which already has considerable influence over Kyrgyzstan and Tajikistan and is trying to consolidate its influence over Kazakhstan, Uzbekistan and Turkmenistan – and China, which is trying to establish itself as a reliable economic player in the CSCA region with its investments and promises of new energy export routes. Iran and Turkey still remain important regional actors in the Great Game, especially as potential export routes of Central Asian oil and gas both to Western markets and (for Iran) also to China, India and Pakistan. The EU desire for the Nabucco route from the Middle East to be connected also to the hydrocarbon resources of the CSCA region is still in the making, and the pipeline routings so far (the BTC and BTE) constitute only minor solutions.

China will still be a serious competitor to Russia in the CSCA region in the medium and long term. Its prime objective, but also its basic problem, is its increasing dependence on imported energy and its strategy of import diversification. China is literally trying to sit on two chairs at the same time: Russia will most likely become one major supplier of oil and gas to China, and the three hydrocarbon-rich Central Asian states are potential competitors (apart from the Middle East and Africa). There is thus a fundamental dilemma confronting China in the fact that its major future supplier will be Russia (in the Far East) at the same time as China and Russia are competing for the hydrocarbon resources of Central Asia. With respect to China, Russia is thus both a supplier of hydrocarbon resources and a competitor over Central Asian resources.[20] To the extent that resources are running more scarce in the medium and long term, the resource competition in Central Asia may very well force Russia and China into a clinch. This is particularly obvious with respect to Kazakh oil and Turkmen gas. In such a situation, Russia holds some strong cards, the most important ones being that Russia will be able to threaten with an export cut of its Far Eastern oil and gas to China (and redirect it to Japan, the United States and the Pacific region).

History so far shows us that Russia was the modern colonizer of Central Asia in the nineteenth century, and the USSR made Central Asia part of modernity and could benefit from that in the years to come. There is no evident fear in Russia today that China or the United States will become serious contenders to Russia's position in the short or medium term. As a result of the "Great Game" so far, Russia has re-established itself as the major regional power, this time in the energy as much as in the security field (See Nygren 2007; Hill 2004). Russia has been able to defy the political and economic influence of the United States in Central Asia, and in the medium to long term it will do so also with respect to China. There are several reasons for this. First, Russia still has the cultural advantage of knowing the region, its peoples, cultures, leaders and its clan-ridden political systems.[21] Second, Russia still has some advantage from the remnants of the Soviet infrastructure, especially with respect to energy extraction, production, transportation and communications. Third, Russia has a permanent stake in the security situation of the region and is likely to continue its present course to integrate the Central Asian states in its own security sphere. Fourth, Russia is about to win the contest over exit transits of Central Asian gas resources despite some serious attempts by the West to open up alternative export routes. Finally, Russia has supported the Central Asian leaders when they came under attack for their lack of democratic development by the EU and the United States.

Since China has already established itself in the CSCA region, there is thus a potential for a Sino-Russian conflict in the future. The bilateral Sino-Russian relationship has always been a simple (at worst) or mixed (at best) bag and there is still much mutual suspicion on both sides. Russia has a lingering Mongol complex, best seen in the illegal migration issues in the Russian Far East.[22] China, in turn, often complains of such Russian suspicions, but also of actual Russian sales of more advanced weapons to India than to China and more generally China mistrusts Russian interests in the Pacific area (Lo and Rothman 2006: 13,15). The surface-picture of a happy Sino-Russian relationship thus rests on somewhat shaky ground.

The energy agenda of the three clearly speaks in favour of a two-pronged struggle in the future, between Russia and China over the CSCA hydrocarbon resources, leaving the US companies and the United States largely on the sidelines. Recent Chinese actual and prospected oil and gas pipelines from Central Asia to Xinjiang in China will compete both with the Central Asian export pipelines via Russia to Europe, and also with the US supported pipelines to Turkey and the European markets. The most powerful Chinese instrument is the purse, i.e. of buying and investing in Central Asia, while the most powerful Russian instrument is the "transit weapon". One of the effects of the May 2007 gas transit show-down is that Russia can now play the role of "spoiler" in the CSCA region (Bahgat 2002: 310–327). Although there are competing paradigms of Russia's energy policy, this is also relevant for predicting the future of the "Great Game" and of Russian foreign policy in the CSCA region, and as far as pipeline routing is concerned the "Russian Bear" model dominates: Russia believes that its own basic interests are at stake, and Russia is prepared to put up a fight for what it considers to be its own rightful sphere of influence.[23] Russia's role in the new "Great Game" is that of the "imperial overlord" in the CSCA region (Johnson 2005: 275–276; Kleveman 2004: 12). The United States is still a challenger for this position, but China is a much more obvious future threat.

There is no reason to believe that security governance will be a feature of the CSCA region in the medium or even long term, since the dependency relationships in the future Russia-led CSCA region is such as to rather force the Central Asian states into the Russian embrace, with or without their actual consent. Furthermore, all state actors of the region take the most typical Westphalian positions of all – to remain sovereign, domestically as well as internationally. Russia and China are the two external powers of the region that have openly proved themselves of being precisely Westphalian and act accordingly. Even the United States is more Westphalian than most post-modern states given its hegemonic position and policies. The United States will not be seriously involved in the medium-term to long-term competition in the CSCA region, while China will persist for decades, simply because of its relative vicinity and present similarity of security goals with Russia and the Central Asian states. In this, there is an evident competitive situation between Russia and China, where Russia in the end will have the upper hand. Or, in the words of Fiona Hill: "Russia will achieve the economic and cultural predominance in Eurasia that the United States has in the Americas" (Hill 2004: 6). Russia will be the uncontested great power in the CSCA region. The Great Game is about state power and state competition and the two extreme Westphalian great powers of today, Russia and China, are not even likely to transform into post-Westphalian actors in the next half-century.

Notes

1 The first "Great Game" was fought between Britain and Russian colonizers in an attempt to territorially carve up the region, from the South and from the North respectively, and Afghanistan became the unconquerable "fault line" between the two empires, with Britain ruling in India and Pakistan (and later the Middle East) and Russia in Central Asia and the Caucasus.
2 The Shanghai Cooperation Organization is a possible example of institution-building which has strong ingredients of protection against terrorism as well as denial of US influence. It much more resembles a traditional Westphalian state alliance in the making.
3 Mackinder's well-known dictum on the importance of controlling the heartland ("Who rules Eastern Europe commands the Heartland; Who rules the Heartland commands the world-island; Who commands the World-Island commands the World" cited in O'Hara 2004: 143) is popular both in Russia and the United States. To Russia, the Caspian Sea is the heart of the heartland (O'Hara 2004: 147) and to the United States, Central Asia might well be seen as the pivotal point.
4 A typical constellation of states opposing each other are Russia and Iran as against Turkey and the United States (O'Lear 2004: 167). Others are Armenia and Iran against Azerbaijan and Turkey, or between Russia and Turkey (Karasac 2002: 17).
5 Energy is a major instrument in explaining Russia's behaviour in the CSCA region under Putin (see Nygren 2007). Hill has formulated the change: Russia is back on the global strategic and economic map since "it has transformed itself from a defunct military superpower into a new energy superpower" (Hill 2004).
6 Russian official denials that the SCO is directed at the United States have been frequent and in June 2004, Putin emphasized that the focus was the fight against extremism, the threat of drug trafficking, and efforts to increase economic cooperation, (Putin 17 June 2004) and in April 2006, Sergey Ivanov declared that the SCO "is not a military alliance" but had a focus on anti-terrorism activities (Hutzler 2006).
7 There was, however, never any discussion in Russia of establishing a military alliance with China (Cohen 2005). The importance of the exercises was more political than strategic (Lo and Rothman 2006: 12).
8 Oil resources are somewhat less important than gas resources in this respect because of the many alternative sources and the fact that oil transportation is easier and cheaper than the transportation of gas.
9 Russia has the largest proven natural gas reserves in the world – some 30–35 per cent, and among the ten largest proven oil reserves – some 5 per cent, and it is the world's largest gas producer and gas exporter, the second largest oil producer and exporter. Russia also is the world's third largest energy consumer (see Bahgat 2006: 968; Balzer 2005; Fang 2006; Stulberg 2005: 13). In Central Asia, the proven oil reserves are 1.5 per cent and the proven gas reserves 3.5–5 per cent in the world. In absolute terms, oil resources of the Caspian Sea region amount to 17–34 bbl (billion barrels of oil) as

compared to those of the United States (22 bbl) and the North Sea (17 bbl), or some 4 per cent of today's global production (Andrianopoulos 2002: 77; Bahgat 2005: 123; Bahgat 2006: 970). The gas reserves amount to 4.7 tcm (Bahgat 2006: 970). Of the CSCA's oil reserves, Azerbaijan holds 7 bbl, Kazkahstan 9 bbl, Turkmenistan 0.5 bbl. In comparison, Iran holds 130.7 bbl, Iraq 115 bbl, Kuwait 96.5 bbl, Quatar 15.2 bbl, Saudi Arabia 262.7 bbl, UAE 97.8 bbl. Of the CSCA gas reserves, Azerbaijan holds 1.3 tcm, Kazkahstan 1.9 tcm, Turkmenistan 2.9 tcm, in comparison to Iran's 26.7 tcm, Iraq's 3.1 tcm, Kuwait's 1.0 tcm, Quatar's 25.8 tcm, Saudi Arabia's 6.7 tcm, UAE's 6 tcm (Bahgat 2005: 123).

10 The Caspian Sea itself has been seen as the "second Kuwait", (Karasac 2002: 15) but it is not a "new Persian Gulf" (Andrianopoulos 2002: 76). It is not even a new United States, South America or Africa in this respect; the reserves in the CSCA region are not in themselves very impressive compared to world standards (as opposed to resources of the Russian Far East, which are truly impressive).

11 The idea of the TCGP was dead during the Niazov era but was re-invigorated with the death of Niazov in early 2007 (Peucht 2007).

12 Russia even went quite far to persuade Kazakhstan to remain faithful to the "traditional" Russian routes, and not to join the BTC. Nevertheless, Kazakhstan decided to join the BTC export route by transporting oil by tankers to Baku and then to load it into the BTC pipeline. The US has tried to persuade Kazakhstan to build an underwater oil pipeline from Aktau to Baku, to be connected to the BTC pipeline, although rejected by Kazakhstan so far.

13 Five reasons for China to be interested in Central Asia are evident: its energy importance, its importance as a bridge between Asia and Europe, also in transportation, as an opportunity for cooperation, and to help increase stability in Xinjiang (Xing 2001: 152–153).

14 China's own oil resources are expected to last for another 250 years (in today's terms of production), but oil imports are nevertheless needed, and today constitute some 35 per cent. China is also the world's second-largest oil consumer (Fang 2006). This pipeline (the Atasu in Kazakhstan to Alaskankou in China), from western Kazakhstan connects to the Chinese west–east pipeline running from Xinjiang in China to eastern energy-thirsty China. China bought 50 per cent of the three large blocks in the Kazakh Tengiz fields.

15 From 1992, Russia controlled the only two oil pipeline routes from the Caspian Sea area, one running from Kazakhstan north through Russia to the Baltic Sea, and another from Makhachkala in Dagestan (Russian Caspian Sea coast) via Chechnya to Novorossiisk on the Russian Black Sea coast. The CPC was to add to these. However, it is important to note that on the US side, the companies involved in the CPCA region were private ones: Chevron and Mobil. The construction of the 1,700 km pipeline ran up to a staggering total cost of US$2.6 billion put up by Russian, Kazakhstan, Oman and Western oil companies (Lysenko 2002). This cooperative effort with Russian participation has been fairly free of conflict, basically because Russia in the end controls the pipeline (since it runs through Russia).

16 Of the other two Central Asian states, Kyrgyzstan does not have significant oil and gas resources. Tajikistan, on the other hand, is estimated to possess even larger gas reserves but is unable to develop them on its own. In May 2003, Russian Gazprom signed a 25-year agreement to explore and develop new gas fields in Tajikistan.

17 This victory could also be seen in terms of state versus private investments: while Russian, Chinese and Central Asian investments are controlled by the state, US and European companies are private. To the extent that the "Great Game" takes place in the energy field, the United States and Europe are at a structural disadvantage.

18 The most obvious conflict in this respect developed in relations to Uzbekistan after the Andijon events in the summer of 2005, where US criticism of the Uzbek leadership eventually led to the closure of the US airbase.

19 The only caveat here is the future security interests of the United States: a withdrawal into isolationism is always a risk in US foreign policy, although the present hegemonic role contradicts such a development.

20 The Russian decision in late 2004 to build a US$18 billion and 4,200 km long oil pipeline from Irkutsk (in Western Siberia) to Nakhodka (on the Sea of Japan), a pipeline that avoided Chinese territory and was designed to export oil to the entire Pacific region indicated that China had lost (Vazhenkov 2005). Later, however, China's disappointment was alleviated when an extension of the same pipeline down to China was agreed upon. The construction of the first stretch began in 2006 and the entire Eastern Siberia–Pacific Ocean Oil Pipeline – ESPO – with all its port facilities will be finished 2015–20.

21 Russia is, in Stulberg's words, "well positioned to impose neo-colonial solutions to regional energy security" (Stulberg 2005: 2).

22 Even Putin speaks of the "empty Russian Far East" (Lo and Rothman 2006: 6, 9). Russia has largely been in charge for at least two centuries. One may remember the Russo-Japanese war of 1904–5, the First World War, the Second World War, and, one might add, the Cold War with its "near-war" between Russia and China in 1969 all testifying to the territorial instability of the Russian Far East.

23 The Kuwaitization model, the Liberalization model, the Rent-seeking model, the Russian Bear model, and the Pluralistic school model (Johnson 2005: 258ff.).

6 Children and post-conflict security governance

Alison M. S. Watson[1]

This chapter examines the feasibility of creating an effective security governance framework in a post-conflict environment that takes children into full consideration. Standard state-based governance rules are currently inadequate for dealing with issues of human security in general, and of children in particular. The UN and other security actors, particularly the EU, need to take these policy and legal shortcomings into consideration when planning security governance missions. Redressing this need requires a reworking of the underlying assumptions of the institutional governance agenda in a way that takes human security more seriously. The erosion and irrelevancy of the rules of war, particularly in conflicts within societies that are without effective domestic governance, have resulted in unwarranted suffering among civilians. International law and the methods used to deal with these conflicts must adopt a post-Westphalian conception of sovereignty in place of the state-centric views of security currently embodied in public international law. This perspective requires a reconsideration of how security is conceptualized and who or what might be classified as the relevant referent objects of security in today's world. The EU – as well as other actors involved in governance missions – also needs to recognize fully the potential contribution of non-state actors to security governance, particularly non-governmental organizations (NGOs) that work with marginalized groups, such as children, in the post-conflict stabilization of societies.

Children may play significant roles in both the maintenance of conflict and the creation of peace, yet a consideration of their impact is largely ignored apart from in the most general of ways. Despite existing domestic and international legal frameworks *and* the recognition by organizations such as the World Bank that a large population of young people in an unstable economic environment will have a negative impact upon long-term societal security children, and those adults acting on their behalf, remain marginalized. The reasons for this marginalization reflect perceptions of the child as an agential actor, which in turn are linked to cultural and social norms regarding the nature of childhood itself. Such perceptions are a hindrance to security governance, and as such must be addressed with policy changes over both the short- and long-term. Doing so might not simply involve a reworking of the security governance agenda, but also a wider analysis of the efficacy of the security studies discourse as a whole.

The new rules of the game

The last decade has seen an increasing disaffection with security approaches that do little to engage either with those issues that may make conflict most intractable or with those 'states' whose capacity to provide sovereign protection for their citizens has been fundamentally undermined. The liberal western democratic model is seen as the 'ideal' and represents, as Thomas Risse-Kappen notes, a set of behaviours where

> Decision-makers in democratic polities who have been socialised in the norms governed by liberal states are likely to communicate their intentions in the international realm by referring to these very norms. When they encounter fellow democrats, a collective understanding of these norms can be readily established, providing a common basis for further communication of peaceful intentions. Leaders of democratic states communicating their peaceful intentions to each other can always validate their claims by pointing to the peaceful resolution of conflicts inherent in their domestic structures.
>
> (1995b: 501)

However for those states or failing states 'hobbled by economic adversity, outrun by globalization, and undermined from within by bad governance' (Axworthy 2001: 19), the traditional Western-centred security discourse no longer adequately explains the conditions that exist on the ground in much of the world. In cases such as these, e.g. Darfur, the international community has often demonstrated its inability either to protect civilians from the abuse of their own national governments or to find a viable long-term solution that will allow those affected by conflict the chance to rebuild their lives.[2] Moreover, arguably, the discourse has never really reflected the true nature of such states anyway, but rather a Western liberal interpretation of them. This has resulted in 'the prevalence of particular ways of thinking about, acting upon and (re)presenting post-colonial states which, in turn, facilitated some polices while marginalizing others' (Bilgin and Morton 2002: 56–57). The result has been the recognized need for the new critical discourses that have emerged and which concentrate upon the 'social construction of security'. These argue for a widening of the term (Väyrynen 2004: 133–134), as a result of which, new actors and issues have entered into the security discourse. As Oliver Richmond notes (2004): 'in this "post-Westphalian" system ... identity, representation, and human security issues are priorities, displacing, though not replacing, the hegemony of the state as sole authority and actor'. Human security elevates the person – either individually or collectively – over the state as the primary security referent (Newman 2001: 239). However, as James A. Sperling notes in the introduction to this volume, the post-Westphalian system of which human security is an integral part, engenders both great strength and great vulnerability with 'the ever expanding spectrum of interaction providing both greater levels of collective welfare than would otherwise be possible, alongside the greater level of threat that is a result'. Moreover the notion of 'human security' itself has become institutionalized such that it has sometimes become yet another symbol of liberal democratic stricture as opposed to a real opportunity for dialogue on those issues that may lead to the continuation of conflict. Thus there is no real decision yet made regarding whether 'human security' is a term filled with 'empty rhetoric' or whether it has indeed, as its supporters suggest, become a 'rallying cry [that] has chalked up significant accomplishments, including the signing of an anti-personnel land mines convention and the ... creation of the criminal court' (Paris 2001: 87).

Some authors have suggested that broadening the security agenda does little to change the nature of security itself. As Keith Krause and Michael C. Williams have noted (1997: 35), this is well illustrated in Robert Dorff's rejection of Charles Kegley's attempts to broaden the security agenda. While Dorff agrees that economic, ecological and social questions represent issues of real concern, he denies that they represent security issues:

> There is no conceptual thread in the Kegley list that holds them all together except that they are 'problems'. This is not to downplay the serious nature of some of these problems, but 'problems' is not a concept.... 'Problems' provides us with no ordering of reality that we can use to create a common understanding of what it is that we are talking about and the range of possible policy approaches to addressing these problems.

On the other hand, others see human security, and the broadening of the security agenda that comes with it, although imperfect, as a valuable indicator of the need for a fundamental rethinking of security in the face of so-called new wars and their increasingly disproportionate impact upon civilians, who continue to make up the majority of the victims, either because of deliberate targeting or the inability to distinguish between combatants and non-combatants (Kaldor 2006: viii). In the case of children, the impact of this 'blurring of the line' continues to be devastating and represents a major challenge to effective security governance.

Children and security governance

The traditional state-centric security paradigms are analytically indifferent to the countless number of children killed as the result of disease, civil war, environmental degradation and famine (Owen 2004: 347). Figures suggest that around 26,500 children aged five and under die every day for reasons related to poverty, hunger, and easily preventable illnesses, whilst more than two million children have died as a direct result of armed conflict over the last decade and at least another six million children have been permanently disabled or seriously injured during that time. Moreover, an estimated 20 million children have been forced to flee their homes as a result of war or the abuses of war and live either as refugees or as part of the internally displaced within their own borders.[3] Given such figures, it is no surprise that the most widely accepted piece of international human rights legislation in history is the United Nations Convention on the Rights of the Child (UNCRC), signed in 1989 and since ratified by almost every country in the world. The UNCRC forms part of a body of international legislation that provides the current framework for the protection of children in the international system. Some measures relate directly to those children who actually participate in armed conflict of one form or another, while others relate to the protection of civilian victims. This differentiation is highly indicative of the fact that during wartime children may assume a variety of different roles, any number of which may class a child as either victim or perpetrator. Often separated from (or abandoned by) their parents or orphaned, they are vulnerable to recruitment by rebel, and sometimes national, army groups. Such groups may provide the basic food and shelter that separated children require, thus providing a social welfare function that may not be offered anywhere else. This contemporary blurring of the boundaries between combatant and non-combatant violates public international law and the traditional Clausewitzian logic of war it draws upon; it creates

'Zones of ambiguity' where neither peace nor war prevails in the traditional sense. The state apparatuses are often collapsed and the vacuum is filled with different kinds of actors. The border between combatants and non-combatants becomes murky, and the 'non-combatants' contribute to warfare in many ways (such as providing medical services, food and shelter).

(Vayrynen 2004: 135)

Although often absent from the mainstream historical record, children's participation in violent conflicts has been noted in events as diverse as the nineteenth century Commune riots (immortalized in the character of Gavroche in Victor Hugo's *Les Miserables*), the stereotypical image of the US Civil War drummer boy, and child soldiers defending Berlin in the final days of World War II or participating in wars of national liberation. It is however the scale of their use in modern times that is without precedent (Honwana 2005). Estimates suggest that there are currently around 300,000 children taking direct part in around 30 conflicts worldwide, with the accelerating proliferation of small arms having undoubtedly expanded their numbers. Their involvement may range from engaging in peripheral, if provocative, activities such as stone throwing or rioting. They may also provide logistical support roles such as ferrying supplies or conveying messages to other parts of the group. At the other end of the spectrum, however, it must be acknowledged that a disturbing number of children do become involved in more violent activities. In Columbia alone, it has been reported that there are around 6,000 children fighting for rebel armies and the militia, whilst in perhaps the most well-documented example, children are used in a variety of ways by the Tamil Tigers, including their recruitment to suicide bombing squads – the Black Tigers and the Birds of Freedom – where normally young people between the ages of 14 and 16 are chosen. There are also, of course, examples of the use of children – those under the age of 18 – as suicide bombers in Palestine.

The involvement of children in such events may be compulsory, forced or voluntary. When compulsory or forced, they may find themselves linked to specific acts of terror and violence, such as having to kill family members or friends in acts designed to ensure their permanent alienation from family, home, and community life. They may also suffer some of the worst forms of child abuse, such as forced labour and sexual slavery as well, of course, as being subject to the constant threat of death. For a significant number of children involved in conflict, however, their recruitment is, arguably, voluntary. In Liberia, for example, children were among the first to join the armed factions, and in the Palestinian intifada, children have often acted as the catalyst for violence. For children living their lives in communities characterized by ongoing and often long-term violence, there may seem little or no choice but to join in the violence.

Groups are often able to recruit children because they have been socialized to take part in much the same way as the political socialization of children takes place more generally. They also manage to recruit by peer group pressure, by providing a sense of empowerment, and by emphasizing the nobility of fighting for a 'just cause'.[4] This dynamic is often discussed in recent analyses of Islamist groups, but the idea of the noble child warrior is not new; Western society is not immune to the honouring of noble patriotic youth who have died in the cause of the defence of their society's values.[5]

It must also be said that children may not only go to war, but may also be significant in the process of peace. Peace is often made in their name, but they are an important catalyst in other ways and may be able to take an active role in creating peace and in ensuring its sustainability. The Children's Peace Movement in Columbia, for example, began a series of peace negotiations by the mid-1990s that were spearheaded by the Conciliation Commission comprised of prominent civic and religious leaders. Although it was much more successful as a civil society effort than anything that the government had managed to achieve, the peace movement as a whole remained weak and fragmented until the Children's Movement for Peace was instigated. It began with a number of young people working in isolation and grew into a significant social movement that demanded an end to violence in Columbia and the right to peace. It evolved without a formal structure – there is no official leadership and anyone under the age of 18, working to improve the quality of life in a community affected by violence, can be considered as a member. The significance of the Children's Peace Movement as peace advocates was recognized in its nomination for a Nobel Peace Prize. Children can of course also break the peace if inadequate attention is given to their needs. Peace agreements represent only the beginning of the post-conflict process and some of the most pressing and long-term issues that post-conflict societies face are very much linked with children and their childhoods. Before examining post-conflict interventions in greater detail, it is first necessary to examine the existing international institutional framework as it relates to the child, and to demonstrate why the significance of the child should be recognized.

The institutional framework

There are a number of legal mechanisms that, taken together, provide the current framework for the protection of children in the international system. Some relate directly to those children who actually participate in armed conflict of one form or another, while others relate to the protection of civilian victims. Protocol no. 1 to the 1949 Geneva Conventions, which entered into force on 7 December 1979, and which relates to the protection of victims of international armed conflicts, for the first time makes it illegal for the parties to the conflict to allow the direct participation of children under 15 in the hostilities. This provision, very similar to the UNCRC, article 38, paragraph 2, asserts: 'State parties shall take all feasible measures to ensure that persons who have not attained the age of 15 years do not take direct part in the hostilities.' Also after much consideration, as well as intensive lobbying campaigns from NGOs, the drafters of the UNCRC set the age of recruitment at 15, adding that the oldest children should be selected first. In February 2002, a protocol to the Convention came into force that raises the age at which governments may send soldiers into battle to 18. Other non-state groups, including terrorist groups, more prone to use child soldiers, are prohibited from recruiting or deploying those under the age of 18 as combatants. The age of 15 still remains significant, however. With the establishment of the International Criminal Court (ICC), article 8 of the ICC statute defines the conscription, enlistment, or use in hostilities of children under the age of 15 years as a war crime. The statute also included other important measures to protect children in armed conflict: recognizing intentional attacks on educational institutions as a war crime; providing special arrangements for children as victims and witnesses; and exempting children below the age of 18 from prosecution by the court. However, the existence of the ICC Statute and the UNCRC does not necessarily mean much. Both the ICC Statute and the UNCRC have a number of fatal flaws that become particularly obvious when considering the role of children in the types of conflict that may be characterized as 'new wars'.

First, the inability to monitor the participation of children in armed conflict leaves the ICC statute potentially ineffective. In the majority of situations, a government will deny involvement in an internal armed conflict as classified by the 1949 Geneva Conventions or the 1977 Additional Protocols, believing that such a denial will prevent the application of international humanitarian law. Denial of internal armed conflict status defines the situation as one of internal conflict, thus placing it outside the scope of groups such as the International Committee of the Red Cross (ICRC). The option of definitional subterfuge, in turn, makes monitoring governmental activity much more difficult. Moreover, monitoring and preventing non-state groups from using children as soldiers is much harder even than is the case for governments. Thus the recruitment of children, by both state and non-state actors, continues without much international observation. A fundamental problem here is that, at the domestic level, governments are often unable and unwilling to deal with the problem of recruitment of children. National laws that prevent child recruitment are often not enforced whereas enforcement efforts, when attempted, are ineffective because the government may be either unable or unwilling, for whatever reason, to regulate recruitment in armed opposition groups. Other problems include inadequate or non-existent birth registration. However, a legal provision requiring governments to institute a program of universal birth registration would provide a safeguard by preventing recruiters from drafting children who they claim are older than they are.

Even if it has been recognized by the international community that child combatants have taken part in an internal armed conflict, difficulties may still remain. Specifically, if the presence of child combatants is denied by the parties involved, then frequently no organization or government is willing to put at risk an often fragile peace in order to ensure that children who participated in the conflict receive appropriate post-conflict attention. This was the case in Mozambique, where the use of children was effectively overlooked as part of the peace process, despite the knowledge that children had been employed as soldiers. Under these conditions, the issue of child combatants is something that may be talked about behind closed doors, but not openly confronted. Child combatants are usually not discussed in cease-fire negotiations, and thus are often excluded from the process of what, in UN parlance, is termed as DDR: *Disarmament* (the collection of weapons within conflict zones and the safe storage or disposal of these weapons); *Demobilization* (the formal registration and release of combatants from duty, providing assistance to help them meet immediate needs, and transporting them back to their homes or communities); and *Reintegration* (the process of helping former combatants return to civilian life and readjust both socially and economically). However, once a conflict has ended it is important that children are given the opportunity to recover and deal with whatever long-term physical or psychological damage has been inflicted upon them by their wartime experiences. Indeed, the UNCRC guarantees that children should be provided with psychosocial recovery and social reintegration following such experiences. Sierra Leone's 1999 Peace Agreement, though flawed, was the first such pact to recognize the needs of child soldiers and to plan for their demobilization and reintegration into community life.

A third fatal flaw in the existing legal framework is that there is a conflict between the provisions of the UNCRC and the provisions of the ICC. The upholding and enforcement of the provisions of the Convention on the Rights of the Child depend on the good will of parties to it. Admitting the use of child combatants is tantamount to admitting that a war crime has been committed. Finally, and perhaps most significantly, although the UNCRC, on the whole, does not limit its applicability to governments, it does not make its applicability to non-state parties explicit in article 38, so non-state groups can argue that they are not bound by its terms.

Despite what would appear to be an extensive international legal framework – so crucial to the protection of human security – children continue to slip through the gaps. Determining how and why they do so is important for effective security governance to emerge for a number of reasons. First, an inordinate amount of coverage has examined the significance of terrorism to our contemporary characterization of security. Children are very much a part of this dynamic, but an under-examined one. As Peter Singer notes (2005: 25–26):

> The fact that one of the first US servicemen to die in Afghanistan was shot by a 14-year-old sniper was little discussed in the media. US troops continue to face child soldiers in Afghanistan, the youngest on record being a 12-year-old boy captured in 2004 after a Taliban ambush.... During the invasion that toppled Saddam Hussein's regime, American troops engaged Iraqi child fighters in at least three cities. The trend has grown during the insurgency with children serving as everything from snipers to front-line fighters in the fighting in Falluja.

Children are critical in the 'war on terror', yet policymakers choose to concentrate instead on the standard security apparatuses that surround them. As Singer again tellingly notes (2005: 25–26):

> Focusing solely on the leadership of terrorist organisations is not enough; it misses the larger socio-economic context that enables their recruiting techniques. An equally pressing problem is the environment of violence, humiliation and lack of opportunity that surrounds many children in troubled regions. This is heightened by failing education systems and economic stagnation across many parts of the world. Change these and we begin to change the present trends of terrorism.

Yet, more than this, it is recognized that, in general, young people are significant in the creation of an environment of sustainable peace, particularly in those societies where young people form a significant portion of the overall population. As Henrik Urdal (2004: 2) noted in a report published by the World Bank, there is:

> Robust support for the hypothesis that youth bulges increase the risk of domestic armed conflict, and especially so under conditions of economic stagnation, ... [providing] evidence that the combination of youth bulges, and poor economic performance can be explosive.

In a similar vein, Hart *et al.* (2004: 591) examine how youth bulges may be linked to societal instability, highlighting in particular that:

> Limited civic knowledge and heightened civic participation were developmental markers for the political activity that is characteristic of that witnessed in a 'youth bulge', results that have been linked to a number of conflicts throughout history, as well as in the contemporary system.

Unfortunately, however, although the significance of a youth bulge to the stability of a post-conflict environment is a recognized phenomenon, there remains little that is done in terms of the specific targeting of aid in order to deal with this.

Rather, it is expected that when aid is given, its benefits will eventually trickle down to the youth population. This has been recognized by the International Labour Organization in its request for more targeted and integrated national policies and programmes fostered by international aid, that aim at reaching the most vulnerable youth and reintegrating them back into civil society to the individual and collective benefit of all.[6] It was also recognized by UNICEF in its 2005 call to governments, community leaders and agencies to tap into the under-utilized resource of a large youth population and give adolescents and young people a chance to contribute positively to the reconciliation and reconstruction of their communities.[7] Unfortunately, however, writers so often concentrate on the negative elements of a youth bulge, rather than upon the fact that they 'can also foster system-sustaining civic activity' such as was the case in the civil rights movement in the United States (Hart *et al.* 2004: 591). Moreover, even within the academic discourse surrounding post-conflict aid, there is often little mention of the particular significance of a large youth population, and the financial requirements for the successive implementation of assurance policies. Those that do often tend to concentrate on issues surrounding education, and issues of rehabilitation, that are necessarily focused on the future of youth, rather than upon the instability, or indeed the positive impact, that a large youth population may potentially bring to the present.

Neither has the significance of youth been recognized in any regularized way in either the UN or the EU, where there are few specific policies that argue for the primacy of aid to youth in a post-conflict environment, although there is evidence that, for the EU at least, this picture may be changing. Indeed, the case of the EU is particularly interesting in that, despite an acknowledged interest in social policy and the role of the 'citizen', its conception of citizenship is one that for the majority of its lifetime has been fundamentally based upon the notion of 'citizen-as-worker', rather than upon any particularly humanitarian notion of the need for the realization of rights. This may be understandable, but it is short-sighted given that the EU is probably in a better position than any other group of states to create the security governance agenda, and to treat youth as key actors in the societal arena during the institutionalization of democratic norms. For this reason it is heartening that that there are now EU initiatives in place, such as the 2006 recognition of the need to emphasize the place of children in armed conflict in European Security and Defence Policy, and the recognition by the European Commission in 2005 that[8] 'a particular priority must be effective protection of the rights of children, both against economic exploitation and all forms of abuse, with the Union acting as a beacon to the rest of the world'.

The first stage of this strategy was the adoption of the communication 'Towards an EU Strategy on the Rights of the Child' in July 2006, which was structured around seven specific goals, namely:

> Capitalising on existing EU policies and structures; promoting children's rights in EU relations with partner countries; incorporating children's rights into all EU policies and programmes identifying future priorities and launch-

ing a broad public consultation to develop a long-term children's rights strategy; improving awareness of (*i*) children's rights and (*ii*) EU action in this field; training staff to increase their expertise on children's rights; and, improving cooperation and consultation between stakeholder bodies.[9]

Nevertheless, this still remains a very institutionally based model. Advocacy by children has not been a topic of vital concern when considering security governance, largely because when the discourse is centred around the place of the adult, little thought is given to the agency of the child either as peace-maker or peace breaker (Honwana and Boeck 2005), or as victim or perpetrator. It is to these issues that we now turn.

A goodbye to childhood

According to article 1 of the UNCRC, a child means every human being below the age of 18 years unless, under the law applicable to the child, majority is attained earlier. But this conception of what childhood means is a historically and culturally limited conception, and is very much constructed on the model of a child who stays home, under parental jurisdiction, until they have left for full-time education. Under such circumstances children are effectively separated from adults, both in society and under international law. Partly this comes from the development of Western law. During the Middle Ages, the germ of a set of new ideas about childhood developed, at the heart of which was the belief in a prolonged, innocent, childhood that was fundamentally separate from the nature of adulthood. Outside of this Western intellectual norm, childhood did not necessarily exist as something separate. Up to the present day, the difficulties regarding the nature of childhood itself continue to exist – and the age of majority as mentioned in the UNCRC remains problematical. In some societies, for example, majority is attained on marriage, whilst for others indicators of puberty are the gauge to measure whether or not the transition to adulthood has taken place. Childhood, similarly to gender, is therefore a social construction and entails all the stereotypes that result. Whether children are perceived as a threat or a gift at any particular time has a lot to do with the way adults construct them at that time as opposed to any real difference in a child's behaviour. In a certain sense we are therefore expecting too much from international law. Just as gender issues do not relate in the same way to all women, issues related to childhood do not relate equally to every child. Thus creating one set of laws that is specifically for children may in actuality mean that the child is considered as being an actor over which we have obligations, but that the child itself does not have rights. This is seen perhaps most obviously in article 12 of the UNCRC which states that:

> The child who is capable of forming his or her own views [should have] the right to express those views freely in all matters affecting the child, the views of the child being given due weight in accordance with the age and maturity of the child.[10]

The latter appears to presuppose that children have some form of right to actual participation as opposed to mere representation (at the same time recognizing that children of different ages have different abilities). Such participation was identified by the Committee on the Rights of the Child as one of the fundamental principles of the UNCRC and, although it does not necessarily require that the opinions of the child be automatically approved, it does give children the capacity to influence those decisions that may affect their lives and that, in some sense, they possess agency. As Daniel Holloway and Gill Valentine note (2000: 37):

> Recognition of children's agency does not necessarily lead to a rejection of the appreciation of the ways in which their lives are shaped by forces beyond the control of individual children ... [n]or ... does a recognition of children's agency result in a universal categorization of the category 'child'. Though children are defined in relation to adults, other differences also fracture (and are fractured by) these adult–child relations. Children's identities are classed, racialised, gendered and so on, just as gender, class and racialised identities are cross-cut by adult relations. Moreover, these adult–child relations are constituted in different ways in different times and places.

Of immediate significance here is the whole framing of the agent–structure debate. Roland Blieker (2000: 274–275), for example, argues that the 'notion of structure ... is intrinsically linked to neo-realist, statist and spatial perceptions of world politics'. This also brings out the issue of the types of agency that are attached to different actors. Acknowledging the significance of children within this discourse may thus allow for a fuller understanding of what agency means, and may result in the inclusion of children as 'knowledge agents' whose presence may contribute to the demarcation of the discourse itself. For example, in some senses states are more accepting of the notion that children can acquire 'negative agency' as opposed to 'positive agency'. Thus, children may be held responsible for the crimes that they have committed (negative agency) at an age when it is generally assumed that they are too young to make any particular positive societal contribution (positive agency). This is partly a concern with what Sharon Stephens (1995) has termed 'risky children' – those such as child labourers, child soldiers or even child refugees who need to be controlled in ways that will neither threaten the existing societal order nor indeed cause too much upheaval in the rapidly changing global one. What it is partly true, of course, is a recognition that children as actors do not fit in to the security governance rules that Western states – including EU member-states – have so carefully developed.

Conclusion

This chapter has examined the place of the child in the international system, and specifically in the systems of security governance that the Western liberal tradition has engendered, and of which the EU is a part. Despite the UNCRC, and recent initiatives by the EU, we remain in a place where children are considered as an afterthought, and where their role in conflict is perceived to be a negative one – either because they are victims without agency or because they are perpetrators without moral authority. Either characterization means that their role is consigned to being a minor one. One way to address this is to ensure that the advocacy of NGOs is recognized. Many NGOs work on children's behalf, and should be recognized as containing knowledge that would be useful from the point of view of developing more effective strategies for creating and sustaining peace and social integration. Crucial too is the need for those actors so significant to our contemporary notions of security governance – the UN and the EU in particular – to recognize that it is up to them to set a new agenda and institutionalize new norms, rather than rely upon those derived from the Westphalian order. So far this is something that they have done with only limited authority. Thus, the analytical framework of 'security governance' enables scholars and practitioners to move beyond Westphalia and include non-state actors in their analysis and practice, but this is only an opportunity – much remains to be done. We must recognize that children are fundamental to the post-Westphalian system of governance, not simply because of the potential role that they could play as actors, but also because any system which espouses human security can only really accurately do so if it takes the cause of all of society's constituents as its guide.

Notes

1 The author would like to thank James A. Sperling for his very helpful suggestions on the chapter, and Jean Grugel for her advice on recent policy.
2 Online, available at: www.ascleiden.nl/Library/Webdossiers/Darfur2.aspx (accessed 2 December 2008).
3 Figures taken from 'Child Protection from Violence, Exploitation and Abuse'. Online, available at: www.unicef.org/protection/index_armedconflict.html (accessed 2 December 2008).
4 Although it must be said too that children do not always choose to participate in political conflict simply because their surrounding environment suggests that they should and indeed there are accounts of childhood experiences serving to turn an individual against the group that they would be expected to support. For example, the children of Abu Khaled, a Palestinian militant who had suffered torture and imprisonment, became distrustful of the Palestinian nationalist movement which, as they saw it, had destroyed their father and made all of their lives more difficult as a result.
5 Witness for example, in the UK, the remembrance of those who 'shall not grow old as those who are left grow old', and the mythologizing of youth in words such as Wilfred Owen's 'Anthem for Doomed Youth'.
6 Online, available at: www.ilo.org/public/english/bureau/inf/pr/2006/48.htm (accessed 2 December 2008).
7 Online, available at: www.unicef.org.uk/press/news_detail_full_story.asp?news_id=447 (accessed 4 November 2008).
8 Online, available at: http://ec.europa.eu/external_relations/human_rights/child/index.htm (accessed 17 November 2008).
9 Online, available at: http://ec.europa.eu/external_relations/human_rights/child/index.htm (accessed 17 November 2008).
10 This echoes the reasoning of Martha Nussbaum, who argues that, politically, the assumption must be made that

All children of two human parents are capable of the major functions of human life, unless and until prolonged experience with an individual indicates to us that a different type of functioning is what is appropriate for that individual, as in the case of a very severely mentally handicapped child, who will need special education and may or may not become capable of political functioning.

(Nussbaum 2000: 108)

See also, Nussbaum (1988) 'Nature, Function and Capability', *Oxford Studies in Ancient Philosophy*, suppl. vol. 1: 145–184. Of course, such arguments also raise questions regarding the nature of political rights in the community as a whole.

Conclusion

Farewell Westphalia? The prospects of EU security governance

Charlotte Wagnsson and Jan Hallenberg[1]

What are the prospects for exporting the EU's security culture that makes possible its unique form of security governance? Each author has not only highlighted the unexplored mechanisms and potential for global security governance on the EU model, but has identified the barriers for realizing this novel form of security multilateralism. The EU has established a record of independent agency in both regional and global security, but can this form of security governance actually be projected beyond Europe?[2] Can EU security governance withstand the encroachments and exigencies of a Westphalian world? These questions animate the individual chapters. In the conclusion, we seek to answer those questions, drawing on the empirical evidence provided in the individual chapters, and to assess the validity of James A. Sperling's (post)-Westphalian thesis for understanding the mechanisms and potential of global security governance.

The analytical framework of security governance has a greater capacity to capture vital interaction patterns within the sphere of security today than many other analytical approaches that tend to overlook the significance of non-state actors and other new phenomena in the sphere of security. Security governance is characterized by heterarchy; the interaction of a large number of actors, both public and private, institutionalization that is both formal and informal; relations between actors that are ideational in character, structured by norms and understandings as much as by formal regulations; and, finally, collective purpose (Webber *et al.* 2004: 8). Consistent with the insights of the Copenhagen School of security studies (Buzan *et al.* 1998), security governance gains its conceptual purchase from a broad view of what constitutes security, the process of securitization, the role of non-state actors as agents of threat, and the importance of non-state referents as central components of many security governance systems.

Security governance does more than amalgamate competing theories of international relations and systems of security multilateralism. As compared to regime theory and social constructivism, security governance, as an analytical framework, enables us to go beyond a preoccupation with intra-organizational dynamics or intersubjective understandings of the material capabilities and interests *and* sites our analyses of security on a firmer and richer empirical foundation. Most theorizing on co-operation is restricted to analysing co-operation within and among organizations and states or limited by the straightjacket of rational choice theory. In contrast to integration theory or regime theory, the security governance framework is truly global in scope – it involves a wide range of state and non-state actors, and it spans the various levels of analysis (lateral, horizontal and vertical). Moreover, irrespective of how analytically current other schools within the fields of international relations and security studies may claim to be, most of them tend to take the state for granted as an analytical assumption. It can be argued that in today's world, where non-state actors possess an ever-increasing influence along a broad spectrum of security concerns, this assumption is both flawed and regrettable. This is most easily observable in the post-Westphalian region of EU Europe, where interactions between non-state and state actors are highly developed and essential elements of the more advanced forms of security governance are prevalent.

James A. Sperling suggests in the introduction that states may be placed along a continuum ranging from Westphalian (defined as traditional sovereignty-bound states that confront a rather narrow security agenda, have an egoist definition of the national interest, and act according to the individualist logic of consequentiality) to post-Westphalian states (defined as states that are willing to compromise or abnegate sovereignty, are consequently prone to the institutionalization of security co-operation, act according to a collective logic of appropriateness, and adopt the broadest definition of security). The security governance framework with its ability to take into account a large variety of actors, and with its focus on institutionalized co-operation structured by shared norms, is particularly relevant in post-Westphalian settings.

The EU best represents a post-Westphalian region (cf. Webber *et al.* 2004: 15–19; Sperling 2007). All key features that characterize a security governance system are present in Europe: the European sphere of security involves the interaction of a large number of actors, both public and private, security practises are institutionalized through the EU, relations between actors are ideational in character, structured by – albeit controversial – norms and understandings, and a common purpose is evident in the European Security Strategy (ESS) and is supported by a range of other EU security policy documents and statements. The EU is also deeply committed to spreading 'good governance', which reinforces the prospects of effective regional security governance. As Andrew L. Ross argues in this volume (Chapter 4), the EU represents 'the state of the art for global governance and security governance alike. With the ESDI, CFSP, ESDP and the ESS,[3] security governance within the EU has exhibited potential at the supranational, transnational, and intergovernmental levels'.

How does the EU cope with states and regions that have not yet travelled beyond Westphalia? Where do the major states in the world fall along the Westphalian continuum and with what consequences for the EU export of security governance? It is to these questions we now turn.

(Post-)Westphalia: common rules versus undiluted power

If the EU is the best example of a post-Westphalian actor, Bertil Nygren demonstrates in Chapter 5 that China and Russia are extreme Westphalian actors that 'are not likely to transform in the next half-century'. In Nygren's analysis, Central Asia is consequently not at all ripe for security governance, since the Great Game there is about state power and competition, particularly the traditional threats to statehood and territorial integrity. The Caspian Sea and Central Asian region more generally falls far short of the advanced systems of governance put forward in the introductory chapter, instead it remains 'a Russia-led regional security complex'. Nygren's analysis suggests that the feasibility of governance depends not only on the character of states as either Westphalian or post-Westphalian, but is also issue-area specific. The key to Nygren's argument is that the energy sector is particularly difficult to 'post-modernize' owing to its close link to traditional security concerns. Actors are critically dependent upon energy both for their capacity to sustain a national defence and a strong economy; energy, in other words, is tightly intertwined with the fundamental strategic goal of survival. The Westphalian character both of the Central Asian states and the issue-area renders the 'energy game' in Central Asia exceptionally difficult to institutionalize at a transnational level, and presents a particularly hard case for security governance. Although the wider implications of the absence of security governance in this particular context should perhaps not be exaggerated, the EU can presently do little in terms of security governance in regional contexts dominated by Westphalian states wedded to a traditional security agenda.

The US's lack of engagement in security governance presents a greater threat to the EU system of governance, at least with respect to its dissemination. In Andrew Ross's logic, security governance starts at home. He argues that US neoconservatives and nationalists failed to appreciate global governance and security governance in particular. Moreover, the US was unable to promote good governance globally, because the Bush Administration undercut it domestically. Ross is rather pessimistic as to the prospects of the US moving towards the other post-Westphalian end of the continuum. The election of Barack Obama, despite the promise of domestic renewal and repaired relations with allies, is unlikely to implement a fundamental course correction in American foreign policy more consistent with European sensibilities. If the new Administration were to seek an accommodation with the EU system of security governance, the US must invest 'with others in institutionalized governance arrangements that impart legitimacy to the multilateral use of soft and hard power alike'. For Ross, it will take time for the US and for the global security governance project to recover from the nearly decade-long illiberalism that characterized US foreign and domestic policies.

Neither Russia nor the US can be categorized as post-Westphalian states and both are therefore less prone to contribute to a global system of security governance. But where does this leave NATO? Could NATO exercise governance globally? Rafael Biermann notes that NATO members vary in their post-Westphalian character, which causes clashes of diverging norms on security governance and complicates decision-making and the formation of collective purpose. He exposes the difficulties of transforming NATO from a collective defence arrangement originally conceived with a Westphalian logic into a system of security governance which is more compatible with post-Westphalian thinking.

Biermann demonstrates a process of relative institutional decline; NATO's relevance has diminished for several reasons, most of which stem from exogenous systemic shocks that have altered member-state threat perceptions and security cultures among the member-states. Member-states diverge on the purpose of the alliance; for the US, NATO's utility is mainly as a vehicle for collective defence, peace-building and less demanding combat missions; for most Europeans, it is an alliance restricted to those military purposes where Europe cannot act alone. Biermann's analysis exposes that NATO is torn between Westphalian and post-Westphalian thinking, and this makes its engagement in security governance uncertain, as well as its internal evolvement towards a system of security governance.

The split between post-Westphalian and Westphalian actors in the transatlantic area has implications for the management of security. There are actually two competing European forms of security governance in Sperling's view, namely the EU's post-Westhpalian security community and NATO's Westphalian security community. Post-Westphalian actors like the EU favour multilateral and long-term production of security with the aim of strengthening common rules and norms as a way to curb the external diseconomies of anarchy. Multilateral procedures increase interaction patterns among actors and can serve to stimulate and spread post-modern methods of governance, if successful. This, in turn, might facilitate the spread of the 'security governance logic' and establish the foundation for a system of universal global governance. The evolution of common rules and normative frameworks sustaining collective action in the security sphere requires a long-term perspective that favours multilateralism and the gradual development of stable domestic and international institutions and social structures. The ultimate aim for a strategy of long-term production of security is the emergence of a world inhabited by norm-abiding states that have normatively rejected the use of violence as a conflict resolution mechanism. This strategy requires that states are willing to sacrifice their specific national interests temporarily in favour of generalized norms and the gradual growth of a strong and peaceful international society. This ultimate goal may be distant, but this book reports how steps have begun to be taken in its direction.

Security governance allows us to understand both how 'rules' of security evolve, and how states and organizations produce security 'in practice' (Webber 2004: 25). But it does not account for those state practices that may impede the effective evolution of rules and norms. Inflexible rule-governed behaviour is not always compatible with efficient state action; thus, the self-interested national production of security may deviate from otherwise shared norms and rules. Westphalian states, which aim to protect state interests and principles above all else, may adopt 'flexible' interpretations of common rules or depart from common principles. During the past decade, Westphalian actors – NATO and the US and its closest allies – have on several occasions prioritized the immediate production of security at the cost of fostering a long-term multilateral approach to security. This behaviour reflects the assumption that resolute unilateral action is sometimes required where disorder threatens to destabilize entire regions and generate spill-over effects farther afield. It undermines the logic of security governance based on common rules and understandings, notably multilateralism and the long-term institutionalization of collective action.

The EU embodies a post-Westphalian form of security governance, particularly the presence of a broadened security agenda, an emphasis on human security, multilateralism and international society as well as a preoccupation with the root causes of conflicts and threats. It signifies that security requires long-term engagement rather than swift problem-solving missions.[4] The European Security Strategy reflects a commitment to 'an international order based on effective multilateralism', which signifies adherence to institutionalism, a stronger international society, and a rule-based international order. The strategy commits the EU to international law and to strengthening the UN (Council of the European Union 2003: 10–11).

The tension between the long-term and short-term production of security remains a key obstacle to the evolution of a truly global system of security governance. Can the EU project its approach to long-term security governance and ultimately build a global system of security governance consistent with it? Or would such an effort be futile owing to the global importance and reach of the leading Westphalian states, particularly the US, Russia, and China? If Ross's analysis is correct, it is very likely to take a long time until the US changes its focus on the immediate (and unilateral) production of security in favour of a long-term, norm-abiding multilateral approach. A more comforting assessment of opportunity for globalizing or extending the regional reach of the EU system of security governance suggests that it can succeed, because the American and European modes of governance reinforce security and stability and do not always stand in contradiction to one another. Even a Westphalian state with a predilection for unilateralism can benefit from contributing to multilateral security governance missions in unstable regions of the world; the benefits of participation may be derived from stabilized economies and market opportunities at lower costs derived from burden-sharing and coordination to avoid unnecessary duplication of effort.

Moreover, in Chapter 3, Arita Eriksson demonstrates that 'high risk' military operations producing immediate security benefits and 'low risk' operations targeting long-term security objectives (e.g. norm diffusion and institutionalization) are not opposed, but instead are complementary and reinforcing. Drawing on the international experience in stabilizing the Democratic Republic of Congo (DRC), she identifies two different categories of security governance at work, 'limited' and 'comprehensive' security governance. Both involve a variety of participants and multilevel involvement, but the comprehensive approach reaches deeper into the state and society. Eriksson underscores that short-term military efforts primarily conducted top-down are not prone to contributing to the evolution of long-term security; such efforts must be complemented by long-term engagement such as security sector reform (SSR), the projection of democratic norms, and generous development aid supporting, among others, those two objectives. By this logic, long-term development and immediate production of security are two sides of the same coin. A growing number of actors – Westphalian and post-Westphalian alike – realize this interdependence. Evidence suggests that the risk of civil conflict is lessened by economic growth, good domestic governance, and inclusive democracy (Human Security Centre 2005: 155). If peace-building and reconstruction efforts are to forge long-term stability, basic societal structures have to be altered to avoid a repetition of past conflicts or the creation of new ones. These requirements have implications both for development politics and security politics (Duffield 2001: 15).

Although the EU approximates the post-Westphalian ideal type, it remains somewhat circumscribed owing to traditional perceptions of security linked to its Westphalian heritage and the global milieu into which it is embedded. Alison M. S. Watson pushes the argument further in Chapter 6, highlighting that contemporary governance rules, including those of the EU, are inadequate for meeting the challenge of human security, particularly the security of children in (post-) conflict environments. In Watson's analysis, the security governance agenda, as well as the security studies discourse more generally, needs to be reworked in order to turn marginalized groups into central referent objects of security in theory and practice. Children have been ignored in the security discourse despite their important roles in the maintenance of conflict *or* the creation of peace. If security governance efforts are to contribute efficiently to long-term – or even short-term – security in post-conflict environments, external actors must change their perceptions of children, recognizing their capacity as actors with multifaceted roles in the security sphere.

Watson highlights the risk that 'human security' remains a conceptual container filled with little more than empty rhetoric. She offers appalling figures of the number of children killed every year as a result of civil wars and other violent conflicts that have not been sufficiently addressed by the international community, owing in large measure to the dominant state-centric security paradigm. The EU's engagement for the security of individuals, its commitment to prevention, peace-enforcement and peace-building in different regions, and its recognition of the link between security and development constitute important and undervalued steps away from the state-centric perception of security and overdue steps towards a post-Westphalian paradigm that takes human security more seriously, both rhetorically and in practice. A corollary of this argument is that international actors must recognize children as key actors in the security sphere. The international community's acknowledgement – however gradual and still very partial – that women can play important roles in contributing security in war-torn societies serves as an example that the perception of security and its agents can undergo important changes. Similarly, children are active agents in coercive as well as non-coercive contexts in both the state and the societal arenas. Recognizing the multifaceted roles that children can and do play in societies absent effective domestic governance that would serve the cause of long-term stability and security, Watson argues that 'peace agreements represent only the beginning of the post-conflict process and some of the most pressing and long-term issues that post-conflict societies face are very much linked with children and their childhoods'. One practical implication is that the lead actors in governance missions (states and international organizations) draw more effectively on the work of NGO's that work on the behalf of children and possess valuable knowledge of the essential preconditions for long-term security in a particular society.

Skipping Westphalia?

The clash between the long-term and immediate production of security and the 'ungovernability' of sovereignty-bound states such as Russia and China does not necessarily signify that security governance can only function in a post-Westphalian context. In fact, security governance is mainly carried out by post-Westphalian *and* Westphalian actors in *pre*-Westphalian regions. Both Westphalian and post-Westphalian states have demonstrated a willingness to engage in missions of security governance that aim at stabilizing chaotic pre-Westphalian regions and states, in effect pushing them down the road towards Westphalia. The logic of security governance missions in pre-Westphalian regions are often in tune with Westphalian thinking. Westphalian states tend to regard pre-Westphalian entities as problematic sources of transnational problems and threats such as organized crime, terrorism, and uncontrolled flows of refugees. Non-governance in pre-Westphalian social systems is economically problematic, since the return on investments is unlikely to justify the risk of doing so in unstable states and regions. Economic growth and the delivery of social welfare services, and the external financing necessary to deliver either, are held hostage to endemic political violence, social fragmentation, and resource conflicts in much of Africa. Consistent with the observation made by Thomas Hobbes 350 years ago, in the absence of governance supplied by the modern Westphalian state, 'there is no place for industry; because the fruit thereof is uncertain' (Hobbes 1972 [1651]: 143).

There are two avenues paving the way from pre-Westphalian chaos towards stability. The first avenue is based upon traditional realist logic according to which the exigencies of anarchy and competition force each state to seek its own security. New regimes are perforce required to create and control their own militaries with the capability to ensure security internally and externally. This logic would preclude the emergence of regional or continental stability without the formation of stable, centralized Westphalian states. Briefly, according to this first ideal type, the Westphalian state is necessary to overcome the liabilities of anarchy, despite the latter's status as an inevitable by-product of the Westphalian state system (Waltz 1959). The second avenue for escaping pre-Westphalian anarchy involves a more utopian vision, according to which pre-Westphalian states 'skip' Westphalia and proceed directly to a post-Westphalian form of security governance, regionally and globally. This idea builds upon visionary post-modern security thinking, according to which all actors must be functionally undifferentiated (Waltz 1979). These two avenues are clearly ideal types, but serve as analytical devices that can be used to critically assess the value and aims of specific security governance missions.

Within a post-modern entity such as the EU, states can specialize in the provision of security; some may contribute more militarily, others may offer more development assistance, some may contribute to regional and global stability owing to a seat on the UN Security Council, since they can benefit from the particular strengths of the others. This kind of burden-sharing is becoming more common as, in Elke Krahmann's words 'state legitimacy is no longer based on the monopoly of the provision of national and international security but increasingly on the cost-efficient delivery of security'. She argues that the 'search for cost-efficient security governance encourages geographical and functional specialization among states and nonstate actors' (Krahmann 2005: 537). In applying this kind of post-modern security paradigm to pre-Westphalian milieus, one could – at least theoretically – imagine that security governance operations would aim at encouraging and supporting the construction of institutional and legal structures guaranteeing individual and societal security. 'Host' states would ultimately be reduced to 'post-modern containers of authority'; these states would engage in the constructive interaction with other post-modern actors to provide high levels of welfare and security to its citizenry. A precondition for such an outcome, however, is that governments are sufficiently secure to remove the compulsion to acquire a full spectrum of military and defence capability. If authorities in pre-Westphalian regions choose this alternative avenue, it would nurture processes towards a universal system of security governance and lend empirical support to Alexander Wendt's (1992) insight that 'anarchy is what states make of it'. This scenario does not correspond with contemporary realities, but can serve as a useful analytical exercise that can free us from the boundaries of traditional thinking when considering future avenues away from Westphalia.

If Westphalian sovereignty forms a barrier to broad and sustained security cooperation, as Sperling suggests, it is reasonable to argue that the prospects for a universal system of security governance would be improved if multilateral security governance efforts in pre-Westphalian milieus could help pre-Westphalian authorities to 'skip Westphalia' or at least bypass those Westphalian characteristics that reduce the prospects for collaboration. An important question remains: Is a Westphalian phase inevitable and compulsory for a pre-Westphalian lack of internal stability and domestic governance? Malena Britz and Hanna Ojanen, in their contribution, observe that states have to be 'both bypassed and engaged'. They demonstrate that both the EU and the UN have begun to pay attention to the security of the individual in addition to the security of the state. Incorporation of labels such as 'human security' and the 'responsibility to protect' in official documents are among the first signs that the security discourse is shifting from a preoccupation with traditional state security to a concern with the security of the individual. State security and individual or human security have been treated as virtual polar opposites in the security discourse.[5] Yet, the practice of security governance provides empirical support for the contention that human security and state security need not only be seen as opposites, but could, instead, be viewed as complementary and reinforcing. Security governance missions tend to support non-state actors *and* to build stable states, not only for their own sake, but so that they can warrant the security of the individual. This twofold objective is formidable. By addressing the problem, however, the EU and the UN have taken the first step towards solving the tensions between the countervailing exigencies of the Westphalian and post-Westphalian orders.

The practice of EU global security governance is dependent upon how well the EU can co-ordinate its efforts with other actors in order to lower costs and realize better outcomes. Security governance missions often aim at avoiding or stopping civil wars, protecting individuals, and stabilizing and then reconstructing states and societies. The *Human Security Report* (Human Security Centre 2005) singles out international activism as the single best explanation for the stark decrease in civil wars across the globe since the 1990s: 'the main driver of change has been the extraordinary upsurge of activism by the international community that has been directed toward conflict prevention, peacemaking and peace building'. Yet, these missions are costly and time-consuming. Based on the empirical evidence presented in this volume, it is reasonable to conclude that in order to minimize the expected costs and increase the expected benefits of any given security governance venture, contributing actors – states or institutions – need to increase their co-ordination. It is no easy task to synchronize inter-institutional goals and methods (Krahmann 2003: 20–21). Each institution tends to remain loyal to its own institutional logic and purpose, even if this means placing particularistic interests before the common good. With regard to humanitarian intervention, actors tend to 'compete for reputation' by engaging very publicly (if not ostentatiously) in as many prestigious interventions as possible. Yet, Britz and Ojanen argue that the EU and the UN increasingly interact, because the EU needs the UN as the main partner and arena for global governance, and the UN needs the EU for burden-sharing and for managing the excesses of American power and purpose. They demonstrate that EU governance efforts are helped by co-ordination with the UN, and that these two international actors already exercise interlinked modes of governance which they define as 'interconnected multilateralism'.

In the case of NATO, Biermann's analysis indicates that divergences among member-states regarding the purpose of the alliance might impede its effective participation in multilateral security governance. The transatlantic discourse on NATO is no longer a simple story of traditional tasks and capabilities. Instead, it revolves around norms and institutions, two preoccupations congruent with a security governance approach. It remains to be seen where this debate will take the alliance. Biermann notes that the ever-increasing density and overlap of purpose and interest in Europe, especially among security institutions, have strongly impacted on the present and future relevance of the alliance for Europe. He demonstrates that whereas the late Westphalian United States trusts NATO to handle the tasks of post-Cold War security governance, most Europeans, who acknowledge a broader post-Westphalian security agenda, have been compelled out of necessity to turn to other security organizations. In Biermann's view, NATO's growing irrelevancy to Europe's security concerns indicates NATO's relative decline. The key question is whether the member-states will re-frame their partnership according to post-Cold War necessities. Biermann's chapter indicates that as several member-states travel further beyond Westphalia, so does their inclination to shift towards new strategies and instruments of statecraft more in tune with the EU's post-Westphalian security governance. At what pace are NATO member-states willing to say farewell to Westphalia and how will they handle their internal differences along this journey? The answer has great implications for the EU's future interaction with NATO and for its chances of succeeding in spreading its form of security governance globally.

The success of EU security governance

The chapters in this book confirm Sperling's argument that states fall along a Westphalian/post-Westphalian continuum and that the placement of an individual state along it indicates a propensity for unilateralism or instrumental multilateralism or for normatively-conditioned and institutionalized multilateralism. It seems more difficult to realize security governance in regions dominated by Westphalian actors than in a post-Westphalian region such as the EU. Yet, in pre-Westphalian regions both kinds of actors may join forces in security governance missions that aim towards, or even beyond, Westphalia.

Nygren's chapter exposes that it is also fruitful to classify sectors along the Westphalian/post-Westphalian continuum. If the energy and military sectors are highly Westphalian and difficult to govern, the EU may have greater chances of governing other sectors, such as human rights and development, consistent with post-Westphalian governance. Both provide a more indirect security threat than does a direct military threat to national survival. More generally, there is a growing and overdue need for key actors to collaborate in a post-Westphalian manner on issues related to the security of children. In the best of worlds, children ought to be treated as a transnational interest that unites different categories of actors in a common concern with good governance, internally and regionally. A necessary prerequisite for such a result would be the recognition that children *are* central actors in the security sphere.

Institution-building could also be seen as a 'post-Westphalian' enterprise since it does not necessarily impinge upon the primordial imperative of national survival. The EU is therefore likely to have a bright future with governance projects aimed at disarmament, demobilization and reintegration (DDR) and security sector reform (SSR). The military-industrial sector, in turn, remains Westphalian in most parts of the world, but in Europe it has taken some modest steps towards the post-Westphalian end of the continuum through the creation of the European Defence Agency (see Britz and Eriksson 2008). The environmental sector is likely to be a special case. It can be interpreted as post-Westphalian since actors share a range of common norms and interests. Yet, it often interacts with the energy sector, which is particularly difficult to govern, and affects the global competitiveness of European industry. Even within the EU, states have been reluctant to give up their national energy agendas, which can explain the difficulties of reaching a much needed common energy policy towards Russia.

The applicability of Sperling's four governance policies – prevention, protection, assurance, and compellence – tends to vary depending on both the nature of the actors involved and the issue-area in question. Britz and Ojanen demonstrate that over time the EU and the UN have become 'more alike', engaging in the same activities: persuasive institution-building and conflict resolution (assurance and prevention); and coercive conflict resolution (compellence). Yet, the main instruments of both organizations are prevention and assurance. Britz and Ojanen note that although both organizations have the capacity to exercise compellence, the EU has only done so with a UN mandate. By contrast, Westphalian actors are more likely to stick to coercive instruments and act without a mandate from the international community if deemed necessary. Nygren demonstrates that Westphalian actors tend to use the coercive instruments of protection and compellence in the energy sector. Still, NATO also has a record of placing priority on coercive instruments exercising protection and coercion, particularly when leading the UN-mandated International Security Assistance Force, ISAF, in Afghanistan. In recent years, the Bush administration has a demonstrable record of favouring compellence over prevention, with or without a UN mandate. Afghanistan and Iraq, respectively, are cases on point.

In addition to the degree of post-Westphalianess and the issue-area or policy sector, other factors also impinge upon the feasibility of security governance. Actors must be willing to allocate resources for security governance and be capable of co-ordinating their efforts. The number of actors involved makes a difference; it is often easier to negotiate and reach consensus if only a few are involved. It is, however, much easier to generate the requisite financial resources if many are involved; it may also be easier to convince the local parties to the conflict or sector to adopt the 'right' norms or the 'right' political agenda if pressured by many external actors rather than by a few. Eriksson demonstrates that the key to success is not necessarily to forge consensus on a common problem definition, but that actors are able to work roughly towards the same goal. Norms matter too. Security governance is difficult to achieve if the norms at stake are highly contested and even more so if they are closely intertwined with state interests. The EU has clarified that further co-operation with Russia, for example, hinges on Russian compliance with EU norms and principles; namely the very essence of good governance. Moscow, in turn, has made it clear that it does not wish to be governed (Wagnsson 2008: 131–134, 138–142). Russia, as a former superpower fallen on hard times, is a special case, but its unwillingness to adopt the norms and practices of good governance underscores the limitations on expanding the EU system of security governance and the continuing centrality of sovereignty in much of the contemporary world.

The EU's governance approach has functioned quite well in many areas. It has been rather successful in spreading good governance throughout its neighbourhood, particularly to those states applying for EU membership. The EU has been able to export its favoured norms and principles, thus 'pacifying' its closest neighbourhood and thereby making Europe more secure. The EU is nevertheless forced to adopt an agenda of modest ambition and to stick to the governance techniques of assurance and compellence when involved with Westphalian actors cautious towards governance, particularly when the Union challenges favoured norms.

In sum, there are many obstacles to security co-operation outside the EU, but a number of major states and institutions are deeply involved in security governance efforts around the world, particularly in Afghanistan and in Africa. Thus, the challenges of co-ordination among self-interested actors should also be seen as opportunities for pushing forward the EU governance agenda. Some of these processes have only begun quite recently. With time and an ever increasing number of experiences from the field, these favoured methods will become refined, tuned and, with success, institutionalized.

Can EU security governance 'go global'? Britz and Ojanen view the EU as exercising governance *internally, regionally* (through influence on outsiders) and *globally* (through intervention and leadership), but conclude that only the UN's mode of governance can be termed *universal* by virtue of its exclusive authority to mandate the use of force. Eriksson identifies the EU's governance in the DRC as an example of global governance, because it is a venture beyond the regional EU sphere of interest and a range of global actors co-operate. Moreover, the EU provides 'a focal point for universal security efforts, a link between the involvement of the international community and the local authorities'. She observes a variety of *functions* of security governance in the DRC: the civilian and military missions fulfil perhaps all of the institutional functions of global governance identified by Keohane (2001). They represent a form of 'collective purpose'; they officially aim at limiting the use of violence, managing major disturbances, functioning as a 'guarantee against the worst forms of abuse', and encouraging integration and the coordination of effort in different parts of the system. Based on her finding that there appears to be rather smooth passages between various types of security governance efforts, she concludes that an overall approach to security efforts in relation to the DRC 'may serve as an example of a universal security system at work'. Britz and Ojanen are somewhat more critical of the EU, remarking that it is not a unitary actor and that it sometimes fails to co-ordinate its own activities: there have been occasions where a number of EU member-states and agencies have been present in the same country implementing uncoordinated policies.

Conclusion

The contributions to *European Security Governance: The European Union in a Westphalian World* demonstrate the usefulness of the analytical framework of security governance; it exposes key dynamics in the contemporary security sphere that more traditional approaches fail to capture because of their preoccupation with sovereignty. The concept fills an analytical void that has emerged during processes of globalization and that calls for an altered focus within the fields of security studies and IR. It can do what scholars – whether taking their points of departure from norms, ideas, identities, constructivism or regime theory – often claim to do but seldom accomplish in practice; travel beyond realism, sovereignty and Westphalia. Security governance lacks the realist underpinnings that previous theories have been burdened with. It is time to make use of and further develop a perspective that promises to take other actors into account. The study of security governance remains theoretically undeveloped, but this state of affairs only calls for more research in order to increase its precision and analytical operability.

We have mainly dealt with security governance as a method aimed either at preventing or at ending violent civil conflicts or at stabilizing failed states. It is important to remain aware of the fact that security governance is a comprehensive approach that can be used in other analytical contexts as well. Boin and Rhinard, for example, call for further research on 'transnational governance'; the kind of crisis management policies that handle often sudden or dimly anticipated trans-boundary threats such as 'terrorist attacks, water shortages, critical infrastructure failures, unexpected flows of illegal immigrants, progressive climate change, and new pandemics' (Boin and Rhinard 2008: 2,20). Moreover, in order to deepen the analysis of how security governance functions in practice, future scrutiny of regional security governance should from time to time reverse its analytical focus, turning from actors to problems. Many scholars fail to appreciate one of the particular merits of the security governance framework: it enables a systematic focus on problems rather than on actors. The long established centrality of the state in IR theories still influences scholars to make conventional analytical choices which tend to generate a particular set of questions with a state-centric or institutional bias: how can security governance help advance the interests of a state or an organization? How can a particular institution strengthen its role and status in the international system by participating in security governance missions? We also need studies that take a different – post-modern, constructivist or post-structuralist – approach. Such ventures would begin by identifying a problem – a conflict, a failed state, an issue-area – that requires multilateral management, and then followed by a critical line of enquiry: Who acts and how? This approach would provide an opportunity to ask new questions: What threats or problems need to be contained or solved? What are the referent objects of security? Who or what is in need of protection? What methods or forms of governance are the most effective in meeting specific security threats?

In conclusion, this volume demonstrates that security governance is already at work beyond post-Westphalian contexts, and provides support for Sperling's post-Westphalian hypothesis. We argue that the EU is on its way towards exporting its model of security governance globally and that its missions in pre-Westphalian regions could be interpreted as the very first signs of a universal system of security governance that could, if successful, provide a model for future international interventions. The EU promotes its approach using key concepts that fit into a framework of security governance, such as 'human security' and 'effective multi-lateralism'. Yet, the persistence of Westphalia circumscribes the EU's arena of action. The feasibility of governance depends primarily upon the degree of 'Westphalianness' of both the actors involved and the issue-area, and secondarily upon a number of other critical factors. In a world still preoccupied with polarity and relative power, the EU's export of security governance most likely depends on what path the current hegemon – and any future hegemon – chooses to pursue.

Notes

1 The authors wish to thank James A. Sperling, Maria Hellman, Kjell Engelbrekt, Malena Britz and Arita Eriksson for constructive criticisms of previous versions of this concluding chapter.
2 Engelbrekt and Hallenberg present evidence of the EU's capacity – and limitations – as a global actor in the sphere of security in Engelbrekt and Hallenberg (eds) 2008.
3 ESDI = European Security and Defence Identity; CFSP = Common Foreign and Security Policy; ESDP = European Security and Defence Policy; ESS = European Security Strategy.
4 Human security is framed as a 'philosophy underlying the EU's approach to security' (Ferrero-Waldner 2006). Conflict prevention, crisis management and human rights have been defined as 'priority issues' (Ferrero-Waldner 2004). There is a widespread understanding within the EU that international crime and terrorism are interlinked with wars and instabilities in war-torn, underdeveloped societies. The Union has consequently established and strengthened a 'root cause' approach with regards to terrorism (Council of the European Union 2003: 1, 16).
5 For an overview of the debate on human security, see Paris (2001) and a special issue of *Security Dialogue* (2004). For an example of the debate on the EU and human security, see Kaldor *et al.* (2007) and Matlary (2008).

Bibliography

Adler, E. and Barnett, M. (1998a) 'A Framework for the Study of Security Communities', in Adler, E. and Barnett, M. (eds), *Security Communities*, Cambridge, UK and New York: Cambridge University Press.

—— (eds) (1998b) *Security Communities*, Cambridge, UK and New York: Cambridge University Press.

A European Way of Security. The Madrid Report of the Human Security Study Group comprising a Proposal and Background Report (2007) Madrid, 8th November, 2007. Online, available at: www.lse.ac.uk/Depts/global/PDFs/Madrid%20Report%20Final%20for%20distribution.pdf (accessed 31 March 2008).

A Human Security Doctrine for Europe. The Barcelona Report of the Study Group on Europe's Security Capabilities. Presented to EU High Representative for Common Foreign and Security Policy Javier Solana, Barcelona, 15 September 2004 (2004) (Convenor: Mary Kaldor). Online, available at: www.lse.ac.uk/depts/global/studygroup/studygroup.htm.

Alibekov, I. (2004) 'Kazakhstan Tilts toward Russia', *Eurasia Insight*, 18 February 2004.

Anderson, B. (2006) *Imagined Communities: Reflections on the Origin and Spread of Nationalism*, revised edition, London and New York: Verso.

Andrews, D. M. (2004) 'The Atlantic Alliance after Iraq', Fiesole: European University Institute, working paper, RSCAS 2004/08.

—— (2005) *The Atlantic Alliance Under Stress*. Cambridge, MA: Cambridge University Press.

Andrianopoulos, A. (2002) 'The Economics and Politics of Caspian Oil', *Journal of Southeast European and Black Sea Studies*, 3(3): 76–91.

Ash, G. T. (2001) 'Europe at War', *New York Review of Books*, 20 December, 48(20): 68.

Axworthy, L. (2001) 'Human Security and Global Governance: Putting People First', *Global Governance*, 7: 19–23.

Bacevich, A. (2005) *The New American Militarism: How Americans Are Seduced by War*, Oxford: Oxford University Press.

Background (2006) 'EU support to the DRC during the election process', DRC Elections 2006 RDC/02/EN June 2006.

Bahgat, G. (2002) 'Pipeline Diplomacy: The Geopolitics of the Caspian Sea Region', *International Studies Perspectives*, 3(3): 310–327.

Bailes, A. J. K. (2005) 'Introduction. Global Security Governance: A World of Change and Challenge', *SIPRI Yearbook 2005: Armaments, Disarmament and International Security*, Stockholm: SIPRI, 1–27.

Barnett, M. and Duvall, R. (2005) 'Power in Global Governance', in Barnett, M. and Duvall, R. (eds) *Power in Global Governance*, Cambridge, UK and New York: Cambridge University Press.

—— (eds) (2005) *Power in Global Governance*, Cambridge, UK and New York: Cambridge University Press.

Belton, C. (2006) 'Caspian Great Game Back On', *Eurasia Insight*, 5 May.

Berenskoetter, F. (2004) 'Mapping the Mind Gap: A Comparison of US and European Security Strategies', *Security Dialogue*, 36(1): 71–92.

Berenskoetter, F. and Giegerich, B. (2006a) 'From NATO to ESDP? Analyzing Shifts in German Institutional Preferences', paper presented at the annual meeting of the International Studies Association, San Diego, 22 March.

—— (2006b) 'What "War on Terrorism" are we Talking About? A Response to Alistair Shepherd', *International Politics*, 43(1): 93–104.

Biermann, R. (1997) *Zwischen Kreml und Kanzleramt. Wie Moskau mit der deutschen Einheit rang*, Paderborn: Schöningh.

—— (2006) *Lehrjahre im Kosovo. Das Scheitern der internationalen Krisenprävention vor Kriegsausbruch*, Paderborn: Schöningh.

—— (2008a) 'Towards a Theory of Inter-Organizational Networking: The Euro-Atlantic Security Institutions Interacting', *Review of International Organizations*, 3(2): 151–177.

—— (2008b) 'Rivalry Among International Organizations: The Downside of Institutional Choice', paper prepared for the conference Internationale Beziehungen und Organisationsforschung: Stand und Perspektiven, Munich Center on Governance, University of Munich, 18–19 September.

Biersteker, T. (2005) 'State, Sovereignty and Territory', in Carlsnaes, W., Risse, T. and Simmons, B. A. (eds) *Handbook of International Relations*, London: SAGE, 157–176.

Bilgin, P. and Morton, A. D. (2002) 'Historicising Representations of "Failed States": Beyond the Cold-War Annexation of the Social Sciences?', *Third World Quarterly*, 23(1): 55–80.

Biscop, S. (2005) *The European Security Strategy: A Global Agenda for Positive Power*, Aldershot and Burlington, VT: Ashgate.

Blagov, S. (2007) 'Russia Celebrates its Central Asian Energy Group', *Eurasia Insight*, 16 May. Online, available at: www.eurasianet.org/departments/insight/articles/eav051607.shtml.

Blank, S. (2004) 'Russia Mulls Measures to Check Chinese Influence in Central Asia', *Eurasia Insight*, 29 July.

—— (2005) 'Focus of Central Asia's Geopolitical Contest Set to Shift to Kyrgyzstan', *Eurasia Insight*, 5 December.

Blieker, R. (2000) *Popular Dissent, Human Agency and Global Politics*, Cambridge, UK: Cambridge University Press.

Bobbitt, P. (2002) *The Shield of Achilles: War, Peace, and the Course of History*, New York: Anchor Books.

Boin, A. and Rhinard, M. (2008) 'Managing Transboundary Crises: What Role for the European Union?', *International Studies Review*, 10(1): 1–26.

Bolton, J. (2007) *Surrender is Not an Option*, New York: Threshold Editions.

Boutros-Ghali, B. (1992) 'An Agenda for Peace: Preventive Diplomacy, Peacemaking and Peace-keeping', report of the Secretary-General pursuant to the statement adopted by the Summit Meeting of the Security Council on 31 January 1992.

—— (1995) 'Supplement to an Agenda for Peace', position paper of the Secretary-General on the occasion of the fiftieth anniversary of the United Nations, United Nations General Assembly Council.

Bradford, Jr, C. I. and Linn, J. F. (eds) (2007) *Global Governance Reform: Breaking the Stalemate*, Washington, DC: Brookings Institution Press.

Brenner, M. (2002) 'Europe's New Security Vocation', Washington, DC: National Defense University. Online, available at: www.ndu.edu/inss/McNair/mcnair66/McN66.pdf (accessed 26 September 2007).

Bretherton, C. and Vogler, J. (2006) *The European Union as a Global Actor*, 2nd edition, London and New York: Routledge.

Britz, M. and Eriksson, A. (2008) 'Analyzing the EU's shared strategy', in Engelbrekt, K. and Hallenberg, J. (eds) *The European Union and Strategy: An Emerging Actor*, London and New York: Routledge, 56–70.

Brussels (2003a) 'Declaration by the Presidency on Behalf of the European Union on the Conclusion of the Inter-Congolese Dialogue', 9 April, 8300/03 (Presse 113) P 46/03.

—— (2003b) 'Remarks by Javier Solana, High Representative for the CFSP, to the Press on the Preparations to Deploy an EU Military Mission in the Democratic Republic of Congo (DRC)', 4 June, S0123/03.

—— (2003c) 'Javier Solana, EU High Representative for the CFSP, to Visit the African Great Lakes Region and the United Nations 15–18 July 2003', 11 July 2003, S0144/03.

Bull, H. (1995) *The Anarchical Society: A Study of Order in World Politics*, second edition, New York: Columbia University Press.

Buzan, B. (1983) *People, States and Fear: The National Security Problem in International Relations*, Chapel Hill: The University of North Carolina Press.

Buzan, B. and Wæver, O. (2003) *Regions and Powers: The Structure of International Security*. Cambridge, UK: Cambridge University Press.

Buzan, B., Wæver, O. and Wilde, J. de (1998) *Security: A New Framework for Analysis*, Boulder, CO and London: Lynne Rienner.

Carothers, T. (2008) 'An Unwanted League', *Washington Post*, 28 May: A13.

Carter, A. B., Perry, W. J. and Steinbruner, J. D. (1992) *A New Concept of Cooperative Security*, Washington, DC: Brookings Institution Press.

Charillon, F. (2004) 'Sovereignty and Intervention: EU's Interventionism in its "Near Abroad"', in Carlsnaes, W., Sjursen, H. and White, B. (eds) *Contemporary European Foreign Policy*, London, Thousand Oaks and New Delhi: SAGE Publishers, 252–264.

Checkel, J. T. (1998) 'The Constructivist Turn in International Relations Theory', *World Politics*, 50(2): 324–348.

Chinkin, C. (2004) 'European Security Strategy: An International Law Framework with Respect to International Peace and Security', background paper for the Barcelona group, Centre for the Study of Global Governance. Online, available at: www.lse.ac.uk/Depts/global/StudyGroup/LegalPaper.htm.

Cogan, C. G. (2001) *The Third Option: The Emancipation of European Defense, 1989–2000*, Westport, CT: Praeger.

Cohen, A. (2005) 'Military Maneuvers Cement Chinese–Russian Rapprochement', *Eurasia Insight*, 24 August.

Commission on Global Governance (1995) *Our Global Neighborhood*, New York: Oxford University Press.

Council Common Position (2003) 'Concerning European Union Support for the Implementation of the Lusaka Ceasefire Agreement and the Peace Process in the Democratic

Republic of Congo (DRC) and Repealing Common Position 2002/203/CFSP', 8 May 2003/319/CFSP.

Council Decision (2003) 'On the Launching of the European Union Military Operation in the Democratic Republic of Congo', 12 June 2003, 2003/432/CFSP.

Council Joint Action (2003) 'On the European Union Military Operation in the Democratic Republic of Congo', 5 June 2003/423/CFSP.

—— (2004) 'On the European Union Police Mission in Kinshasa (DRC) Regarding the Integrated Police Unit (EUPOL Kinshasa)', 9 December 2004/847/CFSP.

—— (2005) 'On the European Union Mission to Provide Advice and Assistance for Security Sector Reform in the Democratic Republic of the Congo (DRC)', 2 May 2005/355/CFSP.

—— (2006a) 'Amending and Extending Joint Action 2005/355/CFSP on the European Union Mission to Provide Advice and Assistance for Security Sector Reform in the Democratic Republic of the Congo (DRC)', 25 April 2006/303/CFSP.

—— (2006b) 'On the European Union Military Operation in Support of the United Nations Organisation Mission in the Democratic Republic of the Congo (MONUC) During the Election Process', 27 April 2006/319/CFSP.

—— (2006c) 'Amending and Extending Joint Action 2004/847/CFSP on the European Union Police Mission in Kinshasa (DRC) Regarding the Integrated Police Unit (EUPOL 'Kinshasa') Extension into 2007', 7 December 2006/913/CFSP.

—— (2007a) 'Amending Joint Action 2005/355/CFSP on the European Union Mission to Provide Advice and Assistance for Security Sector Reform in the Democratic Republic of the Congo (DRC)', 27 March 2007/192/CFSP.

—— (2007b) 'On the European Union Mission to Provide Advice and Assistance for Security Sector Reform in the Democratic Republic of the Congo (DRC)', 12 June 2007/406/CFSP.

—— (2007c), 'On the European Union Police Mission Undertaken in the Framework of Reform of the Security Sector (SSR) and its Interface with the System of Justice in the Democratic Republic of the Congo (EUPOL RD Congo)', 12 June 2007/405/CFSP.

—— (2007d) 'Amending Joint Action 2007/405/CFSP on the European Union Police Mission Undertaken in the Framework of Reform of the Security Sector (SSR) and its Interface with the System of Justice in the Democratic Republic of the Congo (EUPOL RD Congo)', 20 December 2007, 2008/38/CFSP.

Council of the European Union (2003) 'A Secure Europe in a Better World: The European Security Strategy', 12 December 2003.

—— (2006a) Council Conclusions on the Democratic Republic of Congo (2744th External Relations Council meeting, Brussels, 17 July 2006).

—— (2006b) Press Release 12286/06 Extraordinary Council Meeting, General Affairs and External Relations Council, Brussels, 25 August 2006.

Council on Foreign Relations (2004) 'Renewing the Atlantic Partnership', report of an independent task force, New York: Council on Foreign Relations Press.

Cox, M. (2005) 'Beyond the West: Terrors in Transatlantia', *European Journal of International Relations*, 11(2): 203–233.

Daalder, I. and Kagan, R. (2007) 'The Next Intervention', *Washington Post*, 6 August 2007: A17.

Daalder, I. and Lindsay, J. (2007) 'Democracies of the World, Unite', *American Interest*, 2(3): 5–15.

Daalder, I. H. (2003) 'The End of Atlanticism', *Survival*, 45(2): 147–166.

Dembinski, M. (2005a) 'Die Beziehungen zwischen NATO und EU von "Berlin" zu "Berlin Plus": Konzepte und Konfliktlinien' in Varwick, J. (ed.) *Die Beziehungen zwischen NATO und EU*, Opladen: Verlag Barbara Budrich, 61–80.

—— (2005b) 'Eine Zukunft für die NATO?', *HSFK-Standpunkte 6,* Frankfurt: Peace Research Institute.

Deutsch, K. W., Burrell, S. A. and Kann, R. A. (1957) *Political Community and the North Atlantic Area: International Organization in the Light of Historical Experience,* Princeton: Princeton University Press.

Diehl, J. (2008) 'A "League" by Other Names', *Washington Post*, 19 May: A17.

Dombrowski, P. and Ross, A. L. (2006) 'The "New Strategic Triangle" and the U.S. Grand Strategy Debate', in Hallenberg, J. and Karlsson, H. (eds) *Changing Transatlantic Security Relations: Do the US, the EU and Russia Form a New Strategic Triangle?* London and New York: Routledge: 146–166.

—— (2007) 'The Political Economy of the U.S. Grand Strategy Debate Revisited', a paper presented at the 2007 Annual Conference of the International Security and Arms Control Section of the American Political Science Association and the International Security Studies Section of the International Studies Association on 'Global Security Challenges: When New and Old Issues Intersect', Montreal, 19–20 October.

Duffield, J. S. (1994–5) 'NATO's Functions after the Cold War', *Political Science Quarterly*, 109(5): 763–787.

Duffield, M. (2001) *Global Governance and the New Wars the Merging of Development and Security*, London: Zed Books.

Duke, S. (1994) *The New European Security Disorder*, New York: St. Martin's.

Eberwein, W.-D. (1995) 'The Future of International Warfare: Toward a Global Security Community?', *International Political Studies Review*, 16(4): 341–360.

Eggen, D. and White, J. (2008) 'Memo: Laws Didn't Apply to Interrogators', *Washington Post*, 2 April: A01.

Eide, E. (2004) 'Introduction: The Role of the EU in Fostering "Effective Multilateralism"', in Eide, E. (ed.) *'Effective Multilateralism': Europe, Regional Security and a Revitalised UN,* Global Europe, Report 1, The Foreign Policy Centre, British Council and the European Commission, in association with Wilton Park. Online, available at: http://fpc.org.uk.

Eilstrup-Sangiovanni, E. and Verdier, D. (2005) 'European Integration as a Solution to War', *European Journal of International Relations*, 11(1): 99–135.

Ekengren, M. (2007) 'The External–Internal Dimension of Security and Terrorism' in Spence, D. (ed.) *The European Union and Terrorism*, London: John Harper Publishing.

Ekengren, M., Matzén, N. and Svantesson, M. (2006a) 'Solidarity or Sovereignty – EU Cooperation in Civil Protection', *Journal of European Integration*, vol. 28, no. 5, December.

—— (2006b) 'The New Security Role of the European Union: Transnational Crisis Management and the Protection of Union Citizens', Stockholm: Swedish National Defence College Acta B35.

Engdahl, O. and Hellman, C. (eds) (2007) 'Responsibility to Protect', research report, Stockholm: Swedish National Defence College.

Engelbrekt, K. and Hallenberg, J. (eds) (2008) *The European Union and Strategy: An Emerging Actor*, London and New York: Routledge.

Eriksson, A. (2006) *Europeanization and Governance in Defence Policy: The Example of Sweden*, Studies in Politics 117, Stockholm: Department of Political Science, Stockholm University.

—— (2008) *Analyzing EU Defence Integration through Problem Definition*, Studies in Security 6, Stockholm: Swedish National Defence College.

EU Council Secretariat (2005) 'The European Union's engagement towards stability and security in the Democratic Republic of Congo (DRC)', RDC/00 (initial) 23 May 2005, Background.

EUPOL (2006) 'EUPOL Kinshasa The first European Police mission in Africa', press document, October.

Eurobarometer 35 (1991) June, Brussels: Commission of the European Communities.

European Commission (2003) *The European Union and the United Nations: The choice of multilateralism*, communication from the Commission to the Council and the European Parliament: Brussels, 10.9.2003, COM(2003) 526 final.

European Defence Agency (2007) 'European–United States Defence Expenditure in 2006'. Online, available at: www.eda.europa.eu/WebUtils/downloadfile.aspx?fileid=356.

European Union (2003) 'A Secure Europe in a Better World: European Security Strategy', Paris: The EU Institute for Security Studies.

EUSEC RD Congo Mission (2007) 'The EUSEC RD CONGO Mission – Information Document', information document, October.

Evans, G. (1994) 'Cooperative Security and Intrastate Conflict', *Foreign Policy*, 96: 3–20.

Falk, R. (2002) 'Revisiting Westphalia, Discovering Post-Westphalia', *Journal of Ethics*, 6(4): 311–352.

Fang, B. (2006) 'The Great Energy Game' *U.S. News and World Report*, 9 September.

Feiser, J. (2003) 'Finding a New Central Asian Doctrine of Lucid Flexibility', *Eurasia Insight*, 15 July.

Ferrero-Waldner, B. (2004) 'Address to the European Parliament', 5 October 2004. Online, available at: http://ec.europa.eu/commission_barroso/ferrero--waldner/speeches/speeches/ephearing_051004_en.htm, (accessed 29 January 2009).

—— (2006) 'The EU's Role in Protecting Europe's Security', conference on Protecting Europe: Policies for Enhancing Security in the European Union, 30 May 2006. Online, available at: http://europa.eu/rapid/pressReleasesAction.do?reference=SPEECH/06/331&format=HTML&aged=1&language=EN&guiLanguage=en, (accessed 29 January 2009).

Findlay, T. (2002) *The Use of Force in UN Peace Operations*, Stockholm: Sipri/Oxford: Oxford University Press.

Freedman, L. (2003) *The Evolution of Nuclear Strategy*, 3rd edition, Houndmills, Basingstoke: Palgrave Macmillan.

Gaddis, J. L. (1989) 'Hanging Tough Paid Off', *Bulletin of the Atomic Scientists*, 45(1): 11–14.

—— (2004) *Surprise, Security, and the American Experience*, Cambridge, MA, and London: Harvard University Press.

Gawdat, B. (2006) 'Europe's Energy Security: Challenges and Opportunities', *International Affairs*, 82(5): 961–975.

Gelb, B. A. (2006) 'Russian Oil and Gas Challenges', *CRS Report for Congress RL3321*.

Gerven, W. van (2005) *The European Union: A Polity of States and Peoples*, Stanford: Stanford University Press.

Gheciu, A. (2005) *NATO in the 'New Europe'. The Politics of International Socialization after the Cold War*, Stanford: Stanford University Press.

Gilpin, R. (1977) 'Economic Interdependence and National Security in Historical Perspective', in Knorr, K. and Trager, F. N. (eds), *Economic Issues and National Security*, Lawrence, KN: The Regents Press of Kansas, for the National Security Education Program, 19–98.

—— (1981) *War and Change in World Politics*, Cambridge, UK: Cambridge University Press.

Ginsberg, R. H. (2001) *The European Union in International Politics: Baptism by Fire*, Lanham, MD: Rowman and Littlefield.

Gowan, R. and Brantner, F. (2008) 'A Global Force for Human Rights? An Audit of European Power at the UN', *Policy Paper*, European Council on Foreign Relations, London.

Graham, K. and Felício, T. (2005) 'Regional Security and Global Governance: A Proposal for a 'Regional–Global Security Mechanism' in Light of the UN High-Level Panel's Report', *Egmont Paper 4*, Royal Institute for International Relations (IRRI-KIIB), Brussels.

Grindle, M. S. (2007) 'Good Enough Governance Revisited', *Development Policy Review*, 25(5): 553–574.

Gulati, R. and Gargiulo, M. (1999) 'Where Do Interorganizational Networks Come From?', *American Journal of Sociology*, 104(5): 1439–1493.

Haass, R. N. (2006) 'The New Middle East', *Foreign Affairs*, 85(6): 2–11.

Haftendorn, H. (2002) 'NATO III', *Internationale Politik* (transatlantic edition), 3(3): 29–34.

Haftendorn, H., Keohane, R. O. and Wallander, C. (eds) (1999) *Imperfect Unions: Security Institutions over Time and Space*, Oxford and New York: Oxford University Press.

Hanrieder, W. F. (1978) 'Dissolving International Politics: Reflections on the Nation-State', *American Political Science Review*, 72(4): 1276–1287.

Harnisch, S. and Maull, H. (eds) (2001) 'Introduction' in Harnisch, S. and Maull, H. (eds) *Germany as a Civilian Power? The Foreign Policy of the Berlin Republic*, Manchester: Manchester University Press.

Hart, D., Atkins, R., Markey, P. and Youniss, J. (2004) 'Youth Bulges in Communities: The Effects of Age Structure on Adolescent Civic Knowledge and Civic Participation', *American Psychological Society*, 15(9): 591–597.

Hawkins, D. G., Lake, D. A., Nielson, D. L. and Tierney, M. J. (2006) 'Delegation under Anarchy; States, International Organizations, and Principal-Agent Theory', in Hawkins, D. G., Lake, D. A., Nielson, D. L. and Tierney, M. J. (eds), *Delegation and Agency in International Organizations*, Cambridge, UK: Cambridge University Press, 3–37.

Heisbourg, F. (2000) 'Europe's Strategic Ambitions: The Limits of Ambiguity', *Survival*, 42(2): 5–15.

Hellmann, G. and Wolf, R. (1993) 'Neorealism, Neoliberal Institutionalism, and the Future of NATO', *Security Studies*, 3(1): 3–43.

Herz, J. (1957) 'The Rise and Demise of the Territorial State', *World Politics*, 9(4): 473–493.

Hewson, M. and Sinclair, T. J. (eds) (1999) *Approaches to Global Governance Theory*, Albany, NY: State University of New York Press.

Higgott, R. (2005) 'The Theory and Practice of Global and Regional Governance: Accommodating American Exceptionalism and European Pluralism', *European Foreign Affairs Review*, 10(4): 575–594.

Hill, F. (2004) 'Energy Empire: Oil: Gas and Russia's Revival', London, UK: The Foreign Policy Centre, September.

Hippel, K. von (2004) 'NATO, EU and ad hoc Coalition-led Peace Support Operations: The End of UN Peacekeeping or Pragmatic Subcontracting?', *Sicherheit und Frieden/ Security and Peace*, 22(1): 12–18.

Hirschman, A. (1970) *Exit, Voice and Loyalty: Responses to Decline in Firms, Organizations and States*, Cambridge, MA: Harvard University Press.

Hobbes, T. (1972 [1651]) *Leviathan*, London: Collins Clear-Type Press.

Holloway, S. and Valentine, G. (2000) *Children's Geographies: Playing, Living, Learning*, London: Routledge.

Holmes, S. (2007) *The Matador's Cape: America's Reckless Response to Terror*, Cambridge, UK and New York: Cambridge University Press.

Holsti, K. J. (1991) *Peace and War: Armed Conflicts and International Order, 1648–1989*, Cambridge, UK: Cambridge University Press.

Holzgrefe, J. L. (2003) 'The Humanitarian Intervention Debate', in Holzgrefe, J. L. and Keohane, R. O. (eds) *Humanitarian Intervention: Ethical, Legal, and Political Dilemmas*, Cambridge, UK: Cambridge University Press.

Honwana, A. (2005) *Child Soldiers in Africa*, Philadelphia: University of Pennsylvania Press.

Honwana, A. and Boeck, F. de (eds) (2005) *Makers and Breakers: Children and Youth in Postcolonial Africa*, Trenton, NJ: Africa World Press.

Holsti, K. J. (1996) *The State, War, and the State of War*, Cambridge, UK and New York: Cambridge University Press.

Hopf, T. (1998) 'The Promise of Constructivism in International Relations Theory', *International Security*, 23(1): 171–200.

Howorth, J. (2000) 'Britain, France and the European Defence Initiative, *Survival*, 42(2): 33–55.

—— (2007) *Security and Defence Policy in the European Union,* Houndmills, Basingstoke and New York: Palgrave Macmillan.

Human Security Centre (2005) *Human Security Report 2005*, Oxford: Oxford University Press. Online, available at: www.humansecurityreport.info/HSR2005_PDF/Part5.pdf.

Hurd, I. (1999) 'Legitimacy and Authority in International Politics', *International Organization*, 53(2): 379–408.

Hurrell, A. (2007) *On Global Order: Power, Values, and the Constitution of International Society*, Oxford and New York: Oxford University Press.

Hutzler, C. (2006) 'Shanghai Group to Hold War Games', *Eurasia Insight*, 27 April.

Hyde-Price, A. (2001) *Germany and European Order: Enlarging NATO and the EU*, Manchester: Manchester University Press.

—— (2004) 'European Security, Strategic Culture, and the Use of Force', *European Security*, 13(4): 323–343.

Ignatieff, M. (2007) 'Getting Iraq Wrong: What the War Has Taught Me about Political Judgment', *New York Times Magazine*, 5 August: 26–29.

Ikenberry, G. J. (1996) 'The Myth of Post-Cold War Chaos', *Foreign Affairs*, 75(3): 79–91.

—— (1998–9) 'Institutions, Strategic Restraint, and the Persistence of American Postwar Order', *International Security*, 23(3): 43–78.

—— (2001) *After Victory: Institutions, Strategic Restraint, and the Rebuilding of Order After Major Wars*, Princeton: Princeton University Press.

—— (2004) 'Liberalism and Empire: Logics of Order in the American Unipolar Age', *Review of International Studies*, 30(4): 609–630.

International Commission on Intervention and State Sovereignty (ICISS) (2001) *Responsibility to Protect*, ICISS report, Ottawa.

Iwashita, A. (2004) 'A 4,000 Kilometre Journey along the Sino-Russian Border', Sapporo, Hokkaido: Slavic Research Center.

Janusz, B. (2005) 'The Caspian Sea Legal Status and Regime Problems' report, London: Chatham House August 2005 (REP BP 05/02).

Jervis, R. (1983) 'Security Regimes', in S. D. Krasner (ed.) *International Regimes*, Ithaca and London: Cornell University Press: 173–194.

—— (1985) 'From Balance to Concert: A Study of International Security Cooperation', *World Politics*, 38(1): 58–79.

—— (2002) 'Theories of War in an Era of Leading Power Peace', *American Political Science Review*, 96(1): 1–14.

Johnson, D. (2005) 'EU–Russian Energy Links: A Marriage of Convenience?', *Government and Opposition*, 40(2): 256–277.

Jonson, L. (2004) *Vladimir Putin and Central Asia: The Shaping of Russian Foreign Policy*, London, New York: I. B. Taurus.

Kagan, R. (2004) *Of Paradise and Power: America and Europe in the New World Order*, New York: Alfred A. Knopf.

Kahler, M. and Lake, D. A. (2003) 'Globalization and Governance', in Kahler, M. and Lake, D. A. (eds) *Governance in a Global Economy: Political Authority in Transition*, Princeton, NJ: Princeton University Press.

Kaim, M. (2006) *Pragmatismus und Grand Strategy: Die NATO-Debatte in den Vereinigten Staaten*, Berlin: German Institute for International and Security Affairs, SWP-Studie S 31.

Kaldor, M. (2006) *New and Old Wars: Organized Violence in a Global Era,* Cambridge, UK: Polity Press.

—— (2007) 'Human Security: A New Strategic Narrative for Europe', *International Affairs*, 83(2): 273–288.

Karagiannis, E. (2003) 'The US–Iranian Relationship after 11 September 2001 and the Transportation of Caspian Energy', *Central Asian Survey*, 22(2/3): 151–162.

Karasac, H. (2002) 'Actors of the New "Great Game", Caspian Oil Politics', *Journal of Southern Europe and the Balkans*, 4(1): 15–27.

Karns, M. and Mingst, K. (2004) *International Organizations: The Politics and Processes of Global Governance*, Boulder, CO and London: Lynne Rienner.

Kelsen, H. (1948) 'Collective Security and Collective Self-Defense under the Charter of the United Nations', *American Journal of International Law*, 42(4): 783–796.

Keohane, R. O. (1984) *After Hegemony: Cooperation and Discord in the World Political Economy*, Princeton: Princeton University Press.

—— (1989) *International Institutions and State Power: Essays in International Relations Theory*, Boulder, CO: Westview Press.

—— (2001) 'Governance in a Partially Globalized World', *American Political Science Review*, 95(1): 1–13.

—— (2002) 'Introduction: From Interdependence and Institutions to Globalization and Governance', in R. O. Keohane *Power and Governance in a Partially Globalized World*, London and New York: Routledge, 1–23.

Keohane, R. O. and Nye, Jr, J. S. (eds) (1970–1) *Transnational Relations in World Politics*, Cambridge, MA and London: Harvard University Press.

—— (2001) 'Governance in a Globalizing World', in R. O. Keohane *Power and Governance in a Partially Globalized World*, London and New York: Routledge, 139–218.

Kingdon, J. W. (1995) *Agendas, Alternatives and Public Policies*, 2nd edition, Stanford, CA: Addison Wesley Longman.

Kirchner, E. J. (2006) 'The Challenge of European Union Security Governance', *Journal of Common Market Studies*, 44(5): 947–968.

—— (2007a) 'European Security Strategy versus National Preferences' in Kirchner, E. J. and Sperling, J. A. (eds) *Global Security Governance: Competing Perceptions of Security in the 21st Century*, London and New York: Routledge.

—— (2007b) 'Regional and Global Security: Changing Threats and Institutional Responses', in Kirchner, E. J. and Sperling, J. A. (eds) *Global Security Governance: Competing Perceptions of Security in the 21st Century*, London and New York: Routledge: 3–22.

Kirchner, E. J. and Sperling, J. A. (2002) 'The New Security Threats in Europe: Theory and Evidence', *European Foreign Affairs Review*, 7(4): 423–452.

—— (2007a) *EU Security Governance*, Manchester: Manchester University Press.

—— (eds) (2007b) *Global Security Governance: Competing Perceptions of Security in the 21st Century*, New York and London: Routledge.

Kjaer, A. M. (2004) *Governance*, Cambridge, UK and Malden: Polity Press.

Klevemann, L. (2004) 'Oil and the New Great Game', *Nation*, 16 February: 11–14.

Kolodziej, E. A. (2005) *Security and International Relations*, Cambridge, UK and New York: Cambridge University Press.

Kooiman, J. (2000) 'Societal Governance: Levels, Modes, and Orders of Social-Political Interaction' in Pierre, J. (ed.) *Debating Governance: Authority Steering, and Democracy*, Oxford: Oxford University Press.

Koremenos, B., Lipson, C. and Snidal, D. (2001) 'The Rational Design of International Institutions', *International Organization*, 55(4): 761–799.

Krahmann, E. (2003) 'Conceptualizing Security Governance', *Cooperation and Conflict*, 38(1): 5–26.

—— (2005a) 'Security Governance and Networks: New Theoretical Perspectives in Transatlantic Security', *Cambridge Review of International Affairs*, 18(1): 15–30.

—— (2005b) 'American Hegemony or Global Governance? Competing Visions of International Security', *International Studies Review*, 7(3): 531–545.

Krasner, S. D. (1983) 'Structural Causes and Regime Consequences: Regimes as Intervening Variables', in Krasner, S. D. (ed.) *International Regimes*, Ithaca, NY and London: Cornell University Press, 1–21.

—— (1995–6) 'Compromising Westphalia', *International Security*, 20(3): 229–251.

—— (1999) *Sovereignty: Organized Hypocrisy*, Princeton: Princeton University Press.

—— (2001) 'Abiding Sovereignty', *International Political Science Review*, 22(3): 229–251.

Krause, K. and Williams, M. C. (1997) 'From Strategy to Security: Foundations of Critical Security Studies', in Krause, K. and Williams, M. C. (eds) *Critical Security Studies: Concepts and Cases*, Minneapolis: University of Minnesota Press.

Krauthammer, C. (2002–3) 'The Unilateral Moment Revisited', *National Interest*, 70: 5–17.

Krickovic, A. (2007) 'Is SCO New Warzaw Pact or Modern-day Holy Alliance?', *Radio Free Europe/Radio Liberty Newsline*, 22 August, end note.

Krugman, P. (2007) 'Hired Gun Fetish', *New York Times*, 28 September: A27.

Kumar, K. (1992) 'The Revolutions of 1989: Socialism, Capitalism, and Democracy', *Theory and Society*, 21(3): 309–356.

Kupchan, C. A. and Kupchan, C. A. (1991) 'Concerts, Collective Security, and the Future of Europe', *International Security*, 16(1): 114–161.

—— (1995) 'The Promise of Collective Security', *International Security*, 20(1): 52–61.

Kupchan, C. A. and Trubowitz, P. L. (2007) 'Dead Center: The Demise of Liberal Internationalism in the United States', *International Security*, 32(2): 7–44.

Kupchinsky, R. (2007) 'Gas OPEC Moves Closer to Becoming Reality', *Radio Free Europe/Radio Liberty Energy*, 6 February.

Laitinen, I. (Brig. Gen, Executive Director of Frontex) (2008) Seminar organized by the Finnish Institute of International Affairs together with the Stefan Batory Foundation in Helsinki on 15 September.

Langer, W. L. (1950) *European Alliances and Alignments*, 2nd edition, New York: Random House.

Layne, C. (2006) *The Peace of Illusions: American Grand Strategy from 1940 to the Present*, Ithaca, NY and London: Cornell University Press.

Lebow, R. N. and Risse-Kappen, T. (eds) (1995) *International Relations Theory and the End of the Cold War*, New York: Columbia University Press.

Leffler, M. P. (1992) *A Preponderance of Power: National Security, the Truman Adminis- tration, and the Cold War*, Stanford: Stanford University Press.

Lipson, C. (2003) *Reliable Partners: How Democracies have Made a Separate Peace*, Princeton: Princeton University Press.

Lisbon Treaty (2007) *The Treaty of Lisbon amending the Treaty on European Union and the Treaty establishing the European Community, signed in Lisbon on 13 December 2007*. Consolidated version online, available at: http://eur--lex.europa.eu/JOHtml.do?ur i=OJ:C:2007:306:SOM:EN:HTML.

Liska, G. (1962) *Nations in Alliance: The Limits of Interdependence*, Baltimore: Johns Hopkins University Press.

Lo, B. and Rothman, A. (2006) 'China and Russia: Common Interests, Contrasting Perceptions' *CLSA Asian Geopolitics Special Report*, May.

Lukin, A. (2003) *The Bear Watches the Dragon: Russia's Perceptions of China and the Evolution of Russian–Chinese Relations since the Eighteenth Century*, London, New York: M. E. Sharpe.

Lundestad, G. (1986) 'Empire by Invitation? The United States and Western Europe, 1945–1952', *Journal of Peace Research*, 23(3): 263–277.

Lysenko, I. (2002) 'Caspian Sea Consortium: "Balance of Regional Interests"', *International Affairs*, 48(2): 34–40.

McCalla, R. B. (1996) 'NATO's Persistence after the Cold War', *International Organization*, 50(3): 445–475.

Mandelbaum, M. (2002) *The Ideas That Conquered the World: Peace, Democracy, and Free Markets in the Twenty-first Century*, New York: Public Affairs.

—— (2005) *The Case for Goliath: How America Acts as the World's Government in the 21st Century*, New York: PublicAffairs.

Manners, I. (2002) 'Normative Power Europe: A Contradiction in Terms?', *Journal of Common Market Studies*, 40(2): 235–258.

Mansfield, E. D. and Snyder, J. (2007) *Electing to Fight: Why Emerging Democracies Go to War*, Cambridge, MA: MIT Press.

March, J. G. and Olsen, J. P. (1989) *Rediscovering Institutions: The Organizational Basis of Politics*, New York: Free Press.

—— (1998) 'The Institutional Dynamics of International Political Orders', *International Organization*, 52(4): 943–969.

Martin, L. L. and Simmons, B. A. (1998) 'Theories and Empirical Studies of International Institutions', *International Organization*, 52(4): 729–757.

Matlary Haaland, J. (2008) 'Much Ado about Little: The EU and Human Security', *International Affairs*, 84(1): 131–143.

Mayer, J. (2008) *The Dark Side: The Inside Story of How the War on Terror Turned into a War on American Ideals*, New York: Doubleday.

Mearsheimer, J. (1990) 'Back to the Future: Instability in Europe after the Cold War', *International Security*, 15(1): 5–56.

—— (1994–5) 'The False Promise of International Institutions', *International Security*, 19(3): 5–49.

Menon, A., Forster, A. and Wallace, W. (1992) 'A Common European defence?', *Survival*, 34(3): 98–118.

Mérand, F. (2008) *European Defence Policy: Beyond the Nation State*, New York: Oxford University Press.

Meyer, C. O. (2006) *The Quest for a European Strategic Culture: Changing Norms on Security and Defence in the European Union*, Houndmills, Basingstoke: Palgrave Macmillan.

Michel, L. G. (2003) 'NATO Decisionmaking: Au Revoir to the Consensus Rule?', *Strategic Forum 202*, Washington, DC: National Defense University. Online, available at: www.au.af.mil/au/awc/awcgate/ndu/sf202.pdf.

Milward, A. S. (1992) *The European Rescue of the Nation-State*, Berkeley: University of California Press.

Moravcsik, A. (2003) 'Striking a New Transatlantic Bargain', *Foreign Affairs*, 82(4): 74–89.

Most, B. A. and Starr, H. (1980) 'Diffusion, Reinforcement, Geopolitics, and the Spread of War', *American Political Science Review*, 74(4): 932–946.

Müller, P. S. and Lederer, M. (2005) 'Introduction: Challenging Global Governance' in Lederer, M. and Müller, P. S. (eds) *Criticizing Global Governance*, New York and Basingstoke: Palgrave Macmillan.

Myers, J. and Soligo, R. (2004) 'Re-evaluating U.S. Strategic Priorities in the Caspian Region: Balancing Energy Resource Initiatives with Terrorism Containment', *The Energy Dimension in Russian Global Strategy*, Baker Institute Study, October.

Newman, E. (2001) 'Human Security and Constructivism', *International Studies Perspectives*, 2: 239–251.

Nicolaïdis, K. (2007) 'Trusting the Poles? Constructing Europe through Mutual Recognition', *Journal of European Public Policy*, 14(5) 682–698.

Nolan, J. E. (ed.) (1994) *Global Engagement: Cooperation and Security in the 21st Century*, Washington, DC: Brookings Institution Press.

Novosseloff, A. (2004) *EU–UN Partnership in Crisis Management: Development and Prospects*, New York: International Peace Academy. Online, available at: www.ipacademy.org.

Nowak, A. (ed.) (2006) 'Civilian Crisis Management: The EU Way', *Chaillot Paper 90*, Paris: EU Institute for Security Studies.

Nussbaum, M. C. (1988) 'Nature, Function and Capability', *Oxford Studies in Ancient Philosophy*, suppl. vol. 1: 145–184.

—— (2000) 'Aristotle, Politics and Human Capabilities: A Response to Antony, Arneson, Charlesworth, and Mulgan', *Ethics*, 111(1): 102–140.

Nuttall, S. (1998) 'Two Decades of EPC Performance' in Regelsberger, E., De Schoutheete de Tervarent, P. and Wessels, W. (eds) *Foreign Policy of the European Union: From EPC to CFSP and Beyond*, Boulder, CO: Lynne Rienner.

Nye, Jr, J. S. (1990) *Bound to Lead: The Changing Nature of American Power*, New York: Basic Books.

—— (2002) *The Paradox of American Power: Why the World's Only Superpower Can't Go it Alone*, New York: Oxford University Press.

—— (2004) *Soft Power: The Means to Success in World Politics*, New York: Public Affairs.

Nye, Jr, J. S. and Donahue, J. D. (eds) (2000) *Governance in a Globalizing World*, Washington, DC: Brookings Institution Press.

Nygren, B. (2007) *Rebuilding of Greater Russia: Putin's Foreign Policy towards the CIS Countries*. London and New York: Routledge.

—— (2008a) 'The EU's Democratic Norm Project for Eurasia – Will the Beauty Tame the Beast?', in Engelbrekt, K. and Hallenberg, J. (eds) *The European Union and Strategy – an Emerging Actor*, London and New York: Routledge.

—— (2008b) 'Using the Gas Sector to Reintegrate the CIS', *Problems of Post-Communism*, 55(4): 3–15.

OCHA (2008a) General Information about OCHA. Online, available at: http://ochaonline. un.org (accessed 14 October 2008).

—— (2008b) *OCHA in 2008: Office for the Coordination of Humanitarian Affairs. Activities and Extrabudgetary Funding Requirements*. Online, available at: http://ochaonline. un.org (accessed 14 October 2008).

O'Hara, S. L. (2004) 'Great Game or Grubby Game? The Struggle for Control of the Caspian', *Geopolitics*, 9(1): 138–160.

Ojanen, H. (2005) 'The EU and the UN: A Shared Future', *FIIA Report 13/2005*, Helsinki: The Finnish Institute of International Affairs.

—— (2006) 'The EU's Responsibility for Global Security and Defence', in Vogt, H. and Mayer, H. (eds) *A Responsible Europe? Ethical Foundations of EU External Affairs*, Houndmills, Basingstoke and New York: Palgrave Macmillan.

—— (2007) 'Inter-organizational Relations: The New Facet of European Security Policy', in Forsberg, T., Kivimäki, T. and Laakso, L. (eds) *Europe in Context. Insights to the Foreign Policy of the EU*, Helsinki: Finnish International Studies Association, Publications, 1: 105–119.

Oldberg, I. (2007) 'The Shanghai Cooperation Organisation: Powerhouse or Paper Tiger?', FOI Base Data Report, FOI-R – 2301-SE, June.

O'Lear, S. (2004) 'Resources and Conflict in the Caspian Sea', *Geopolitics*, 9(1): 161–186.

O'Rourke, B. (2005) 'China's Growing Regional European Links Seen as Benefiting Region', *Eurasia Insight*, 28 January.

Ortega, M. (2007) 'Building the Future: The EU's Contribution to Global Governance', *Chaillot Paper 100*, Paris: The EU Institute for Security Studies.

Osgood, R. E. (1962) *NATO: The Entangling Alliance*, Chicago: University of Chicago Press.

Osiander, A. (2001) 'Sovereignty, International Relations, and The Westphalian Myth', *International Organization*, 55(2): 251–287.

Ostrom, E. (1990) *Governing the Commons: The Evolution of Institutions for Collective Action*, Cambridge, UK and New York: Cambridge University Press.

Owen, J. M. (1994) 'How Liberalism Produces the Democratic Peace', *International Security*, 19(1): 87–125.

Owen, T. (2004) 'Human Security – Conflict, Critique and Consensus: Colloquium Remarks and a Proposal for a Threshold-based Definition', *Security Dialogue*, 35(3): 373–387.

Pannier, B. (2008a) 'Gazprom Deal Imperils Hopes for Trans-Caspian Pipeline', *Radio Free Europe/Radio Liberty Energy*, 17 March.

—— (2008b) 'Presidential Summit to Explore Gas Options', *Radio Free Europe/Radio Liberty Energy*, 19 May.

—— (2008c) 'Beijing Flexes Economic Muscle across Region', *Radio Free Europe/ Radio Liberty Energy*, 29 May.

Paris, R. (2001) 'Human Security Paradigm Shift or Hot Air', *International Security*, 26(2): 87–102.

Pershin, K. (2003) 'Iraq War Prompts Most Central Asian Leaders to Reevaluate US Ties', *Eurasia Insight*, 4 April.

Petman, J. (2000) 'Alueellisten järjestelmien uusi rooli globaalissa turvallisuusjärjestelmässä' (The New Role of Regional Systems in the Global Security System), *Ulkopolitiikka*, 37(3): 41–57.

Peucht, J.-C. (2007) 'Turkmenistan: New President Modifying Niazov's Neutrality Policy', *Radio Free Europe/Radio Liberty Energy*, 11 May.

Pew Research Center for the People and the Press (2003) 'America's Image Further Erodes, Europeans Want Weaker Ties: A Nine-country Survey', March 18. Online, available at: *http://people-press.org/reports/display.php3?ReportID=175* (accessed 19 May 2008).

Pierre, J. (2000a) 'Introduction: Understanding Governance', in Pierre, J. (ed.) *Debating Governance: Authority Steering, and Democracy*, Oxford: Oxford University Press.

—— (ed.) (2000b) *Debating Governance: Authority Steering, and Democracy*, Oxford: Oxford University Press.

Pond, E. (2004) *Friendly Fire: The Near-death of the Transatlantic Alliance*, Washington, DC: Brookings Institution Press.

Posen, B. R. (2007) 'Stability and Change in U.S. Grand Strategy', *Orbis*, 51(4): 561–567.

Posen, B. R. and Ross, A. L. (1996–7) 'Competing Visions for U.S. Grand Strategy', *International Security*, 21(3): 5–53.

Pouliot, V. (2006) 'The Alive and Well Transatlantic Security Community: A Theoretical Reply to Michael Cox', *European Journal of International Relations*, 12(1): 119–127.

Powell, R. (1991) 'Absolute and Relative Gains in International Relations Theory', *American Political Science Review*, 85(4): 1202–1220.

Prins, G. (2005) 'Lord Castlereagh's Return: The Significance of Kofi Annan's High Level Panel on Threats, Challenges and Change', *International Affairs*, (London), 81(2): 373–391.

Putin, V. (2001) statement 15 June 2001, Zayavlenie Presidenta Rossiiskoi Federatsii V. V. Putin na itogam sammita 'Shangaiskogo Foruma', Shanghai. Online, available at: http:// president.kremlin.ru/events/234.htlm (accessed June 2005).

—— (2002) press conference 7 June, Sovmestnaia press konferentsiia s Presidentom Kazakhstana Nursultanov Nazarbaevom, Moscow. Online, available at: www.kremlin. ru/appears/2002/06/07/1000_type63380_28943.shtml (accessed June 2005).

Rees, G. W. (1998) *The Western European Union: Between Transatlantic Solidarity and European Integration*, Boulder, CO: Westview.

Reichard, M. (2006) *The EU–NATO Relationship: A Legal and Political Perspective*, Aldershot: Ashgate.

RFE/RL Radio Free Europe/Radio Liberty Newsline (2002) 7 June.

—— (2006) 9 May.

—— (2002) 22 January.

Rhodes, E. (2003) 'The Imperial Logic of Bush's Liberal Agenda', *Survival*, 45(1): 131–154.

RIA Novosti (Russian News and Information Agency Novosti) (2008) 17 January. Online, available at: http://en.rian.ru/russia/20080117/97148666.html.

Richmond, O. P. (2001) 'Post-Westphalian Peace Building: The role of NGOs', *Martin Journal of Conflict Resolution*, article 3.

Risse, T. (1995) *Cooperation among Democracies: The European Influence on U.S. Foreign Policy*, Princeton: Princeton University Press.

—— (2004) 'Beyond Iraq: The Crisis of the Transatlantic Security Community', in Held, D. and Koenig-Archibugi, M. (eds) *American Power in the Twenty-first Century*, Cambridge, UK: Polity Press, 214–240.

Risse-Kappen, T. (1995a) *Cooperation among Democracies: The European Influence on U.S. Foreign Policy*, Princeton, NJ: Princeton University Press.

—— (1995b) 'Democratic Peace – Warlike Democracies? A Social Constructivist Interpretation of the Liberal Argument', *European Journal of International Relations*, 1(4): 491–517.

Rosamond, B. (2005) 'Conceptualising the EU Model of Governance in World Politics', *European Foreign Affairs Review*, 10(4): 463–478.

Rosenau, J. (1992) 'Governance, Order, and Change in World Politics', in Rosenau, J. and Czempiel, E.-O. (eds) *Governance without Government: Order and Change in World Politics*, Cambridge, UK: Cambridge University Press.

—— (1997) *Along the Domestic–Foreign Frontier: Exploring Governance in a Turbulent World*, Cambridge, UK: Cambridge University Press.

—— (2000) 'Governance in a Globalizing Space', in Pierre, J. (ed.) *Debating Governance: Authority Steering, and Democracy*, Oxford: Oxford University Press.

Ross, A. L. (2005) 'What is to be done with U.S. Predominance? Grand Strategy Choices and Challenges', in Lloyd, R. M. (ed.) *A Nation at War: Reconciling Ends and Means*, Newport: Naval War College, 35–39. Online, available at: www.nwc.navy.mil/nsdm/A_Nation_at_War.pdf.

—— (2008) 'A Progressive European Union, a Problematic United States: An Exceptional Experiment Contends with American Exceptionalism', in Engelbrekt, K. and Hallenberg, J. (eds) *The European Union and Strategy: An Emerging Actor*, London and New York: Routledge: 167–183.

Ross, D. (2007) *Statecraft: And How to Restore America's Standing in the World*, New York: Farrar, Straus and Giroux.

Ruggie, J. G. (1996) *Winning the Peace: America and World Order in the New Era*, New York: Columbia University Press.

—— (1998) *Constructing the World Polity: Essays on International Institutionalization*, London and New York: Routledge.

—— (2007) 'American Exceptionalism and the U.S. Role in the World', in Halperin, M. H., Laurenti, J., Rundlet, P. and Boyer, S. R. (eds) *Power and Superpower: Global Leadership and Exceptionalism in the 21st Century*, New York: The Century Foundation Press, 17–22.

Russett, B. M. and Oneal, J. (2001) *Triangulating Peace: Democracy, Interdependence, and International Organizations*, New York: W. W. Norton.

Sandholtz, W. and Stone Sweet, A. (eds) (1998) *European Integration and Supranational Governance*, Oxford: Oxford University Press.

Schimmelpfennig, F. (2008) 'Transatlantic Relations, Multilateralism and the Transformation of NATO' in Bourantonis, D., Ifantis, K. and Tsakonas, P. (eds) *Multilateralism and Security Institutions in an Era of Globalization*, London: Routledge.

Schmidt, J. R. (2006–7) 'Last Alliance Standing? NATO after 9/11', *Washington Quarterly*, 30(1): 93–106.

Schori, P. (2005) 'Painful Partnership: The United States, the European Union, and Global Governance', *Global Governance*, 11(3): 273–280.

Schweller, R. (1998) *Deadly Imbalances: Tripolarity and Hitler's Strategy of World Conquest*, New York: Columbia University Press.

Security Dialogue (2004) 35(3), September.

Sepehri, V. (2007) 'Iran: Politicians Support Establishment of Natural-Gas Cartel', *Radio Free Europe/Radio Liberty Energy*, 6 February.

Shane, S., Johnston, D. and Risen, J. (2007) 'Secret U.S. Endorsement of Severe Interrogations', *New York Times*, 4 October: A1 and A22–A23.

Shanks, C., Jacobson, H. K. and Kaplan, J. H. (1996) 'Inertia and Change in the Constellation of International Governmental Organizations, 1981–1992', *International Organization*, 50(4): 593–627.

Sheehan, J. J. (2008) *Where Have All the Soldiers Gone? The Transformation of Modern Europe*, Boston: Houghton Mifflin.

Shepherd, A. (2006) 'Irrelevant or Indispensable? ESDP, the "War on Terror" and the Fallout from Iraq', *International Politics*, 43(1): 71–92.

Silber, L. and Little, A. (1995) *The Death of Yugoslavia*, London: Penguin Books.

Singer, P. (2006) *Children at War*, Berkeley and Los Angeles: University of California Press.

Sinnott, R. (1997) 'European Public Opinion and Security Policy', *Chaillot Paper 28* Paris: WEU (today EU) Institute for Security Studies.

Siverson, R. M. and Starr, H. (1990) 'Opportunity, Willingness, and the Diffusion of War', *American Political Science Review*, 84(1): 47–67.

Sjursen, H. (2004) 'On the Identity of NATO', *International Affairs*, 80(4): 687–703.

—— (ed.) (2006) *Civilian or Military Power? European Foreign Policy in Perspective*, London and New York: Routledge.

Smith, H. (1994) 'Prospects for Peacekeeping', in Smith, H. (ed.) *International Peace Keeping: Building on the Cambodian Experience*, Canberra: Australian Defence Studies Centre.

Smith, K. (2005) 'Beyond the Civilian Power EU Debate', *Politique Européenne numéro 17, automne 2005*: 63–82.

Smith, T. (2007) *A Pact with the Devil: Washington's Bid for World Supremacy and the Betrayal of the American Promise*, New York and London: Routledge.

Solana, J. (2003) S0148/03 Intervention by Javier Solana, EU High Representative for the Common Foreign and Security Policy. Public meeting of the UN Security Council on the Democratic Republic of Congo, New York, Friday 18 July.

—— (2007) United Nations Security Council, presentation by Javier Solana, EU High Representative for the CFSP, on the Democratic Republic of Congo/EUFOR, New York, Tuesday, 9 January.

Special Eurobarometer 146 (2001) Public Opinion and European Defence (by Philippe Manigart), July 2001. Online, available at: http://ec.europa.eu/public_opinion/archives/ebs/ebs_146_summ_en.pdf (accessed 16 May 2008).

Sperling, J. A. (2003) 'Eurasian Security Governance: New Threats, Institutional Adaptations', in Sperling, J. A., Kay, S. and Papacosma, S. V. (eds) *Limiting Institutions? The Challenge of Eurasian Security Governance*, Manchester: Manchester University Press, 3–26.

—— (2004) 'The Foreign Policy of the Berlin Republic: The Very Model of a Postmodern Major Power?', *German Politics*, 12(3): 1–34.

—— (2007) 'Regional or Global Security Cooperation? The Vertices of Conflict and the Interstices of Cooperation' in Kirchner, E. J. and Sperling, J. A. (eds) *Global Security Governance: Competing Perceptions of Security in the 21st Century*, New York: Routledge, 263–286.

—— (2008) 'State Attributes and System Properties: Security Multilateralism in Central Asia, Southeast Asia, the Atlantic and Europe', in Bourantonis, D., Ifantis, K. and

Tsakonas, P. (eds) *Multilateralism and Security Institutions in an Era of Globalization*, London: Routledge.

Sperling, J. A. and Kirchner, E. J. (1998) 'Economic Security and the Problem of Cooperation in Post Cold War Europe', *Review of International Studies*, 24(2): 221–237.

Sperling, J. A., Kay, S. and Papacosma, S. V. (eds) (2003) *Limiting Institutions: The Challenge of Eurasian Security Governance*, Manchester: Manchester University Press.

Stephens, S. (1995) *Children and the Politics of Culture*, Princeton: Princeton University Press.

Stone Sweet, A., Sandholtz, W. and Fligstein, N. (2001) *The Institutionalization of Europe*, Oxford: Oxford University Press.

Stulberg, A. N. (2005) 'Moving beyond the Great Game: The Geoeconomics of Russia's Influence in the Caspian Energy Bonanza', *Geopolitics*, 10: 1–25.

Syroezhkin, K. (2002) 'Central Asia between the Gravitational Poles of Russia and China', in Rumer, B. (ed.) *Central Asia: A Gathering Storm*, New York and London: M. E. Sharpe, 169–207.

—— (2005) 'Russia: On the Path to Empire?', in Rumer, B. (ed.) *Central Asia: A Gathering Storm*, New York and London: M. E. Sharpe, 93–129.

Tardy, T. (2005) 'EU–UN Cooperation in Peacekeeping: A Promising Relationship in a Constrained Environment', in Ortega, M. (ed.) 'The European Union and the United Nations: Partners in effective multilateralism', *Chaillot Paper 78*, Paris: EU Institute for Security Studies.

Taylor, A. J. P. (1954) *The Struggle for Mastery of Europe, 1848–1918*, Oxford: Clarendon Press.

Teló, M. (2006) *Europe: A Civilian Power? European Union, Global Governance, World Order*, Basingstoke and New York: Palgrave Macmillan.

Transatlantic Trends (2006) German Marshall Fund and Compagnia di San Paolo (2006). Online, available at: www.transatlantictrends.org/ (accessed 18 May 2008).

—— (2007) German Marshall Fund and Compagnia di San Paolo (2007). Online, available at: www.transatlantictrends.org/ (accessed 19 September 2007).

United Nations Economic and Social Commission for Asia and the Pacific (undated) 'What is Good Governance?'. Online, available at www.unescap.org/pdd/prs/ProjectActivities/Ongoing/gg/governance.pdf (accessed 29 September 2007).

United Nations Secretary-General (2005) 'In Larger Freedom: Towards Development, Security and Human Rights for All', report A/59/2005. Online, available at: www.un.org/largerfreedom/ (accessed 31 March 2008).

UNHCR (United Nations High Commissioner for Refugees) (2008). Online, available at: www.unhcr.org/news/NEWS/48f475732.html (accessed 26 October 2008).

Urdal, H. (2004) 'The Devil in the Demographics: The Effect of Youth Bulges on Domestic Armed Conflict, 1950–2000', *Social Development Papers*, Washington, DC: IBRD.

Väyrynen, T. (2004) 'Gender and UN Peace Operations: The Confines of Modernity', *International Peacekeeping*, 11(1): 125–142.

Vazhenkov, R. (2005) 'Pumping Peril to the Pacific', *Moscow Times*, 31 May.

Vershinin, A. (2007) 'Russian, Central Asia Strike Crucial Gas Pipeline Deal in Blow to Western Hopes', Associated Press. Online, available at: www.signonsandiego.com/news/world/20070512-1113-centralasia-russia.html.

Vinogradov, S. and Wouters, P. (1996) 'The Caspian Sea: Quest for a New Legal Regime', *Leiden Journal of International Law*, 9: 87–98.

Wagnsson, C. (2008) *Security in a Greater Europe: The Possibility of a pan-European Approach*, Manchester: Manchester University Press.

Wallace, W. (1999) 'Europe after the Cold War: Interstate Order or Post-sovereign Regional System?', *Review of International Studies*, 25(5): 201–224.

Wallander, C. A. (2000) 'Institutional Assets and Adaptability: NATO after the Cold War', *International Organization*, 54(4): 705–735.

Wallander, C. A. and Keohane, R. O. (1999) 'Risk, Threat, and Security Institutions', in Haftendorn, H., Keohane, R. O. and Wallander, C. E. (eds) *Imperfect Unions. Security Institutions over Time and Space*, Oxford: Oxford University Press, 21–47.

Wallander, C. A., Haftendorn, H. and. Keohane, R. O. (1999) 'Introduction', in Haftendorn, H., Keohane, R. O. and Wallander, C. E. (eds) *Imperfect Unions. Security Institutions over Time and Space*, Oxford: Oxford University Press, 1–18.

Walt, S. (1987) *The Origins of Alliances*, Ithaca: Cornell University Press.

—— (1997) 'Why Alliances Endure or Collapse', *Survival*, 39(1): 156–179.

Waltz, K. (1959) *Man, the State, and War: a Theoretical Analysis*, New York: Columbia University Press.

—— (1979) *Theory of International Politics*, Reading, MA: Addison-Wesley.

—— (1993) 'The Emerging Structure of International Politics', *International Security*, 18(2): 44–79.

Ward, M. D. and. Gleditsch, K. S. (1998) 'Democratizing for Peace', *American Political Science Review*, 92(1): 51–61.

Warrick, J. (2008) 'CIA Tactics Endorsed in Secret Memos: Waterboarding Got White House Nod', *Washington Post*, 15 October: A01.

Webber, M. (2002) 'Security Governance and the "Excluded" States of Central and Eastern Europe', in Cottey, A. and Averre, D. (eds) *New Security Challenges in Central and Eastern Europe: Securing Europe's East*, Manchester: Manchester University Press, 43–67.

—— (2007) *Inclusion, Exclusion and the Governance of European Security*, Manchester and New York: Manchester University Press.

Webber, M., Croft, S., Howorth, J., Terriff, T. and Krahmann, E. (2004) 'The Governance of European Security', *Review of International Studies*, 30(1): 3–26.

Weber, S. (1992) 'Shaping the Postwar Balance of Power: Multilateralism in NATO', *International Organization*, 46(3): 633–680.

Weiss, T. G. (ed.) (1993) *Collective Security in a Changing World*, Boulder, CO and London: Lynne Rienner Publishers.

Wendt, A. (1992) 'Anarchy is What States Make of It: The Social Construction of Power Politics', *International Organization*, vol. 46(2): 391–325.

—— (1999) *Social Theory of International Politics*, Cambridge, UK: Cambridge University Press.

Whitman, R. G. (1998) *From Civilian Power to Superpower? The International Identity of the European Union*, Basingstoke: Macmillan.

Wiebes, C. and Zeeman, B. (1983) 'The Pentagon Negotiations March 1948: The Launching of the North Atlantic Treaty', *International Affairs*, 59(3): 351–363.

—— (1992) 'Eine Lehrstunde in Machtpolitik', *Dokumentation: Vierteljahreshefte für Zeitgeschichte*, 40(3): 413–423.

Wilson, J. L. (2004) *Strategic Partners: Russia–Chinese Relations in the Post-Soviet Era*, New York and London: M. E. Sharpe.

Wolfers, A. (ed.) (1959) *Alliance Policy in the Cold War*, Baltimore: Johns Hopkins University Press.

—— (1963) *Discord and Collaboration: Essays on International Politics*, Baltimore: Johns Hopkins University Press.

Worldviews (2002) *American Public Opinion and Foreign Policy*, Chicago Council on Foreign Relations and the German Marshall Fund (eds). Online, available at: www.worldviews.org/ (accessed 18 May 2008).

Xing, G. (2001) 'China and Central Asia', in Allison, R. and Jonson, L. (eds) *Central Asian Security: The New International Context*, London and Washington, DC: Royal Institute of International Affairs and Brookings Institution Press.

Yearbook of International Organizations 2006/07 (2006) Geneva: Union of International Associations.

Yost, D. S. (2007) 'NATO and International Organizations', *Forum Paper 3*, Rome: NATO Defense College.

Young, O. R. (1999) *Governance in World Affairs*, Ithaca: Cornell University Press.

Ziegler, A. H. (1998) 'European Public Perceptions of the Atlantic Alliance: Implications for Post-Cold War Security Policy', research paper submitted to NATO. Online, available at: www.nato.int/acad/fellow/96–98/ziegler.pdf (accessed 16 May 2008).

Index

natural disasters 26, 28–9, 34, 39n2
natural resources 97
neighbourhood policy 34
neighbouring countries 70–1
neo-isolationists 91
neoliberal 40; institutionalists 86, 93n18
Netherlands 50
networking 5; horizontal 53
non-combatants 116
non-discrimination 86
non-governmental organizations 30, 39n8, 44, 71, 114, 119, 125, 133
non-member states 27; inclusion of 34
non-state groups 119
normative power 34, 62
norms 5, 8–9, 49, 63, 81–2, 85, 89, 137; of childhood 114; creation 23, 35; diffusion 47, 69, 72; diverging 129; international 32, 85; liberal democratic 40; national 10; socially accepted 11
North America 4
North Atlantic 83
North Korea 98
North Korea Six-Party Talks 54
nuclear energy 6, 50; energy cooperation 104; weapons 48

Obama, Barack 129; administration 90–2
off-shore balances 91
Office for the Coordination of Humanitarian Affairs 29
oil and gas 96, 98; export 105–6; natural gas 111n9; resources 112n16
oil pipelines 103–6, 110; Caspian Sea routes 112n15; Nabucco 104, 109
oil tankers 112n12
Operation Enduring Freedom 54, 56
opinion polls 47
Organization for Economic Cooperation and Development (OECD) 75n8
Organization for Security and Cooperation in Europe (OSCE) 53, 83
organizations 21–3, 25, 29, 35–6; global 30
organized crime 27, 34, 36, 133
overseas missions 32

Pakistan 94, 99, 109
Palestine 117; Intifada 118
participants 63–4, 69, 71–2, 74; in security governance *70*
participation 80, 84
partnership 45–7, 57
Partnership for Peace 47, 100

peace 49, 87; advocates 118; agreements 29, 132; building 51, 58, 83, 132, 135; enforcement 28–9, 83; international 19, 24, 26; mission 98; operations 20, 31; process 63, 118; sustainable 121
peacekeeping 11, 25, 28, 29, 83
peacemaking 83, 135
peer group pressure 118
persuasion 7, 58, 80, 89; instruments 7, 23, 72; security strategies 2
Petersberg tasks 5, 25–6, 39n3
pipeline 95, 104; delivery disturbances 105; gas pipeline 103–4, 106; routes 103, 110
piracy 38n1
Poland 51
police 31, 37, 39n8, 65; missions 63, 68
policy 21, 36; disagreements 40; illicit choices 80; instruments 7, 8
political socialization of children 118
political systems 20, 34, 53
Portugal 50
post-2001 United States 14, 40, 89, 97, 98, 99, 107, 108
post-Cold War 40, 59n7, 90; debate 47; Europe 57; security governance 42, 54, 135; security risks 52
post-colonial states 115
post-conflict attention 120; stabilization of societies 114
post-war 3; rise of Europe 50
post-Westphalian 45, 52–3, 73–4, 79, 80, 82–3, 114, 127–9, 131, 133, 135; challenge 95; context 139; EU 50; political union 89; states 1–3, 6, 8, 10, 13, 20, 128–9; system 9, 13, 115, 125; thinking 130; world 86
post-Westphalian security 44; community 9–14, 15n9, 20, 45, 49, 52, 90; governance 94, 136
post-Westphalianness 137
post-World War II 86–7, 91; liberal order 93n18
postmodern 49; security 134
power 86–7, 96–7; centralization of 85; disequilibria 4; distribution 10; economic 108; hard 2, 45, 91; politics 98
pre-emptive strikes 31, 88
prevention 7–8, 136
pre-Westphalian 74, 134; regions 133
Primakov period 98
private security companies 44
problems 64, 66, 69, 72–3; management 61; transnational 133

For Product Safety Concerns and Information please contact our EU
representative GPSR@taylorandfrancis.com
Taylor & Francis Verlag GmbH, Kaufingerstraße 24, 80331 München, Germany